DYNAMISM

DYNAMISM

*The Values That Drive
Innovation, Job Satisfaction,
and Economic Growth*

EDMUND PHELPS

RAICHO BOJILOV

HIAN TECK HOON

GYLFI ZOEGA

Harvard University Press

Cambridge, Massachusetts
London, England
2020

First printing

Library of Congress Cataloging-in-Publication Data
Names: Phelps, Edmund S., author. | Bojilov, Raicho, 1982- author. | Hoon,
Hian Teck, author. | Gylfi Zoega, author.
Title: Dynamism : the values that drive innovation, job satisfaction, and economic
growth / Edmund S Phelps, Raicho Bojilov, Hian Teck Hoon, Gylfi Zoega.
Description: First. | Cambridge, Massachusetts : Harvard University Press,
2020. | Includes bibliographical references and index.
Identifiers: LCCN 2019054529 | ISBN 9780674244696 (cloth)
Subjects: LCSH: Technological innovations. | Entrepreneurship. | Job satisfaction. |
Individualism. | Economic development.
Classification: LCC HC79.T4 P54 2020 | DDC 338/.064—dc23
LC record available at https://lccn.loc.gov/2019054529

Dedicated to the memory of the late Paul Samuelson,
giant of economic theory

It is better to have a model with inexact foundations that gives you a good grip to handle reality than to wait for better foundations or to continue to use a model with good foundations that is not usefully relevant to explain the phenomena that we have to explain.

—PAUL A. SAMUELSON

CONTENTS

II. THE ROOTS AND BENEFITS OF INNOVATION

III. TWO APPLICATIONS OF ROBOTS

PREFACE

The existing body of economic theory, largely formed over the 20th century, has come to be an impressive machine for analysis. Yet there is now a feeling among many people that it has not fully grasped the forces and channels behind some of the important developments in the modern world. There is also a feeling in the profession that corrections to some of its mistakes are needed if it is to help society understand this world.

Several economists and noneconomists have pointed—some of them long ago—to human desires and satisfactions missing from or intentionally excluded from standard economic theory: Nietzsche on overcoming obstacles, Bergson on vitality and personal growth, Veblen on the instinct called workmanship, Sen on developing our capabilities, Frydman on forecasting consistent with Knightian uncertainty, Robb on "action that is for itself," and my work on the joy of creating.

Yet the economic models used to address public issues or theoretical questions continue to overlook these desires and satisfactions right up to the present time. Two premises of the standard theory are striking in their disregard of those desires and satisfactions, and both premises have to do with what goes on in the workplace.

One of these premises is the supposition that the reward of work is *solely pay*. But there is an abundance of evidence against that. In America, it is very clear that work is central to a meaningful life—as shown gloriously in the film *Shane*. The American Dream, held by many, is best interpreted as the hope of succeeding at something in that life—a hope realized in *A Star Is Born* and dashed in *On the Waterfront*.

In such an economy, conceiving a new thing or new method, imagining an unseen possibility, and exploring the unknown are apt to be the most deeply rewarding sort of work experience. When many of these experiences disappear from some jobs over much of the country, there is a sense of deprivation: some of the meaningfulness of work is lost.

The few attitudinal surveys stretching over a long span provide evidence of the meaningfulness that work has held for a great many people. Asked by Ipsos-Reid whether they enjoy their work so much they "have a hard time putting it aside," 51 percent of interviewees said "yes" in its earliest survey, conducted in 1955. Asked by Roper whether "work is the most important thing . . . or is it leisure?" 48 percent said "work" in its earliest year, 1975. Asked by Gallup whether they are "satisfied or dissatisfied" with their job or the work they do, 86 percent said "satisfied" in its earliest year, 1966. These data say something about who Americans were in those times and who they are today.

Lamentably, the subsequent surveys show a steep decline in job satisfaction starting in the 1970s and continuing to the last surveys around 2000. (The General Social Survey reports that "life satisfaction" has trended down since 1990—this in spite of a rise in household income.) This must be explained. Conceivably that decline is explained—in part, at any rate—by a substantial contraction of annual aggregate innovation. But what is the main force driving innovation? That brings us to the other problematic omission in the standard theory.

The other premise is the supposition that the source of innovation is *solely scientists*. In that view, economic advance is the insightful and fortunate commercial applications of scientific discoveries—applications seen as chosen by knowledgeable entrepreneurs. This would mean that the phenomenon of sustained economic growth, which sprang up early in the 19th century and had spread through most of the West by the century's end, and the subsequent slowdown of this economic growth, which started around 1970 and has since spread through the West, are simply a result of a rise and fall in the rate of scientific advance.

It is true that corporations in some industries of an economy may have R&D departments seeking to identify commercial applications that seem promising enough to be worth designing and marketing—thus helping the firm decide new products and methods to launch on the market. But these departments are not the *origin* of sustained economic advance any more than capital investment is the origin of sustained growth.

It is also true that Silicon Valley has created high-flying start-ups that rely on technological advances in computing and telecommunications. But apart from a brief episode in the late 1990s, the contribution of these companies to the economy as a whole has been minor, their mighty propaganda machines notwithstanding.

With *Mass Flourishing*, which appeared around six years ago, a competing hypothesis on innovation has arisen. There are nations in which ordinary people from "the grass roots on up," having backgrounds in various businesses and having acquired insights into the businesses where they work, come to possess the *capability* to use their acquired know-how to conceive better methods and new things. Further, if such a nation possesses the necessary modern values, these people will have the *desire* to develop those methods and things—thus, market forces permitting, to generate indigenous innovation. That is dynamism—the desire and capacity to generate indigenous innovation. And being engaged in this innovative activity is at the core of modern life. High job satisfaction, the exhilaration of new possibilities, and consequently economic progress are the fruit.

The fundamental purpose of this book is to test this modernist theory against the standard theory driven by exogenous scientific discovery and then to consider the implications of the results for some of the concerns of the present day.

Mass Flourishing presented a *historical* explanation of the rapid, sustained growth of productivity that broke out in a small number of Western nations over the 19th century and the accompanying "flourishing" in those nations—meaningful work, self-expression, and personal growth. Then it presented an explanation of the losses of prosperity and flourishing in one nation after another over the past five decades. These explanations imply a rise and fall of modern values.

But was all this right, or was the older view somehow better in some ways? Economics will not point us to the road we need to take and may point us to wrong roads if we misunderstand the roots of innovation.

This book measures values directly through surveys and estimates their effects through statistical methods. With the tests done and the results in, we can have a better understanding of the main cause of the secular decline—of the losses of growth and flourishing. Then we can begin to address the sense of a void that is felt in much of the West.

DYNAMISM

Introduction

A Theory of Innovation, Flourishing, and Growth

Edmund Phelps

With the dawning of the 20th century, economics—from Wicksell in 1898 and Schumpeter in 1911 to Pigou and Ramsey in the 1920s and Samuelson and Solow in the 1940s to the 1980s—went beyond the static theory of prices and quantities, begun in the 19th century by Ricardo and generalized by Walras, to a theory of the economy's development through time: the path of its capital stock and labor force, the path of the profit rate and the wage, and the growth of its productivity.[1]

That advance has been a central part of economics for decades. Besides providing better foundations for previously existing fields, it opened up new fields for analysis such as household saving and labor supply, business investment, exchange rates, and capital accumulation.[2] Most striking, perhaps, was Schumpeter's 1911 book going beyond the classical view of a nation's development as simply its capital formation—investment and saving—to its innovation and entrepreneurship.

This "neoclassical" theory was nevertheless criticized as omitting features of a *modern* economy. In 1921, Frank Knight observed that firms making investment decisions typically faced "uncertainty" and J. M. Keynes wrote of "unknown" probabilities.[3] In 1936, Keynes argued that, contrary to the neoclassical theory, markets cannot generally have the understanding needed to reach an equilibrium path, so the economy may drift into a slump or boom. In that event, he believed that monetary or fiscal policy could pull the economy back toward normal.⁴ Yet neoclassical theory remains the standard on *growth*—also wage and profit rates.

The most critical deficiency of this standard growth theory is its failure to recognize the core of modern life, of which Knightian uncertainty is just a part.⁵

Critical Shortcomings of the Standard Theory

In the standard economics, true economic growth—defined as growth of total factor productivity, a weighted average of labor productivity and capital productivity—comes out of a machinelike economy driven by "technical progress" (to use Solow's term)⁶ that is solely or predominantly *exogenous* to the economy.⁷ This "progress" is the driving force: although some nations may maintain a higher level of productivity than some others, *no nation can maintain a growth rate of productivity faster than the "rate of technical progress."*⁸ Technical advances with commercial applications prompt businesspeople with acumen and zeal to start new enterprises or reorganize existing ones in the expectation of profiting from the new step.

Schumpeter and others in the German Historical School thought that this "technical progress" arose from the *discoveries* made by the world's "scientists and navigators," which may have been true enough of Schumpeter's Austria. Such discoveries were viewed as the *prime mover* while entrepreneurs undertook the commercial applications that a discovery made possible. This became the standard theory's explanation of *innovations*—what Schumpeter called *Neuren* (new things). In his thinking, there were no people *inside* a nation's economy who might be conceiving "new things" and thus potentially contributing to a nation's innovation and growth—no *indigenous* innovation.⁹

But it is doubtful that these elements of the standard theory fit at all well the highly modern societies emerging in the past 200 years: largely the societies that developed in the 19th century—mainly in Britain and America, later Germany and France. Some points are suggested by the humanities, anthropology, and other social studies.

First, people in general—not just "scientists and navigators"—are capable of having *original ideas,* and many of these ideas (not only those of artistic people) might have commercial applications—just as scientific ideas might. Indeed, virtually every industry has had workers, managers, or others that hit upon new ideas at one time or another. Anthropologists have long believed that humankind has that faculty, and now there is evidence of that. Nicholas Conard and his team, exploring a South German cave once inhabited by some early *Homo sapiens,* found a functioning flute.[10] If humankind has such remarkable talent, it seems possible that society, if willing, could institute an economy that permits and encourages the formation of new ideas, thus fueling innovation and economic growth.

Second, there is far more to a nation's economy than growth. It is fair to say, painting with a broad brush, that the standard theory depicts people's wants as entirely material: no more than their consumption (including collective goods) and leisure. Such a theory may have described life in a mercantile economy, like that in 18th-century England, but it omits the *experiential* dimension central to a modern economy—conceiving and trying out new ways and new things. In the standard theory, a person's life is reduced to simply getting the best terms—finding where revenues are highest or the cost lowest.

Furthermore, the standard theory views the participant as atomistic, hence having no sense of impacting on the quantity or quality of any product supplied. Thus working life lacks any exercise of free will and hence any pursuit of the good life. The theory sees us as being robots from nine to five. That feeling is not the norm in a modern economy, however. There, the experience of acting on an idea of one's own gives people a sense of *agency*—a feeling that they are making a difference in some small part, at any rate.

Because the standard theory does not recognize these dimensions, it can explain neither the *intercountry differences* in nations' economic performance, material and nonmaterial, nor the *rise and fall* of this performance.

Regarding intercountry differences in *material* performance, the standard theory implies that productivity tends to be equalized, as capital and technologies flow to countries where they are scarcer. The data, though, show that, among G7 countries, productivity is far below what the theory would suggest in Britain and Germany while far above it in America.[11] Conceivably, a country might keep ahead of the others if it had superior "entrepreneurship," but Schumpeter made such an argument awkward for Schumpeterians with his insistence—in keeping with his theory—that the commercial opportunities opened up by discoveries were "obvious," hence obvious to all.[12]

As for *nonmaterial* performance, the standard theory says nothing about any systematic intercountry differences either, since it does not see differences in the nature of countries' economic experience. The data show that a measure of nonmaterial performance, mean job satisfaction, is high in Switzerland, Denmark, and Austria while low in Spain, Germany, and Italy.

Regarding intertemporal differences in economic performance, it is clear that the standard theory, having no predictive model of what it terms "technical progress," does not explain them either. It is *not capable* of explaining such developments, material or nonmaterial. And there is a world of change to explain: historical evidence and recent studies show the rise of a *secular exhilaration* (the opposite of secular stagnation) in several nations, one after another, over the 19th century and a *secular stagnation* in one nation after another toward the end of the 20th. It is a serious failing of this prevailing theory that it offers no explanation whatsoever for either the exhilaration or the stagnation.[13]

How then to explain how a nation may gain—or lose—some of its economic performance, material and nonmaterial, *relative* to other nations and, for that matter, relative to its own past? Clearly, we will have to go inside the nations we are studying if we want to understand differences among them in what society wants to gain from its economy and in what it is able to gain. We will need to identify and gauge forces in society that help to explain how a nation might become able to innovate on its own.

A few theorists sought to show how a nation's economy might play a wider role than Schumpeter conceived in the development of innovations—some going so far as to speak of *endogenous* growth in contrast to Schumpeter's exogenous growth. In the 1960s, theorists (virtually all of us with ties to RAND) delved into the commercial application of scientific advances.[14] Kenneth Arrow built a model of productivity gains through "learning by doing."[15] Richard Nelson and others wrote of "technological advances" through "industrial research" and the "diffusion" of new methods.[16] In the 1980s, Paul Romer built a model in which successive variants of an original product line are introduced.[17] In the 1990s, Philippe Aghion and Peter Howitt analyzed a model in which "research activities"—with probabilistic results—generate random sequences of quality-improving innovations.[18] A 1990 model by Romer contains events labeled "new ideas."[19]

We have to go beyond this—and in more than one way. We need to find forces that will produce *sustained* growth. Certainly, learning models do not if there are not new things to be learned. Industrial research teams seeking a commercial application of some scientific discovery appear to be creatures of Schumpeterian advances. (As Nelson said, industrial research would wind down if scientists closed shop.)[20] Successive product lines do not constitute sustained growth either. "Research activities" and "new ideas" are a black box. The spark and the fuel are not described.

While, in modern economies and somewhat less-than-modern ones, organized corporate R&D—activities such as researching for new applications, learning by doing, and solving problems—may yield an occasional productivity gain or new product, no evidence has been presented to suggest that *sustained* innovation, growth, and job satisfaction are to some degree explained (in the statistical sense) by these activities. It is safe to say that these activities cannot have been the source of the productivity explosion of the past 200 years.

We also need to take into account the new ideas of *ordinary people* and the wellspring of those ideas. Even if some statistical correlations should be found, to view the organized research activities of technicians in companies and government offices as fundamental to innovation, thus job satisfaction and growth, does not get to the bottom of things: it is a blinkered view of what individuals, inside or outside companies, are capable of conceiving and doing—*with or without* advancing scientific knowledge—and what things they want to do for their satisfaction. Thus, the existing "endogenous growth theory" is inherently missing key dimensions in human possibilities: the same ones missing in the standard theory.

The thesis expounded in this introduction and to be tested in the body of this monograph takes a different view. Its fundamental premise is that people from all walks of life, not just scientists and lab technicians, possess inborn *powers to conceive* "new things," whether or not scientists have opened up new possibilities. And a modern society allows and even encourages people to *act on* newly conceived things—to create them and try them—which stimulates people to conceive the new. The whole nation might be on fire with new ideas.

The implication is that, whatever Schumpeterian innovation may be occurring, in highly innovative nations, much of that innovating is *indigenous*: it springs from the powers of originality and creativity among large numbers of people working in the nation's economy.

In this thinking, a nation may possess the *dynamism*—an appetite and capacity, a desire and capability—needed to create innovations and a willingness as a society to accept their introduction into the economy.[21] Of course, such a nation may encounter obstacles—external ones such as wars or climate and internal ones such as regulation and bureaucracy. In general, though, the more of that dynamism a nation possesses, the more apt it is to attempt and succeed at innovating. Of course, current conditions, such as the general business outlook or political turmoil, may not warrant the attempt.

The next section points to major evidence of the sources and the rewards of this dynamism, drawing on histories of indigenous innovation in modern times—the early 19th century to the present age.[22] These sources and rewards are tied up with the personal values that came to the fore in those times: the willingness to attempt innovation may be tied to developing conceptions of the "good life." This theory has grown out of work beginning soon after the founding of the Center on Capitalism and Society in 2001 and culminating in my book *Mass Flourishing*, published in 2013. (Work on the present volume has led to a better understanding of many matters, but the basic thesis to be tested is unchanged.)

The Rise of Dynamism and the Impetus of Values

There were forerunners of *Mass Flourishing*, of course. Two scholars stand out for their accounts of the unprecedented economic performance that developed in large parts of the West over the 19th century.

In his first book, *The Process of Economic Growth*, the economic historian Walt Rostow, looking at centuries past, noticed that economic growth had always been episodic, and the rare outbreaks were typically reversed until, in the 19th century, there were—in his inspired term—"take-offs into sustained growth": Britain and America around 1815, Germany and France around 1870.[23] Countries busy copying the new methods and products passing the market test in a "lead economy"—the Netherlands and Italy, for example—saw their own growth rates pulled up. (The further they were outstripped by the leaders, the faster they grew.)[24]

In any nation where it took hold, this growth was immensely powerful. It transformed the nation from agricultural to industrial, from rural to urban, and from trading to producing. New cities sprouted up and new ways of life arose.

In a vivid portrait, *The Birth of the Modern: World Society 1815–1830*, the eminent historian Paul Johnson introduces us to many of the vast number of people whose originality and daring were characteristic features of the modern life that arose in Britain and to a lesser extent in America and continental Europe. Writing about hundreds of innovators—some businesspeople, some scientists, and some artists—he depicts the experimentalism, the learning from mistakes, the curiosity, and the courage to fail that personified the modern people. He also shows us that these people, though gifted for the most part, came mostly from ordinary, not privileged, backgrounds.[25] Johnson was on to something quite important.

Mass Flourishing presents an explanation of this modern life—how it emerged and why it was valued.[26] It points out the new outlook on life—the new attitudes—that permeated Britain and America: going one's own way, seizing one's opportunities, and, as Dickens conveyed, taking control of one's life. The English spoke of "getting on," meaning they were getting somewhere—perhaps getting ahead.[27] Some of these attitudes have been found in contemporary documents by the historian Emma Griffin.[28] My book argues that this new outlook on life spread through much of the West in the 19th century and is reflected by the Romantic movement in music and art. And it, more than anything else, brought about a transformation of the economy.

It was this new spirit that gave rise to an unprecedented *dynamism*. Businessmen might seize unnoticed or neglected opportunities to have better ways to produce existing products or have better-selling products to make—"adaptations," in Hayek's term.[29] There were some adventurers in Renaissance Venice too, but that was nothing like the spread of entrepreneurial pursuits witnessed in the 19th century. Firms of a more entrepreneurial bent were springing up all over the economies of Britain and America. The agglomeration of such firms led to the emergence of more cities (but they were not a driver).[30]

Workers too brought this enterprising attitude to the workplace. The supply of labor—in the working class and middle class—shifted more and more from work that was routine or dull toward work that was challenging, hence engaging, in offices, yards, and shops. Employees might be keeping an eye out for better ways to do their job or organize their work. This new workplace was important. Marshall, observing in 19th-century England, thought so: "The business by which a person earns his livelihood generally fills his thoughts during by far the greater part of those hours in which his mind is at its best; during them his character is being formed by . . . his work . . . and by his relations to his associates in work."[31] Thus, both demand and supply brought people to the new kind of workplace. It was a subject of discussion for decades, from Tocqueville[32] to the young Marx.[33]

But, far more important, the new outlook brought a spirit of *imaginativeness* to people in the economy. Some people might be dreaming up a new product, other people might be conceiving a new way to produce, and still others might be thinking up a new market for an existing product. Everyone was looking for a new way to do something, a new thing to do, or a new thing to use.

It was not a "trading economy" led by enterprising merchants and entrepreneurs that had arrived. It was an "innovation economy"—an economy built by a modern society. At its core was a "vast *imaginarium*"—a space for conceiving, creating, marketing, and perhaps adopting the new. Hume, decades ahead of his time, was its first philosopher: he saw the necessity of imagination for new knowledge, the role of the "passions" in human decisions, and the mistake of counting on past patterns to hold up in the future.[34]

The emergence of this phenomenon must have been breathtaking. While the *adaptation* achieved by "entrepreneurs" could pull an economy to its frontier, or "possibility locus," *innovation* kept on pulling up the frontier itself, and people had no idea when it would come to rest—or *if* it would come to rest. The results were spectacular.

But what was it about this new kind of economy—this new way of work—that made it desired? And why was the necessary fuel present in some nations and not in others?

Fruits of the Dynamic Economies

The takeoffs gradually brought rising *material* rewards. Wages were pulled up by rising productivity. Profits gained kept on exceeding profits lost. More and better food and clothing led to improved health and longevity. In Britain, which kept records, wage rates, which had been up and down since 1500 and depressed from 1750 to 1800 (the years of the First Industrial Revolution), finally "took off"—ultimately growing at the same rate as output per worker. Moreover, workers found a growing number of ways in which to spend their time and money—from theater to sports to pubs. (While it is suggested that pollution and crime in British cities offset much of the wage gains there, a study estimates that, taking account of amenities as well as the disamenities, "city size, on net, is an amenity.")[35] Ultimately, there were invaluable public benefits as well. As revenues rose, governments could take measures to combat disease and boost public health.

Yet for increasing numbers of participants, the material reward—though historic—was not the extraordinary feature of this unprecedented period. Some rewards from the dynamic economy were unprecedented—spread over the breadth of the country from the grass roots on up: there was an explosion of choices, which brought with it a thirst for more choices. Different sorts of jobs kept opening up, different firms kept on entering, and different kinds of goods for use by households kept on turning up. People found this exciting, needless to say. Lincoln, back from his tour of the country in 1858, exclaimed that "young America has a great passion—a perfect rage—for the new."[36] What may explain that "passion" that Lincoln noticed?

The dynamic economy brought with it invaluable *nonmaterial* rewards as well. Even in economies that were *not* dynamic, there were the rewards of learning things, having interchanges of information with others, and simply keeping busy—all of which are nonmaterial in essence and arise from the *experience* of work. Those working in the dynamic economy, however, were in a different world. It was rich in experiences offering nonmaterial rewards that provided a sense of *agency*: people working in a modern economy—most of them at any rate—were *taking responsibility, using their judgment,* and *exercising initiative.* There was also the allure of setting out into the unknown. (We may never know whether Lincoln saw these experiential benefits.)

In the modern societies arising in the 19th century, most people evidently felt a gain from being able to participate in this kind of economy—the excess of benefits over the cost deriving from the inevitable crises and slumps. A great many Americans, for example, did not appear ready at any time to trade away careers offering the prospect of those extraordinary rewards, however uncertain they were thought to be, for a life of security.

Modern Values: The Roots of Dynamism

Much research has ensued on the *effects* of this unprecedented development—less on the *causes*. Why were people in some nations happy to have such an economy in which to pursue their careers—and this in spite of the uncertainty of success—while people in other nations were not? And why do we find today some nations less drawn to such an economy than they once were? In short, what was it in some nations that led to a society willing and able to *provide* an economy with the dynamism to innovate? We might think at first that the spectacular rewards offered by that economy explain its rise. But that would not answer the question of why such a miraculous economy arose over the 19th century in Britain, America, France, and Germany and hardly anywhere else.

The explanation hypothesized here is that a relatively innovative economy tended to be found in nations having (relatively) *modern people*. People are not the same. Even if all countries would have the same nonmaterial rewards had they acquired a modern economy, the people in some countries might have drawn *more satisfaction* from those rewards—and hence be more drawn to a modern economy—than the people in other countries: their appreciation of some or all of the nonmaterial rewards might have been more pronounced. It is possible that the relatively modern people of 19th-century Britain and America had *outsize desires* for some particular satisfactions offered by the modern economies. Several such satisfactions come to mind.

- These "moderns" may have been people who took huge satisfaction in *achieving* something through one's own efforts—and may have taken further satisfaction if the achievement resulted in better terms or more recognition.[37]
- They may have been people who felt huge satisfaction in *succeeding*—an older term for which was *prospering* (from the Latin *pro spere*, meaning "as hoped," "according to expectation"). Successes come in many forms: an office worker winning a promotion for his achievement, a craftswoman seeing her hard-earned mastery result in a better product, a merchant's satisfaction at seeing "his ship come in."[38]

- They may also have been people who took enormous delight in the sense of *flourishing* they got from life's journey—the unfolding of their career, the thrill of voyaging into the unknown, the excitement of the challenges, the gratification of overcoming obstacles, and the fascination with the uncertainties.
- These moderns may also have taken deep satisfaction from *making a difference*—"acting on the world" and, with luck, "making a mark."
- They may also have enjoyed competing alongside colleagues to build a business or to stave off rival firms.

Going deeper, we may form hypotheses about the *values* in society that underlie the desire for some or all of these satisfactions.

The influence of *individualism* on these desires cannot be overestimated. The modernist satisfactions are inherently individualistic. The satisfactions of achieving, succeeding, flourishing, and making a difference are only or mainly one's own satisfactions. (They may extend to those closest to one.) Individualism was first celebrated around the early 16th century—notably by Pico della Mirandola, philosopher of the Renaissance, and Martin Luther, founder of the Reformation—and it spread widely well into the 19th century.

Another key influence is *vitalism*. The dynamic economy appealed to people looking for challenges and opportunities that made them feel alive. It is impossible not to think of innovators as generally full of energy and dedication. The restlessness of Don Quixote in Cervantes's timeless 1605 novel epitomized the vitalism emerging at that time.

The value that might be termed *self-expression* is another influence attracting people to work in an economy of dynamism. In being allowed and perhaps inspired to imagine and create a new thing or a new way, a person can reveal a part of who he or she is.

Mass Flourishing argues that a modern society and the resulting dynamism of its economy bloomed in nations where the humanist values that could fuel the necessary desires and attitudes had reached a critical mass. Figure Intro.1 contains a table of these values and desires.

Testing the Thesis of Dynamism and Its Roots

Before proceeding to test statistical support for this break with the standard theory, it should be acknowledged that although what has been sketched so far is a new *thesis* outside the standard theory, it is not a *theory* in the academic sense, usually a mathematical model.[39] And a formal theory may turn out to have some uses. Interested readers may enjoy the appendix.

This volume's purpose is to test the thesis in *Mass Flourishing*. This has been a three-stage process.

First, there having been no existing time series on indigenous innovation, we have created an econometric model of the types of innovation in a multicountry world with which to estimate time series of *indigenous innovation* (in addition to exogenous innovation and imported innovation) in each of the countries under study. These estimated time series provide estimates of both *intercountry* differences in rates of indigenous innovation in the past and, for each country, *intertemporal* shifts in the rate of indigenous innovation.

Second, we have drawn on attitudinal data from household surveys of the countries under study to test whether intercountry differences in attitudes expressing the modern values of individualism, vitalism, and self-expression largely explain—better than intercountry differences in more familiar dimensions such as institutions do, at any rate—the intercountry differences in economic performance, as measured by a potpourri of variables ranging from the standard (such as fertility and labor force participation) to the modern (such as indigenous innovation and job satisfaction).

Last, this investigation can be seen as a test of the very existence of dynamism. And that is a radical venture, since the literature aiming to explain differences in economic performance does not admit into its framework the existence of dynamism. The prevailing explanation of differences across countries in economic performance is focused instead on the role of institutions—thus paying little or no attention to values.[40]

This is hugely important. Where there is great dynamism, there is also an abundance of its characteristic fruit: achieving, succeeding, prospering, and flourishing. And where it is lacking, there is a joyless society.

Values are subject to change, however. The Renaissance values—referred to here as the "modern values"—that finally attained a critical mass in the 19th century, though initially articulated in much earlier epochs, were not strong enough at first to overcome other values. We must look, then, for evidence that some of the values that fueled the historic dynamism in the West have weakened—and watch for evidence that some competing values have strengthened.

Some discussion may be worthwhile before the statistical investigations of these questions.

Losses of Dynamism? Losses of Modern Values?

Data collected by the Penn World Tables and, recently, by Banque de France show that total factor productivity growth, which had been fast by historical

Figure Intro.1. Societal values and economic performance

MODERN VALUES

Individualism
Thinking for oneself (Luther)
Right to pursue happiness (Jefferson)
Working for one's own ends (Dickens)
A willingness to rely on oneself (Emerson)
Breaking from convention (George Eliot)

Vitalism
Relishing challenges (Cervantes)
Summoning the courage to act (Shakespeare)
Taking initiatives: 'acting on the world' (Hegel)
Competing with others (Cellini, Dumas)
Imagining the new (Hume)
Adventuring (Twain)

Self-Expression
Creating things (Voltaire)
Exploring; experimenting (Goethe)
Voyaging into the unknown (Verne)
Making a mark (Dickens, Thackeray)

TRADITIONAL/ANTI-MODERN VALUES

Family responsibilities
Community solidarity
Staying in a circle of friends
Sharing good fortunes with stakeholders
Service to others and service to society
Material rather than experiential goals
Opposition to dislocation
Opposition to "new money"
Conformism
Moving in lock step
Sense of entitlement
The Law of Jante

TRADITIONAL/CORPORATIST ECONOMIES

Merit Goods: Social Security
Pensions, medical care

Social protection
Job protection, tariff protection

Solidarism
State's concertation with social partners
Company consultation with stakeholders

Nexus between private and public
Clientelism
Patronage, Lobbies

Roles of elites

Dirigisme

A QUALITY LIFE

Amenities
Leisure
Enjoyment of culture
Preservation of traditions
Professional sports competitions
Conservation of environment
Material wealth and income

DYNAMIC ECONOMIES

Dynamism
Desire, capacity and latitude to innovate
Innovative activity: imagination and ingenuity

Economic independence
Abundance of jobs: ease of starting up companies

Prospering
Gaining better terms for what one does through one's own initiative and creativity

Flourishing
Gaining experiential rewards: using one's imagination, satisfying
one's creativity, venturing into the unknown, having the thrill of
discovery

Wide participation
Innovating down to the grassroots

GOOD LIFE

Gaining understanding (Aristotle)
Meeting challenges (Cervantes)
Achieving personal growth (Montaigne)
Voyaging into the unknown (Kierkegaard)
Overcoming obstacles (Nietzsche)
Living fearlessly (William James)
Becoming: personal growth (Bergson)

standards over the years 1950–1970 in America and extraordinarily fast in France and Italy, fell to very slow rates in all four countries over the years 1970–1990, then partially recovered to the earlier rates in America and Britain while slowing further in France and especially Italy. (Germany is a special case.)[41] A longer history offers another perspective: among the large countries that were in the economic lead over much or all of the 20th century—Britain, America, Germany, and France—growth of total factor productivity was markedly slower over the span 1990–2013, and still slower in the span 1970–1990, than it had been in the interwar decades, 1919–1939, and the span 1950–1970, according to the Banque de France estimates.[42]

Popular explanations of this development, in presuming that all or most innovation is Schumpeterian, attribute the slowdowns of total factor productivity to a drying up of commercially usable scientific discoveries—a fall in the *exogenous* "rate of technological progress" driving economic growth in the standard theory.[43] Yet that inference looks questionable: if the slowdowns of total factor productivity—nearly all of which began around 1970, by which time all the countries had recovered from the war, so there were no slowdowns on this account—were the result of a decline of scientific discovery, and thus a slowing of Schumpeterian innovation, slowdowns of total factor productivity would have arrived more nearly at the same time and been more nearly of the same magnitude. But perhaps someone will someday show the presence of forces that prevented the slowdowns from being synchronous and equal. So, contentions that Schumpeterian innovation played a major role cannot be excluded on this account.

Our desire to understand these slowdowns motivates much of this volume. Not all of the statistical findings have direct implications for the slowdowns, of course, and nothing like a "general-equilibrium" time-series model of indigenous innovation is estimated. Yet we can draw from the pieces some plausible, perhaps persuasive, inferences. There are four layers of questions to probe.

If the nations of the West have been suffering from generally slower growth of total factor productivity in recent decades, are the slowdowns attributable to a *structural* slowing of *innovation*, not merely a run of adverse disturbances?

If the nations of the West are indeed in the grip of systematic slowdowns of innovation, are they results of *indigenous* innovation in some or all of the most innovative economies rather than Schumpeterian innovation?[44]

If there have been major losses of indigenous innovation, whether or not there has been some loss of Schumpeterian innovation as well, are these losses of indigenous innovation to a large extent a result of losses in *dynamism*—not merely a run of bad luck by plucky, ever-dynamic would-be innovators?

If there have been serious losses of dynamism, is there evidence of losses in the modern values—or gains in the opposing values—that *Mass Flourishing* argued were the fundamental determinants of the level of dynamism? (It will be an advance in understanding if, instead of attributing the slowdowns to a decline of dynamism *by default,* we can point to deadly sources of a decline of dynamism.)

A few preliminary inferences may be ventured in spite of the complexity of our thesis. It is plausible to think that the nations engaged in high levels of indigenous innovation on top of the rather equal levels of their Schumpeterian innovation, to which all countries had relatively easy access, would have high productivity growth and have reduced productivity growth when indigenous innovation is low.

It is paradoxical, then, that America, Britain, and France, normally the most highly innovative nations in the world, have seen large regions "ravaged by deindustrialization" since the 1970s, to use President Emmanuel Macron's phrase: America's Rust Belt stretching from Appalachia to the Midwest, Britain's West Midlands, and France's Lorraine region. In the old industries of these regions, there appears to have been deep losses of innovation—so deep that *aggregate* innovation slowed in spite of the astonishing innovation in the new, high-tech industries. But the structure of an advanced economy is apt to be complex. One could imagine that the fall of investment and employment in these regions was caused by a change in the structure of innovation rather than a drop of innovation.

To the extent that the thesis here—the good life through innovation and innovation through dynamism—finds empirical support, it may throw light on the *intense dissatisfaction* of many participants in the economies of the West. Certainly, the falloff of dynamism offers an explanation of the severe slowdown of wages. In the view of some commentators, the slowdown of wages in America was deeply disturbing to workers, for they had grown up believing that rising wages would eventually provide them with a standard of living significantly higher than that of their parents.

The thesis may also shed some light on symptoms of discontent with the workplace. Perhaps there has been a significant falloff of the *nonmaterial* rewards of work in those economies—rewards that may have been more gratifying than the material rewards were. It is significant that household survey data have shown over recent decades appreciable losses of reported job satisfaction in most, if not all, of the nations that were once big stars in the innovation firmament—and, roughly speaking, intercountry differences in job satisfaction explain some 90 percent of differences in "life satisfaction."[45]

Lastly, research by Angus Deaton has found a range of pathologies running at uncommonly high levels in America: suicide, opioid addiction, depression, and obesity.[46] It is plausible that these symptoms too—in the countries under study, at any rate—are the effect of losses of dynamism brought about by widespread weakening of the same values that fueled dynamism. The widely commented changes in the nature of jobs—the loss of a sense of *agency,* of the experience of succeeding at something, and of the sense of voyaging into the unknown—could drain much of the meaningfulness of many people's work.

What might explain the significant losses of dynamism? Some observers have called attention to changes in the values expressed by society as early as the 1970s. The American sociologist Christopher Lasch wrote of a "narcissism" among young people in America that has made them self-indulgent.[47] A White House aide, Patrick Caddell, wrote that one is "no longer identified by what one does, but by what one owns."[48] Margaret Thatcher, the prime minister of Britain in the 1980s, said that "life used to be about trying to do something."[49] In his famous "malaise speech," President Jimmy Carter called for a "restoration of American values" and a "rebirth of the American spirit."[50] It is fair to say that Carter and succeeding leaders could not revive the "spirit" on which the economy's dynamism depended since they lacked any *theory* of what that "spirit" depends on. *Mass Flourishing* laid out a thesis on the set of values underpinning the dynamism that has fueled indigenous innovation.

From the perspective of the theory here, it is natural to hypothesize that the losses in dynamism were caused—to a large extent, at any rate—by losses in the *modern values* that had sparked the dynamism at the outset. This hypothesis passes an obvious test: the countries that showed the greatest losses of indigenous innovation—even percentage losses—appear to be the nations in which innovation was once greatest. But looking at values and dynamism in just one cross section of countries does not provide an adequate test of the theory advanced here. Econometric tests must be performed before we can be confident that the theory sketched here—in this introduction—has an important place in our understanding of the rise and decline of indigenous innovation in the West.

If all these observations and explanations are true enough, they invite the inference that Western nations—the nations hit by the slowdown of their own indigenous innovation and the nations hit by losses of innovations to copy from the lead economies—are suffering from a *deficiency* of dynamism and the resulting innovation. Qualifications may be in order and complications may have developed. But no other explanation is apparent.

We come now to the value added of this volume. Of the ten chapters that follow, the first *seven* submit the foregoing body of speculative theory to statistical and econometric tests. (*Mass Flourishing* gave two short chapters to preliminary tests of its thesis, but the present volume is the first to devote a volume to a battery of tests.) Do the results tend strongly to confirm the presence of *indigenous* innovation, not solely Schumpeterian innovation? Do they tend to confirm the reality of *dynamism*—its power when it was at its peak and its power now that much of it has been lost? Do the results confirm the existence of *modern values,* not just traditional ones? And if so, are the nations most endowed with modern values or least possessing traditional ones found to have the *most* indigenous innovation?

In this volume, we also struggle with some of the big economic questions of our time. If we are in the grip of a structural slowdown, is a fall of indigenous innovation the cause? And if so, is it the result of policies and policy failures *or* more the result of a profound loss of dynamism internal to society?

Though these matters are crucial, we cannot end there.

Shifts in the Direction of Innovation: Labor Adding and Labor Multiplying

No sooner did we embark on the battery of tests presented here than we became aware that, besides whatever losses of dynamism may have occurred in some Western nations, there had been a change not only in the rate of innovation but also in the "direction" of innovation—to use a once-familiar term. No one will wonder why we must take up this new development. Many in the public have become alarmed over the redirection of innovation toward advances in artificial intelligence, specifically its effects on jobs and wages—much more alarmed than they were over the slowdown of aggregate innovation that took hold in 1970 and again from 2000 to 2012 up to the present time.

Even if no part of the public was alarmed over the matter, there would nevertheless have been more work to be done. Just as it was high time early in the 2010s to evaluate the standard theory of growth and venture beyond it to propose a new theory of indigenous innovation, it is now high time to evaluate the present understanding of the effects of advances in artificial intelligence, or AI, leading to more sophisticated robots and to develop a theory of what consequences unfold following the introduction of robots into parts of the economy.

A very simple model I sketched in the spring of 2016 suggests that the arrival of squads of robots causes a drop in employment and wage rates—also a drop in prices, for that matter—in the industry or sector that acquires the robots. But, I argued, those are only the immediate effects, not the final result. The reduction of costs brought by such a wave of robots is rather similar to the reduction of costs brought by a wave of foreign workers arriving in some industry of an otherwise closed economy: economics does not predict a permanent fall of wage rates and jobs. As the consequent drop in wage rates spreads throughout the economy, the capital stock can be expected to rise until a new steady state is reached in which jobs initially lost are regained and wage rates regain their former level. In addition, the initial boost in profit rates leads to additional investment until the ratio of capital to human plus robotic labor has regained its former level.

Yet we need to move beyond that simple model to richer ones.

The last three chapters address a kind of innovation that is different from what was the sole kind of innovation until recently. These chapters bring into the picture a kind of innovation that was traditionally called labor saving. It is ironic that these chapters in a volume challenging the standard theory hark back to issues that were raised in the essay "On Machinery" by Ricardo, which prefigured the standard theory, and addressed by Samuelson, whose brilliant work epitomized the standard theory.

These chapters explore the range of consequences that the introduction of robots can have. A crucial distinction is that between robots that, so to speak, add their labor to that of the workers and robots that potentiate the productivity of the workers—"labor-adding" and "labor-augmenting" robots.

In that framework, a single batch of labor-adding robots would have effects much like those just sketched: wages fall and then recover. However, in one such case wage rates show only a partial recovery.

Prospects are much improved when the robots are labor augmenting. The initial impact on wages is ambiguous. But it is unambiguous that the wage rates take a path of unbounded growth.

Our hope is that this introduction will draw readers into the research presented in the ten chapters that follow.

APPENDIX

While a thesis may possess far more richness than a formal model can, models may reveal possible causal interactions or channels that might not otherwise be perceived. However, such models of indigenous innovation do appear to be possible. It took a long time for Schumpeter's thesis to appear in formal models. The first growth model to be built on this thesis was first constructed by Solow:

$$dK_t/dt = s\ Y_t \tag{S1}$$

$$Y_t = A(t)\ F(K_t, L) \tag{S2}$$

Here, growth of aggregate output, Y, is driven by growth of total factor productivity, $A(t)$, which is exogenous—generated by forces *outside* the economy.

Growth models can instead be built on the growth thesis tested in this book. We could replace Solow's forcing function, $A(t)$, with a state variable, $B(N_t)$, measuring the force of cumulative indigenous innovation, N_t, brought by ideas born *inside* the economy.

A model in the spirit of the theory here describes an economy organized around consumer durables, intermediate and finished. In the labor force, homogenous and of size L, a number of participants are generally found engaged in creating new material, thus adding to the stock of *intermediate* capital, K_t. This is the number of participants, ξ_t, struck by ideas for new durables. (They prefer that sort of work to the others available.) The rest of the labor force is employed in producing from the intermediate assets a flow of new durables, thus constantly increasing the stock durables, D.[51]

This system is represented by the following pair of equations:

$$dD_t/dt = F(K_t, L - \xi),\ F_1 > 0,\ F_2 > 0 \tag{1}$$

$$dK_t/dt = G(K_t, \xi),\ G_1 \geq 0,\ G_2 > 0 \tag{2}$$

In equation (1), investment in D is an *increasing* function of both the current stock of undeveloped assets, K, and the portion of the labor force, $L - \xi$, engaged in its production—thus a *decreasing* function of the portion, ξ, creating new assets. In (2), investment in new undeveloped assets may be increasing in the existing stock of these assets and it is *increasing* in the part of the labor force producing additional capital.[52]

The latter model of growth puts people with new ideas into innovation but does not incorporate the possibly shifting values that lie behind the desires to imagine and create new products, just as the Solow model omits any shifting values governing efforts to make discoveries and achieve scientific advances.

Overview of the Chapters

Raicho Bojilov, Gylfi Zoega, and Hian Teck Hoon

Part I: Estimating Innovation—Across Time and across Nations

The first part of the book has three chapters in which the rate of innovation in different countries is estimated and a distinction is made between indigenous and Schumpeterian innovation. Chapter 1 examines recent calculations of the time series of total factor productivity drawn from historical data by the Banque de France, Chapter 2 studies the transmission of innovations between countries, and Chapter 3 focuses on innovation and its transmission during the period of the IT revolution.

Chapter 1: Innovation: The Source of Rapid Growth

This first chapter presents the data used throughout the book in a cross-country comparison of productivity and innovation. The results of the analysis are a set of stylized facts that motivate the rest of our analysis:

- There is a global slowdown in total factor productivity (TFP) growth after the early 1970s with rates close to zero after 2005–2006. The empirical evidence points to a decline in innovation.
- The TFP growth rates of the US and the UK, in particular, recovered only partially during the 1990s and the 2000s, in comparison with the 1930s, 1950s, and 1960s. Thus, the innovations in the IT industry

appear to have failed to lift aggregate innovation and, in turn, TFP growth even in the US or the UK.

- A sizeable proportion of the growth in gross domestic product per capita across countries can be accounted for by TFP growth and, therefore, innovation. This is especially the case for the earlier periods before WWI, the interwar years, and the post-WWII recovery period.
- At the same time, much of the TFP growth is due to catching up with the best practices in the world.
- Countries differ significantly in their ability to catch up with the best practices in the world.
- Early on, the UK was the global TFP leader, but the US managed to catch up and overtake the UK by the early 1930s. With time, a pluralism of innovation leaders emerged.
- Since no country can become a leader only by following, any theoretical or empirical exercise on the data needs to allow for the existence of multiple centers of innovation in the world.

Chapter 2: Sources of Indigenous Innovation and Channels of Its Transmission across Countries

In the early 20th century, there were at least two countries, the UK and the US, that were generating innovation, which afterward spread around the world. Yet most existing empirical analysis of macro- and industry-level productivity trends assume away the possibility of multiple innovation centers.

We propose a general framework for the study of the propagation of innovation (or TFP shocks) through the world and its evolution over time. We then apply the framework to the data and present the empirical results.

We distinguish between the adoption of innovation originating and imported from abroad and indigenous innovation, which is innovation generated by a given country on its own. Our distinction, therefore, allows us to narrow down our focus on the part of TFP in each country that cannot be traced back to innovation somewhere else.

Our results show that before WWII there was no dominant global leader in innovation. In the years before WWI, the main generators of indigenous innovation were the UK, the US, France, and to a lesser extent Germany. In contrast, during the interwar years, indigenous innovation originated mainly from the US and France. The results for continental Europe support the hypothesis that, in the 30 years after the end of WWII, war-torn Europe caught up very successfully and quickly with the technological leader at the time, the US.

Our key contribution in this context is the qualification that the observed rapid TFP growth in continental Europe in the period 1945–1972 is primarily due to catching up to the world technological frontier rather than indigenous innovation.

The estimates present evidence for a global slowdown in TFP growth by almost 2 percent in the period 1972–2011 relative to the preceding period, 1950–1972. After an initial sharp decline during the 1970s, indigenous innovation made a partial recovery in the US, the UK, and, especially, the Scandinavian countries. The decline in indigenous innovation was particularly dramatic in continental Europe, where it never recovered after the initial drop in the 1970s and the 1980s. A striking result, which justifies our emphasis on indigenous innovation, is that the exogenous innovation attributed to scientific discoveries is not of major quantitative importance.

Chapter 3: Indigenous Innovation during the IT Revolution

This chapter focuses on indigenous innovation and, in turn, productivity growth over the period of the IT revolution. First, we compare the average growth rate of indigenous innovation for the period across countries and then examine the country-specific dynamics for the US, the UK, France, Germany, and Japan. Our results show that there has been no structural change in the transmission network for the period after 1990 relative to the preceding post-WWII decades. Moreover, we see that the annual rates of indigenous innovation in the US and the UK have made only a partial recovery during the IT revolution: while higher than the rates for the period 1970–1990, they are still lower relative to the rates witnessed in the postwar years until the late 1960s. Also, our estimates show that the continental European economies and Japan have not experienced even such a moderate recovery. Interestingly, we find that unlike in the glorious 30 years after WWII, these economies have been rather slow in adopting the (IT) innovations originating in the US and the UK.

Part II: The Roots and Benefits of Innovation

This part has four chapters on the roots of innovation in the system of values found in each country and the benefits measured in terms of job satisfaction and labor force participation. Chapter 4 is a case study of successful innovators in Iceland. The objective of the interviews with these innovators is to establish a set of their shared values. In Chapters 5 and 6, we try to relate these values and innovation in a cross section of countries to test the hypothesis that nations that share these values turn out to be innovative. The last chapter in this section, Chapter 7, shows the effect of innovation on job satisfaction and labor force participation.

Chapter 4: A Case Study of Iceland's Successful Innovators

In this chapter, we establish a common set of values and attitudes that characterize the founders of four successful innovating companies. Each company is founded on the basis of an indigenous innovation, not merely the application of new technology. The values detected and determined are then used in subsequent studies on the relationship between values and innovation at the national level.

We interviewed the innovators in order to establish a set of personal and cultural traits that are conducive to innovation. We can summarize them as follows.

- Innovators like the rewarding nature of work, have an interest in working in a highly creative industry, and value financial independence.
- Innovators tend to like uncertainty in the Knightian sense.
- They are able to accept failure and not take it too much to heart.
- Simple laws and regulations—a lack of red tape—help innovating firms, as does easy access to financing and funds.
- A flat organizational structure where employees are not afraid of saying what they think to their bosses is essential for a successful company.
- Another key factor is trust in business relationships.
- It's advantageous to innovate for the world market rather than starting with the home market.
- A culture that is forgiving of failure and appreciative of risk-taking encourages innovation.
- A welfare state—free education and healthcare—may be helpful in protecting an innovator's family from the financial consequences of failure.

Chapter 5: The Force of Values

This chapter studies the relation between values, institutions, and innovation for 20 OECD countries.

We employ the method of canonical correlations to map the relationship between values and innovation. The method makes sense of the cross-covariance matrices of two multidimensional variables. To perform the canonical correlation, we gather together some observed measures into two different variable sets, X and Y, which represent the two multidimensional components of the latent variables, henceforth known as the canonical variables X and Y. The variable X is our measure of values, and the variable Y is our measure of innovation.

Next, we assign weights to the variables within X and Y in order to create two linear combinations, X^* and Y^*, one for each variable set, which maximize the bivariate correlation between the canonical variables. The set of linear combinations, called canonical functions, is chosen to maximize the canonical correlation between the two latent canonical variables X^* and Y^*. Several uncorrelated components or functions can be determined, as in principal components analysis.

We find a strong relationship between a latent variable that captures both values and institutions, on the one hand, and a latent variable measuring economic performance, on the other hand. In particular, we find that trust, the willingness to take the initiative, the desire to achieve on the job, teaching children to be independent, and the acceptance of competition contribute positively to economic performance. Teaching children to be obedient may, in contrast, reduce economic performance. A measure of economic freedom—that captures the paucity of regulations in goods, capital, and labor markets—is positively related to performance. Economic performance is measured by indigenous TFP growth, imported TFP growth, job satisfaction, male labor force participation, and employment. Fertility is also included in this variable as a measure of optimism about the future.

Chapter 6: Individual Values, Entrepreneurship, and Innovation

In this chapter, we relate the annual average growth rates of TFP for the period 1993–2013 for a set of developed economies to an index of modernism, and we find a strong positive correlation between our measure of modernism and economic performance as measured by TFP growth. Naturally, this hardly constitutes a proof of causality, although our empirical strategy is designed to address some of the obvious concerns about endogeneity and reversed causality.

As a first step, we consider individual-level data from a set of developed economies on beliefs, attitudes, and social norms about economic life, which come from the second wave of the World Values Survey. Using these data, we design an index of modernism and an index of traditionalism. Next, we relate the indexes to the annual average TFP growth rates, and to indigenous and imported innovation for our set of developed economies. We document a strong positive association between our index of modernism and our measures of productivity growth and innovation.

Chapter 7: Innovation, Job Satisfaction, and Performance in Western European Countries

This chapter is about the consequences of low rates of innovation in a sample of 16 European countries. In particular, we study the relationship between these low rates of job satisfaction and the labor force participation of men. Job satisfaction has fallen in the EU over this period, as has the labor force participation of men.

We have found that low levels of indigenous innovation are accompanied by low and falling levels of job satisfaction, falling male labor force participation, and less measured happiness.

In a sample that also includes some non-European countries, we find that performance—measured by the rate of indigenous and transmitted innovation, TFP, and the proportion declaring themselves to be very happy—is lower in the continental European countries than in the United States, the UK, Sweden, the Netherlands, Australia, Canada, and Finland.

We conclude that low levels of innovation may be adversely affecting the level of job satisfaction and happiness in many European countries.

Part III: Two Applications of Robots

In this last part of the book, the focus is turned to the introduction of robots into the labor force. We distinguish between robots that replace humans and robots that augment their productivity, then compare and contrast the effects of these two applications on wages and employment. We also compare the effects of robots when capital is constant and when it moves slowly over time. Finally, we explore the effect of robots on the rate of innovation.

Chapter 8: Growth Effects of Additive and Multiplicative Robots alongside Conventional Machines

We address the issue of how to model both the creation and the effects of robots in the context of the neoclassical growth model. Our approach is to model capital as malleable and flexible in its use either as conventional machines—that is, as traditional capital—or as robots. Given its malleability, the current stock of conventional machines can be retrofitted to function as robots once the robotic technology is available. We model two types of robots: additive and multiplicative.

Additive robots can perform the same functions as a human worker and, thus, are perfectly substitutable for a human worker. Denoting the quantity of additive robots by R_A and human labor by H, the total labor force (both robotic and human) is equal to $R_A + H$. The development of artificial intelligence and machine learning has also produced a second kind of robot, which we call multiplicative, that can be described as augmenting labor power. Such AI-enabled robots, or "multiplicative robots," are denoted by R_M. With the introduction of multiplicative robots, total (robotic and human) labor is given by $(1 + R_M)H$.

With the creation of additive robots, we obtain the stark result that real wages are permanently depressed and the (human) labor share of national income asymptotically tends toward zero, although total (human and robotic) labor share of national income tends toward a positive constant. In contrast, we find that with the arrival of multiplicative robots, while the immediate impact is to cause the stock of conventional machines to fall when it is profitable to adopt robots, the real wage need not fall because of an offsetting labor-augmenting effect coming from the multiplicative nature of the robot. The real wage, even if it drops initially, continues to steadily increase along a balanced-growth path as nonhuman wealth grows even in the absence of steady technological progress. The (human) labor share in national income is also a positive constant in the long run.

Chapter 9: Wage Effects of Additive and Multiplicative Robots alongside Factory Buildings and Physical Structures

In contrast to the assumption of Chapter 8 that conventional machines can be instantaneously retrofitted to function as additive or multiplicative robots, this chapter assumes that the cooperating factor is a slow-adjusting asset like factory buildings and physical structures that take time to build. The adjustment cost of such investments is large. We discover that the adoption of robots leads to the stimulation of investment in slow-adjusting nonmalleable capital that complements total human and robotic labor. Such complementary investment, we show, exerts an upward pull on wage levels.

When additive robots are introduced, we show that when it is profitable for firms to adopt the robots in the production process, the real wage gradually declines to reach a permanently lower level even as the price of physical structures jumps up and gradually increases to reach a permanently higher level. Thus, this polar case of additive robots confirms the fear people have that the introduction of robots hurts workers' wage earnings and enriches the owners of nonhuman wealth. In the long run, however, the stock of factory buildings and physical structures increases, thus restoring the real wage.

However, when multiplicative robots are introduced in the other polar case, we show that there are two offsetting effects with a fixed stock of factory buildings and physical structures: a factor-intensity effect (with more effective labor working on a fixed supply of physical structures in the short run), which tends to reduce wages, and a labor-augmenting effect (with multiplicative robots making each worker more effective), which raises hourly pay. We establish the result that if the share of factory buildings and physical structures is less than the elasticity of substitution between physical structures and effective labor, then introducing robots must raise the whole path of real wages. In the long run, the growth of real wages is further propelled by the accumulation of capital taking the form of factory buildings and physical structures.

Chapter 10: Additive Robots, Relative Prices, and Indigenous Innovation

In a two-sector model, we formalize the idea that when an influx of additive robots in the capital goods industry causes the relative price of the capital good to fall, economic incentives are created to make indigenous innovation in the consumer goods sector more profitable. This causes some workers in the economy to shift from participating in production to participating in innovative activity. Consequently, the new wage path must be ultimately rising, as long as innovation in the consumer goods industries continues undiminished, exerting its upward pull on wage rates.

We set up a two-sector model with the characteristic that there is a sector that uses only human labor to produce a capital good before the creation of robots. The capital good is used to produce a pure consumption good. With zero technological progress and zero population growth, the model exhibits a stationary equilibrium with constant wages, consumption per capita, constant relative price of the capital good, and constant stock of conventional machines. With the creation of additive robots, we obtain the result that capital accumulation is stimulated, consumption per capita grows, and the real wage declines to a permanently lower level as the relative price of the capital good permanently declines to a lower level.

We also study a two-sector model where the consumption goods sector produces a good derived from conventional machines working along with a continuum of intermediate inputs produced by imperfectly competitive firms that also use conventional machines as inputs. Indigenous innovation takes the form of improving the quality of these intermediate inputs. We derive two main results: (1) a drop in the relative price of the capital good stimulates indigenous innovation, which acts to boost real wages; and (2) the creation of additive robots spurs investment in conventional machines, which also stimulates indigenous innovation. Thus, once we depart from the first two-sector model to allow for indigenous innovation that raises the productivity of the consumption goods sector, the arrival of additive robots is good for wage growth.

I

ESTIMATING INNOVATION—
ACROSS TIME AND ACROSS NATIONS

1

Innovation

The Source of Rapid Growth

Raicho Bojilov

ABSTRACT This chapter establishes productivity growth and, in turn, innovation as major, if not the most important, sources of growth in gross domestic product (GDP) per capita in the long run. We review the historical development of the main concepts in the study of economic growth and highlight the central role of innovation, along with the difficulties in the measurement of productivity growth on an aggregate level. It turns out that standard economic analysis is ill suited to the study of innovation. We review how our work relates to the only recently emerging literatures on institutions and on economic culture. The chapter concludes with a review of our data sources and a descriptive analysis that leads to a list of stylized facts that motivates the rest of our work.

Introduction

Economists have consistently found that more than 50 percent of economic growth in developed economies cannot be accounted for by accumulation of production inputs, such as labor and capital. Similarly, they have found that between 40 and 60 percent of growth in output per worker across industries in developed economies, the US in particular, has been driven by growth in total factor productivity (TFP), which is defined as the portion of output not explained by the amount of inputs used in production. Thus, much of the observed economic growth cannot be traced back to easily measured and understood forces. Yet persistent differences in TFP are crucial to explaining the observed persistent differences in economic performance.

In this chapter, we provide a brief review of basic growth accounting and then relate our work to the existing literature. In this way, we hope to highlight the main issues that are at stake in our research investigation, in particular the advantages and disadvantages of using aggregate TFP data. Then, we present the data that we use in our cross-country comparison of productivity and innovation. We conclude with a set of stylized facts that motivate the rest of our analysis.

In more detail, a sizeable proportion of the growth in GDP per capita across countries can be accounted for by TFP growth and, therefore, innovation. We find evidence for a decline in productivity across the developed economies after the early 1970s. This trend was only partially mitigated by the IT revolution. Thus, the innovations in the IT industry appear to have failed to lift the aggregate innovation and, in turn, TFP growth even in the US. Also, much of the TFP growth in the first decades after WWII is due to catching up with the best practices in the world, and countries differ significantly in their ability to catch up. Finally, with the help of long TFP series, we show that early on, the UK was the global TFP leader, but the US managed to catch up and overtake the UK by the early 1930s. Since no country can become a leader only by following, any theoretical or empirical exercise on the data needs to allow for the existence of multiple centers of innovation in the world.

1. The Black Box

In 1927, Paul Douglas and Charles Cobb proposed a functional form that captures the salient features of the observed relation between capital, labor, and aggregate output measured as GDP in the US.[1] The two Americans have observed that, over the years, the shares of total output that went to labor and capital remained virtually the same, and they developed a mathematical expression that captured that defining feature of the American macroeconomic life. Their formulation was analytically very useful and yet remarkably simple:

$$Y_t = A_t K_t^{\beta} L_t^{1-\beta},$$

where Y_t stands for output in year t, A_t for overall technological level in year t, K_t for capital in year t, and L for labor in year t. The power represents the share of total output that goes to capital, and the compliment 1 represents the share of total output in the economy that goes to labor as compensation. The overall technological level A_t is known in economic jargon as TFP or multifactor productivity. Of all the ingredients in the formula, TFP is the most mysterious and most intangible one: as the residual in a growth regression, it stands for little more than the ignorance of economists. Nevertheless, there is a general agreement that innovations contribute to the increase in A_t: despite a number of subsequent variations, this formulation has remained a benchmark in the analysis of economic growth not only in the US but across the world.

This benchmark formulation can help us perform a useful exercise in growth accounting. We take the natural logarithm of the formula and obtain:

$$ln(Y_t) = ln(A_t) + \beta ln(K_t) + (1 - \beta)ln(L_t).$$

Taking differences over time, we obtain that, approximately, the growth in output from year to year t is captured by the following expression:

$$g_t^Y = g_t^A + \beta g_t^K + (1 - \beta)g_t^L,$$

where g_t^Y is the growth in total output, g_t^A the growth in the overall technological level, g_t^K the growth in capital, and g_t^L the growth in labor. With the help of national statistics, economists usually have no problem obtaining reasonably accurate measures of output, capital, and workers over time. The one thing that remains unobservable, however, is TFP, A_t. Nevertheless, assuming that they have postulated the correct functional relation between all the ingredients, economists may be able to obtain an estimate of A_t as the residual from a regression of output Y_t on K_t and L_t: through a similar procedure, we can obtain g_t^A as the residual from a growth regression.

The estimated measures of TFP and TFP growth have many limitations. One of them is that these estimated measures do not have natural or meaningful units. Another, more serious limitation is that as residuals from a regression, they capture everything that economists simply cannot measure and explain. Thus, TFP is a black box whose ingredients and inner workings by construction remain hard, if not impossible, to study. Perhaps, to show that the students of the dismal science do have a sense of humor after all, many economists refer to TFP as the Solow residual.

As a consequence, economists have a hard time measuring in the aggregate the level and growth of innovation in an economy. They only know that innovation is one of the ingredients in TFP and that the estimated TFP is an upper bound for the level of innovation. Worse still, the growth literature starting with Barro and Sala-i-Martin (1992) has consistently documented that, for both developed and developing economies, changes in labor and capital in standard growth regressions cannot explain between 40 and 60 percent of observed output growth.[2] In other words, 40 to 60 percent (and sometimes even more) of output growth falls under the category of the Solow residual, or more euphemistically TFP. It turns out that the ignorance of economists is consistently high.

This brief discussion shows that there are challenges to our study of innovation and its dynamics that are rooted deep in standard economic theory. Until recently, economists entertained a rather mechanistic view of the macroeconomy: the elements of economic activity—the growth of TFP, the volume of business investment, employment level, and job satisfaction—are all regarded as determined from initial conditions known as the "state of the economy." Standard models are built to elucidate the mechanics of this determination. On the microeconomic side, the individual is not seen as having a positive role to play either. The standard models of a market economy view the individual participant in the economy as essentially robotic—as if programmed to calculate correct reactions to data, such as prices. Given such a framework, standard economic theory is unable to say anything interesting about innovation, a rather central element of economic life, except for an upper bound on its magnitude. Recent poor economic performance in both Europe and the US has, however, enticed many economists to look beyond the standard tool kit acquired at university. We hope to contribute to this line of research.

We take as given the estimated TFP series for a set of developed economies and study the transmission of TFP shocks across countries and over time. Then we investigate how differences in the defining features of the dynamics of TFP shocks, presumably proxies for innovation shocks, relate to differences in beliefs and attitudes about economic life across countries. Before we delve into our analysis of these issues, we first review the related work, present the data that we use in our empirical work, and summarize the stylized facts that emerge from a simple descriptive analysis of these data.

2. Related Work

Apart from the broad understanding that TFP is related to innovation, economists have only a few insights to offer on its sources and the laws that govern its dynamics. Nelson and Phelps (1966), followed more recently by Aghion and Howitt (1992) and Aghion, Howitt, and Murtin (2011), have made some advances in the understanding of the statistical structure of TFP growth.[3] Intuitively, they define a frontier of best production practices and stipulate that productivity growth in a country, measured by TFP growth, is increasing in the distance between the country's own technological level and the best practices in the world. Other related research includes Amador and Coimbra (2007), Barro (1991), Baumol (1986), Lucas (1988), Romer (1986, 1990), and Sala-i-Martin (1997).[4] Our work follows in the same research tradition, but it departs from the existing literature in several important respects.

We consider a generalized Aghion-Nelson-Phelps framework, which allows us to decompose TFP growth in each country into two components. The first one is the familiar imported innovation, associated with catching up to the best practices in the world. The second component is indigenous innovation, which originates in the country itself and pushes both the best-practice frontier of the country and the world as a whole. Our specification allows us to investigate several issues, from which previous research has abstracted away. First and foremost, we allow each country to generate innovation, which pushes the worldwide technological frontier. Second, we allow innovation to spread across countries at different speeds, depending on the strength of the transmission mechanism between two countries. Consequently, the speed at which an innovation is adopted across the world may depend on the country from which the innovation originates. Third, these generalizations allow us to map out how innovation shocks propagate across the world.

The limitations of aggregate TFP data have stimulated many researchers to use micro-level data to study innovation. Acemoglu, Akcigit, and Kerr (2016) use patent data of 1975–2010 to measure the network of citations across fields, and they find that the growth in the number of patents in a field leads to future innovation in linked fields.[5] Akcigit, Grisby, and Nicholas (2017) show that based on patent data between 1880 and 1940, more geographically connected states are more inventive.[6] Furthermore, based on citation data, Mohnen and Belderbos (2013) describe matrices of intersectoral and international spillover weights in order to study and evaluate the Europe-wide impact of R&D policies.[7] Moser, Voena, and Waldinger

(2014) show that fields with more immigrants experienced faster growth, based on historical citation data of 1880–1940 and 1920–1970.[8]

The recent studies using microlevel data make very important contributions, but the measures used, in particular patents, have their own problems and only provide partial understanding of innovation. For example, the innovations and productivity growth due to the use of patented products after purchase are not measured by patents. Also, industrial secrets are innovations that are not patented. Often, particularly in the past, innovations, such as the internet, were not patented, but they did have a huge positive impact on productivity. In other cases, patents were used to preclude the entry of potential competitors, which is the case with the US patent on airplanes given to the Wright brothers: as a result, the US had to purchase and use French and British airplanes during WWI despite being the country where the modern airplane was first developed. In fact, it was France and then the UK that pioneered commercial rights, rather than the US, precisely because of long judicial battles related to patent rights. Turnover of firms and products also has similar advantages and disadvantages.

We are not dismissing any prior research based on concrete measures of innovation or downgrading its usefulness. In our work, we just follow an alternative route that starts with representative aggregate measures and analyzes their statistical properties across countries and over time. In fact, we regard work on concrete measures of innovation as complementary to our approach rather than as a substitute. Our choice of methodology, factor analysis or spatial econometrics, is predetermined by our choice to investigate the dynamics of TFP measures. There is no universal measure of innovation, and all existing candidates have their pros and cons, depending on the investigated context. We advance a research agenda that aims at exploring the dynamics and spatial dependence of TFP, one of the existing measures, across countries and time to investigate how the dynamics of innovation has changed on a national level.

Our research project is also related to the endogenous growth literature and some recent advances in the study of innovation and automation. The task-based model of Zeira (1998) provides an early simple but elegant way to model automation.[9] The specification model that we consider borrows heavily from Zeira's framework. One important rationale for doing so is that the observed patterns by Kaldor (1961) of stable growth rates and capital shares do not appear to hold any longer in recent decades.[10] Recent important contributions to this expanding literature include Peretto and Seater (2013), Hémous and Olsen (2016), and Aghion, Jones, and Jones (2017).[11] The last two consider a constant elasticity of substitution rather than the Cobb-Douglas technology used by Zeira (1998).[12] In addition to discussing the different ways automation can be introduced in endogenous growth models and the related characterization of the steady states of the economy, these papers also consider the implications of their framework for income inequality between high-skilled and low-skilled workers. Our theoretical and empirical work reexamines the issues highlighted by Baumol (1967), who observed that rapid productivity growth in some sectors relative to others could result in a "cost disease" in which the slow-growing sectors become increasingly important in the economy.[13]

One popular alternative general equilibrium framework posits that the economic institutions in the capital, labor, and product markets have significant effects on the functioning and the performance of the economy. The most important and influential contributions to this literature are Acemoglu, Johnson, and Robinson (2001) and the related subsequent works, including Acemoglu and Robinson (2012).[14] Earlier, Kydland and Prescott (1990) provide a set of stylized facts suggesting a negative relation between taxation on employment and participation.[15] Hoon and Phelps (1997) show that in a closed economy, a shift to increased payroll taxation raises the natural rate of unemployment under some specifications.[16] Yet Hoon and Phelps point out that in a small open economy, in which the interest rate is given by the world rate, the tax shift is neutral for employment. This framework draws strength from plentiful evidence that the economies that have suffered low economic performance since the early 1990s (until 2008 at any rate) happened to be those that had adopted institutions understood to be "bad," such as excessive regulation of labor markets, red tape, controls on capital and trade rows, and so on. For example, Prescott (2004) compares the tax system and government transfers in the US and the EU and relates these differences to the differences in their economic performance.[17] Aghion and Howitt (1998, 2006) provide a more detailed overview of the related literature.[18]

Our approach is related to this strand in the literature and yet differs in two key aspects. First, we attempt to relate the characteristics of an economy to individual attitudes and beliefs. Second, we focus on the conditions for innovation and the proclivity to innovate rather than on protection of property rights, excessive regulation, and the like. The difference may appear subtle at first sight, but it is quite substantial, as will be seen later. The theory of dynamism employed here and introduced in Phelps (2013) builds on the insights of David Hume, Henri Bergson, Friedrich Hayek, and Michael Polanyi.[19] Every individual, Hayek says, has some knowledge called "know-how," which is practical, concrete.[20] It is often inexplicable in formal scientific terms—that is, "personal knowledge." Such knowledge develops on the borderline of the known and the unknown. Bergson (1911) argues that this knowledge is the driving force behind any action, the force of life itself.[21] Thus, in a suitably structured economy, new commercial ideas may emerge as the actors combine their Hayekian know-how with their Humean imagination.

3. Data and Descriptive Analysis

We use data on GDP per capital, TFP, and labor productivity that are generously provided by Bergeaud, Cette, and Lecat (2016), who belong to the research division at Banque de France.[22] Briefly, Bergeaud, Cette, and Lecat (2016) have tried to follow as closely as possible the methodology used to construct the Penn World Tables in order to extend the time series of GDP per capita and TFP as much as possible in the past.[23] Their paper provides a detailed discussion of the related methodology. GDP per capita, labor productivity, and the TFP index are computed for 13 developed countries: Australia, Canada, Finland, France, Germany, Italy, Japan, the Netherlands, Norway, Spain, Sweden, the United Kingdom, and the United States. The data sources from which the productivity indexes are computed are historical and national accounts series, which allows for international comparisons (for example, Maddison 2003).[24] The data are annual and most of them cover the period 1870–2014. The computation of the TFP index relies on three basic series: GDP, labor, and capital. Regarding labor, Bergeaud, Cette, and Lecat (2016) need data on total employment and working time.[25] The capital indicator is constructed by the permanent inventory method applied to each of the two corresponding investment data sets (IE and IB). For this, as much as possible, very long-term information on investment is used. As in Cette, Kocoglu, and Mairesse (2009), the depreciation rates used to build the capital series are 10.0 percent for equipment and 2.5 percent for buildings.[26]

We start with an overview of the main trends in GDP per capita across major developed economies. Figure 1.1 plots the evolution of GDP per capita in the US, the UK, France, Germany, and Japan. It shows that by the beginning of WWI, the US managed to catch up with the UK and the two countries continued to have similar levels of GDP per capita during the interwar period. However, during and after WWII, the growth in US GDP per capita accelerated markedly, which led to a divergence in the paths of the US and the UK. The UK consistently had lower growth rates than the US during the 1960s and the 1970s, and started to converge back to the level of GDP per capita of the US only in the 1990s. Still, the UK achieved only partial convergence. Indeed, the most striking feature of Figure 1.1 is

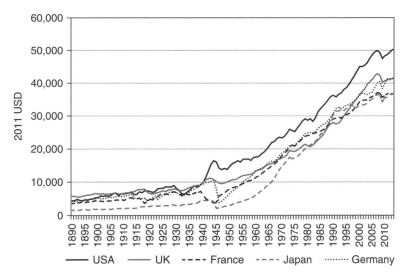

Figure 1.1. Comparison of GDP per capita in France, Germany, Japan, the UK, and the US. *Data source:* Banque de France.

that despite periods of very rapid economic growth, no main economy managed to converge to the US level of GDP per capita during the whole period under investigation. Obviously, the two world wars must be held accountable for some of the differences, but the lack of full convergence even after 60 to 70 years of relative global peace is puzzling.

Next, Figure 1.2 plots the evolution of the corresponding TFP index for the same set of countries. It shows that the US managed to catch up with the UK in terms of TFP only in the 1930s. Moreover, the figure reveals that the main continental European economies converged toward the US in terms of TFP during the whole postwar period, especially during the 1950s and the 1960s. However, the paths of the US and the UK, on one hand, and the paths of France and Germany, on the other, started diverging again after the mid-1990s. Interestingly, Figure 1.2 reveals that most of the spectacular growth in Japanese GDP per capita should be traced back to capital accumulation rather than increase in TFP and, thus, innovation.

Figure 1.3 presents the long-run relation between the cumulative growth of GDP per capita and the cumulative growth of TFP in the US. It reveals that until the mid-1960s the two growth rates shadowed each other closely and were of approximately the same magnitude. After that, GDP per capita grew at a much faster rate than TFP. In fact, we can notice that in the late 1960s and the 1970s, TFP growth actually slowed down. Nevertheless, after the mid-1980s, TFP growth picked up again, but interestingly it

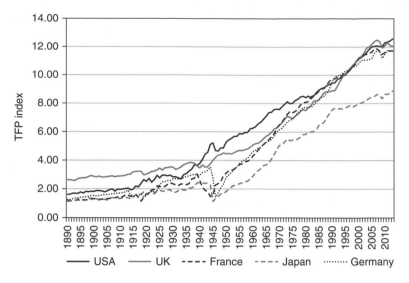

Figure 1.2. Comparison of the levels of the TFP index for France, Germany, Japan, the UK, and the US. *Data source:* Banque de France.

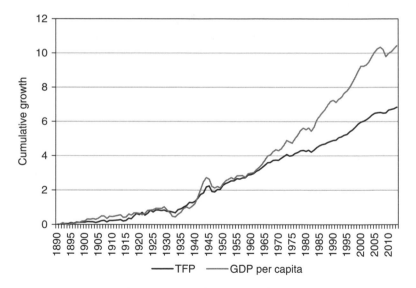

Figure 1.3. Comparison between growth in TFP and growth in GDP per capita for the US. *Data source:* Banque de France.

recovered only partially compared with its performance in the 1950s and the 1960s. The most surprising takeaway from Figure 1.3 is that the best US decades in terms of TFP growth were the 1930s and the 1940s.

The fact that the growth of GDP per capita in the US was higher than the associated TFP growth may be partially accounted for by, for example, the increased contribution of human capital to economic growth. Still, Figure 1.3 captures a key troubling development that we investigate further in the subsequent chapters: TFP growth has slowed down in both absolute and relative terms. Since innovation is incorporated in TFP, the observed dynamics raises the troubling prospect that innovation has actually slowed down since the mid-1960s. Moreover, and somewhat surprisingly, there is no evidence that the IT revolution has caused an unprecedented acceleration in aggregate innovation since the late 1980s. Actually, we record only a moderate recovery to growth rates in TFP that are just below their counterparts for the 1950s and the 1960s and much below the record levels of the late 1930s and 1940s.

Figure 1.4 shows that the slowdown in TFP growth is not a peculiar US phenomenon but rather a global trend in the last 40 to 50 years. It plots the cumulative TFP growth for the US, France, Germany, Japan, and the UK. All five economies experienced an overall slowdown in TFP growth after the early 1970s, with the possible exception of the UK. The UK in fact managed to accelerate its TFP growth for a brief period in the late

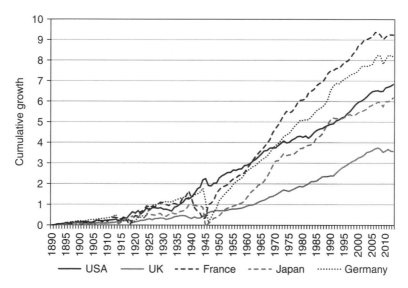

Figure 1.4. Cumulative growth in TFP in France, Germany, Japan, the UK, and the US since 1890. *Data source:* Banque de France.

Table 1.1. Cumulative growth in TFP before WWI, during the interwar years, during the recovery post-WWII, during the post–oil shock decades, and during the IT revolution

Country	Before 1914	1919– 1939	1950– 1970	1970– 1990	1990– 2010	1970– 2013
Canada	0.313	0.228	0.388	0.137	0.160	0.164
Germany	0.240	1.096	1.219	0.554	0.199	0.219
France	0.291	1.166	1.102	0.494	0.194	0.206
Great Britain	0.150	0.216	0.452	0.378	0.355	0.352
Italy	0.200	0.299	1.188	0.382	0.031	0.007
Japan	0.063	0.365	1.810	0.492	0.144	0.174
Sweden	0.604	0.669	0.657	0.198	0.371	0.384
USA	0.201	0.381	0.446	0.243	0.302	0.330

Data source: Banque de France.

1980s and the 1990s to levels that were comparable to the growth rate in the US during the same period. Overall, it seems that the US and the UK fared better than the rest of the lot during the 1990s and the 2000s, as they managed to achieve TFP growth rates that are higher than those of the 1970s and yet a bit lower than those of the 1950s and the 1960s. Most strikingly, TFP growth almost completely vanished in all five economies after 2005–2006. The results for the last 10 years, even preceding the Great Recession, are particularly worrying, since they suggest the drying up of aggregate innovation within each of those developed economies.

Tables 1.1 and 1.2 cut the same data differently. They report the cumulative growth of TFP and GDP per capita, respectively, for a slightly larger set of countries over five well-defined historical periods: the 20 years just before WWI, the interwar years from 1919 to 1939, the post-WWII recovery covering the years from 1950 to 1970, the period of the oil shocks from 1970 to 1990, and the time of the IT revolution from 1990 to 2010. The fact that each period amounts to 20 years allows us to compare growth rates meaningfully.

Tables 1.2 and 1.3 show that the US, as well as all other main economies, experienced its highest rates of growth in GDP per capita and labor productivity, correspondingly, during the "glorious" 30 or 40 years after the end of WWII. Table 1.1 confirms that much of the increase in GDP per capita can be traced back to rapid TFP growth. Furthermore, it highlights that after the end of WWII, all countries experienced their highest TFP growth rates during the 1950s and the 1960s. The table also reveals that most continental European countries actually witnessed higher TFP growth during the period 1970–1990 than during the subsequent decades. Interestingly, even the US, the UK, and Sweden recorded total TFP growth in

Table 1.2. Cumulative growth in GDP per capita before WWI, during the interwar years, during the recovery post-WWII, during the post–oil shock decades, and during the IT revolution

Country	Before 1914	1919– 1939	1950– 1970	1970– 1990	1990– 2010	1970– 2013
Canada	0.692	0.186	0.653	0.507	0.308	0.346
Germany	0.260	1.090	1.792	0.650	0.292	0.339
France	0.362	0.705	1.268	0.623	0.244	0.259
Great Britain	0.229	0.286	0.661	0.619	0.457	0.484
Italy	0.284	0.411	1.958	0.745	0.152	0.096
Japan	0.311	0.541	3.972	1.044	0.170	0.208
Sweden	0.752	0.953	0.913	0.417	0.388	0.409
USA	0.415	0.239	0.581	0.554	0.333	0.387

Data source: Banque de France.

Table 1.3. Cumulative growth in labor productivity before WWI, during the interwar years, during the recovery post-WWII, during the post–oil shock decades, and during the IT revolution

Country	Before 1914	1919– 1939	1950– 1970	1970– 1990	1990– 2010	1970– 2013
Canada	0.591	0.208	0.664	0.311	0.297	0.315
Germany	0.407	1.192	2.036	1.012	0.419	0.394
France	0.466	1.571	1.622	0.985	0.395	0.395
Great Britain	0.211	0.360	0.830	0.677	0.594	0.580
Italy	0.336	0.495	2.288	0.776	0.186	0.165
Japan	0.574	0.726	3.202	1.277	0.507	0.465
Sweden	0.904	0.828	1.258	0.416	0.482	0.502
USA	0.385	0.556	0.628	0.338	0.489	0.498

Data source: Banque de France.

the 1990s and the 2000s that was still substantially lower than the TFP growth for the period of post-WWII recovery. The other interesting aspect of the data is that most countries experienced much higher TFP growth rates during the postwar recovery than the US. Yet it seems that the smaller the gap with the US TFP level, the slower the TFP growth rate became.

We investigate this hypothesis further by plotting the average TFP growth rate for each period against the gap between the corresponding country and the country with the highest TFP level at the beginning of the period. The results are plotted on Figures 1.5–1.9. We add to each plot a simple regression line, along with the associated regression equation and the goodness of fit. The results show that during all investigated periods, there

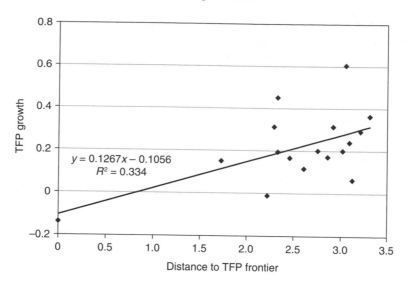

Figure 1.5. Relation between TFP growth and the distance to TFP frontier, pre-WWI period. *Note:* Distance to TFP frontier is defined as the difference between the highest TFP level in the world and the TFP level of each country. *Data source:* Banque de France.

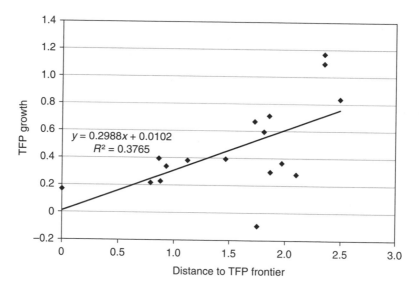

Figure 1.6. Relation between TFP growth and the distance to TFP frontier, interwar period. *Note:* Distance to TFP frontier is defined as the difference between the highest TFP level in the world and the TFP level of each country. *Data source:* Banque de France.

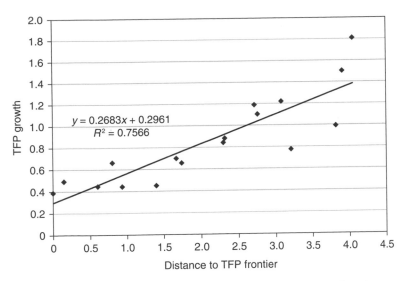

Figure 1.7. Relation between TFP growth and the distance to TFP frontier, post-WWII recovery period. *Note:* Distance to TFP frontier is defined as the difference between the highest TFP level in the world and the TFP level of each country. *Data source:* Banque de France.

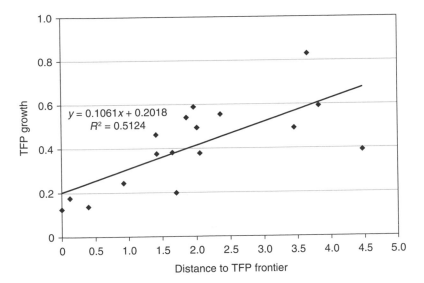

Figure 1.8. Relation between TFP growth and the distance to TFP frontier, post–oil shock period. *Note:* Distance to TFP frontier is defined as the difference between the highest TFP level in the world and the TFP level of each country. *Data source:* Banque de France.

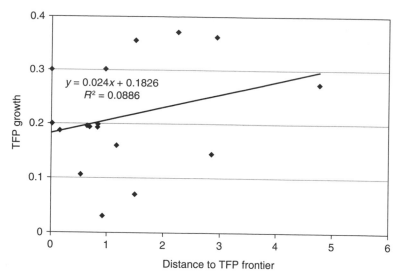

Figure 1.9. Relation between TFP growth and the distance to TFP frontier, IT revolution period. *Note:* Distance to TFP frontier is defined as the difference between the highest TFP level in the world and the TFP level of each country. *Data source:* Banque de France.

is a positive relation between the distance to TFP frontier and TFP growth. Thus, this simple regression analysis suggests strongly that catching up to the best world practices is a major reason for the robust growth in TFP and GDP per capita after WWII. Nevertheless, the plots also reveal curious differences across periods. In particular, we find that the catching-up hypothesis seems to account for observed data patterns extremely well from the early 1950s to the late 1980s. The fit to the data is particularly bad for the period after 1990 and before WWI, which suggests that there has not been much of a technological convergence across countries during those times.

4. Stylized Facts

The foregoing descriptive analysis of the data leads to several conclusions that motivate our subsequent modeling and empirical work:

1. There was a global slowdown in TFP growth after the early 1970s, with rates close to zero after 2005–2006. Thus, the empirical evidence points to a decline in innovation.

2. The TFP growth rates of the US and the UK, in particular, recovered only partially during the 1990s and the 2000s, in comparison with their counterparts for the 1930s, 1950s, and 1960s. Thus, the innovations in the IT industry appear to have failed to lift the aggregate innovation and, in turn, TFP growth even in the US or the UK.

3. A sizeable proportion of the growth in GDP per capita across countries can be accounted for by TFP growth and, therefore, innovation. This is especially the case for the period before WWI, the interwar years, and the post-WWII recovery period.

4. Much of the TFP growth at the same time is due to catching up with the best practices in the world.

5. Countries differ significantly in their ability to catch up with the best practices in the world.

6. Early on, the UK was the global TFP leader, but the US managed to catch up and overtake the UK by the early 1930s. Since no country can become a leader only by following, any theoretical or empirical exercise on the data needs to allow for the existence of multiple centers of innovation in the world.

2

Sources of Indigenous Innovation and Channels of Its Transmission across Countries

Raicho Bojilov

ABSTRACT   We present a generalized framework for the decomposition of total factor productivity (TFP) that allows for persistence of innovation shocks in each country over time and for transmission of such shocks across countries. Before WWII, the main generators of indigenous innovation were the US, the UK, and France, while since WWII the US has been largely responsible for generating innovation shocks that are transmitted to other countries.

Introduction

The data patterns presented in Chapter 1 made clear that the analysis of TFP growth and innovation over a long time horizon needs to accommodate for the likely existence of multiple sources of indigenous innovation. At the very least, the data imply that in the early 20th century there were at least two countries that were generating innovation, which afterward spread over the world: the UK and the US. Otherwise, the US would never have been able to catch up and surpass the UK in generating the world's best practices. Yet most existing empirical analysis of macro- and industry-level productivity trends assume away the possibility of a multiplicity of innovation centers. In what follows, we try to address this limitation by proposing a general framework for the study of the propagation of innovation (or TFP shocks) through the world and its evolution over time. Then we explain how our framework can be taken to the data and present the empirical results from such an empirical exercise applied to our TFP data.

We distinguish between the adoption of innovation originating abroad and indigenous innovation, which is innovation generated by a given economy on its own. Both types of innovation can contribute to TFP growth in a country, but global productivity can only grow in the long run if some countries generate indigenous innovation. Our distinction, therefore, allows us to narrow down our focus to the part of TFP in each country that cannot be traced back to innovation somewhere else.

Our results show that before WWII there was no dominant global leader in innovation, and there appear to be two distinct eras: 1870–1914 and 1919–1939. In the years before WWI, the main generators of indigenous innovation were the UK, the US, France, and to a smaller extent Germany. In contrast, during the interwar years, indigenous innovation originated mainly from the US and France. We also find that the US experienced very high productivity growth during WWII. In contrast, since WWII, most innovation has originated in the US, and to a smaller extent in the UK and the Scandinavian countries. Moreover, these countries consistently have had the highest rates of innovation since the end of WWII.

Finally, we note that TFP growth across the world was much higher in 1946–1972 than in 1972–2012 as a result of both higher rates of catching up and higher rates of indigenous innovation.

1. A Tale of Two Farmers

We develop our analytical framework with the help of the proverbial farmers Alice *(A)* and Bob *(B)* of Neverland. Alice and Bob are good neighbors, and they often discuss what they do and how their crops grow. Alice is open to new seeds and crops, new machinery, and new pesticides and fungicides. She even dabbles in crossing plants to create new varieties. Bob, on the other hand, is a bit old-school and frankly does not see much gain or pleasure in playing around with untested things. Also, he sees no point in trying to play God and create his own hybrid plants, which may surpass the quality of what already exists but most likely will not.

Alice's lifelong project was to come up with hybrid carrots that are orange in color. The reader may be a bit surprised, but Alice and Bob live in a country that has always been cut off from the rest of the world, so they did not know that, back in the 17th century, the Dutch already did that. Thus, from time immemorial, Alice and Bob, along with their copatriots, knew only carrots that were pale yellow or dark red. Alice, however, persevered, and one day she somehow managed to successfully cross dark red and yellow carrots to obtain perfectly cheerful and beautifully orange carrots. Everyone in their country went wild with excitement for Alice's orange carrots. They simply looked better, and people even imagined that (therefore) they tasted better. The price of orange carrots went through the roof, as nobody could possibly imagine that they had been stuck eating any other variety of carrots.

It became evidently clear even to Bob that orange carrots were here to stay, and they were quite a profitable crop to grow. After a few years of reflection, one evening during their regular chats at the fence, Bob asked Alice for a few seeds of her hybrid carrots and even inquired about the way she crossed plants. Next spring, Bob made the momentous decision to plant the seeds and start growing orange carrots. The whole episode shook his system of life beliefs so much that eventually he ventured to pursue his childhood dream of creating black tomatoes. He was successful, and his black tomatoes were a great commercial success. Alice, quick to pick up on any new idea, tried to grow black tomatoes, too. Yet it turned out that black tomatoes are a capricious lot and refuse to grow anywhere else but under the specific mixture of soil, sunshine, and humidity that Bob's vegetable garden is known for. Thus, to this day, Bob remains the only one who grows black tomatoes in Neverland.

This simple story serves to illustrate several important points. First, economic innovation does not necessarily involve grand scientific or technological breakthroughs. In many cases, if not most, it does not. As in our story about carrots, economic innovation may be motivated by consumer tastes, such as the color of a vegetable, that have nothing to do with any "objective" scientific properties. Second, economic agents may learn from each other, and in this way innovations spread around. Third, the transmission is likely to happen fast if the economic agents who are involved are on good terms, share a language, have a similar culture, or share beliefs and attitudes. Fourth, there may be reasons why even successful innovations fail to be adopted widely, such as idiosyncratic production conditions or consumer tastes.

We can express the gist of our story about Alice and Bob in simple mathematical terms. Let the log productivity of Alice and Bob in year t be denoted T_{At} and T_{Bt} respectively. The corresponding annual growth rates in productivity are then ΔT_{At} and ΔT_{Bt}. We define the innovation that each farmer makes in year t as η_{it}, where $i = A, B$, and postulate that such innovation has a positive effect on productivity growth. If our friends Alice and Bob were on bad terms and, therefore, never shared any seeds or information about each other's farms, innovations would not spread around, so productivity growth is:

$$\Delta T_{At} = \eta_{At};$$

$$\Delta T_{Bt} = \eta_{Bt}.$$

Recall that initially Bob was very suspicious of novelties, so

$$\Delta T_{Bt} = \eta_{Bt} = 0.$$

However, we do know that Alice and Bob are friends, so they talk to each other and exchange ideas and seeds. Thus, there is some transmission of innovation between them. At the time when Bob adopted Alice's innovations but did not generate any innovations of his own, the foregoing growth formulas change somewhat:

$$\Delta T_{At} = \eta_{At};$$

$$\Delta T_{Bt} = \theta_{AB}\eta_{AT-1},$$

where θ_{AB} is a coefficient that represents the extent to which Bob successfully implements Alice's past innovations. We impose no restrictions on the magnitude of this coefficient. For example, $\theta_{AB} > 1$ means not only that Bob picked up Alice's ideas but also that he eventually became an even better producer of orange carrots because, for example, the soil of his farm was better suited to growing the new variety. Conversely, $\theta_{AB} < 1$ would imply that Bob adopted Alice's innovation, but the innovation had a smaller impact on Bob's productivity either because he did not master the new innovation as well as Alice or because his land was poorly suited to the implementation of Alice's innovation.

It may also happen that the overall impact of Alice's innovations on Alice's productivity takes more than a year to reach its full effect. Thus, in a given year, Alice's productivity is affected not only by this year's innovations but also by innovations of the past:

$$\Delta T_{At} = \sum_{k=1}^{t} \alpha_{Ak}\eta_{Ak},$$

where the coefficients α_{Ak} capture the effect of innovation in year k on Alice's productivity in year t. Similarly, we can arrive at a slightly more general formulation for Bob's productivity growth:

$$\Delta T_{Bt} = \theta_{AB} \sum_{k=1}^{t-1} \theta_{ABk} \beta_{Ak} \eta_{Ak},$$

where the coefficients β_{Ak} capture the effect of Alice's innovation in year k on Bob's productivity in year t.

Recall, however, that Bob finally became a successful innovator himself. In this most general setting, the preceding formulas become:

$$\Delta T_{Bt} = \sum_{k=1}^{t} \beta_{Bk} \eta_{Bk} + \sum_{k=1}^{t-1} \theta_{ABk} \beta_{Ak} \eta_{Ak},$$

where the first summation represents the contribution of past and present innovation shocks to Bob's productivity growth in year t; and the second term is the already familiar contribution to Bob's productivity growth of Alice's past innovation shocks. The coefficients β_{Bk} capture the effect of Bob's innovation in year k on Bob's productivity in year t. We get an identical expression for Alice:

$$\Delta T_{At} = \sum_{k=1}^{t} \alpha_{Ak} \eta_{Ak} + \sum_{k=1}^{t-1} \theta_{ABk} \alpha_{Bk} \eta_{Bk}.$$

We also pointed out that some of the innovations may be difficult, if not impossible, to spread around the world—that is, there may be innovations that remain idiosyncratic to the market. We operationalize this concept by assuming that

$$\eta_{it} = \eta_{it}^{T} + \eta_{it}^{NT},$$

for $i = A, B$, where η_{it}^{T} is a transmissible shock and η_{it}^{NT} is a nontransmissible innovation shock. Under this specification of the innovation shocks, we can obtain more general formulas for the evolution of productivity:

$$\Delta T_{At} = \sum_{k=1}^{t} \alpha_{Ak}^{T} \eta_{Ak}^{T} + \sum_{k=1}^{t} \alpha_{Ak}^{NT} \eta_{Ak}^{NT} + \sum_{k=1}^{t-1} \theta_{BAk} \alpha_{Bk} \eta_{Bk}^{T};$$

$$\Delta T_{Bt} = \sum_{k=1}^{t} \beta_{Bk}^{T} \eta_{Bk}^{T} + \sum_{k=1}^{t} \beta_{Bk}^{NT} \eta_{Bk}^{NT} + \sum_{k=1}^{t-1} \theta_{ABk} \beta_{Ak} \eta_{Ak}^{T}.$$

Note, in particular, that we allow the impact of transmissible and nontransmissible innovation shocks to vary within a country.

2. General Model

Formally, we consider a set of countries J and study the annual growth of TFP of country i for year t, denoted ΔT_{it}. Our goal is to decompose the growth into a set of factors:

$$\Delta T_{it} = \sum_{j=1}^{J} \left(\sum_{k=1}^{t} \theta_{ijk} \alpha_{jk} \eta_{jk} \right) = \sum_{j=1}^{J} \sum_{k=1}^{t} \psi_{ijk} \eta_{jk},$$

where η_{jk} denotes innovation shock for country j in year k. The expression $\left(\sum_{k=1}^{t} \theta_{ijk} \alpha_{jk} \eta_{jk} \right)$ is the weighted sum of the relevant past innovation shocks in country j: the coefficient θ_{ij} is the impact of the best-practice shocks in country j on the TFP growth in country i. Simplifying expressions, one obtains that $\psi_{ijk} = \theta_{ij} \alpha_{jk}$ captures the marginal effect of an innovation shock in country j during period k on country i. In the special case of the own-country impact, the marginal effect of an innovation shock in country i in period k on itself is denoted ψ_{iik}.

For conceptual reasons, we consider TFP growth as the sum of two components: indigenous and imported innovation. We define indigenous innovation in country i to be the weighted sum of all of its past innovation shocks that still affect productivity growth at time t:

$$\Delta T_{it}^{I} = \sum_{k=1}^{t} \psi_{iik} \eta_{ik}.$$

The past and present innovation shocks from abroad that affect productivity in country i are defined as imported innovation:

$$\Delta T_{it}^{M} = \sum_{j \neq i} \sum_{k=1}^{t} \psi_{ijk} \eta_{jk}.$$

Thus, TFP growth is the sum of indigenous and imported innovation:

$$\Delta T_{it} = \Delta T_{it}^{I} + \Delta T_{it}^{M}.$$

This formulation of innovation transmission across countries generalizes some popular specifications that have been used extensively in the past empirical literature. For example, the preceding literature has often postulated the existence of a technological leader, usually the US, whose innovation activity determines the technological frontier, while all other countries differ in their ability to catch up. In the context of the current framework, this specification boils down to a restriction on the coefficients ψ_{ijk}. Specifically, if the US has index $j = 1$, it implies that

$$\psi_{ijk} = 0 \text{ for all } i \text{ and all } j > 1;$$

$$\psi_{i1k} > 0 \text{ for all } i \text{ and all } j = 1.$$

Alternatively, a world of autarky in which each country innovates but there are no technological spillovers across borders amounts to the restriction that $\psi_{ijk} = 0$ for all $i \neq j$.

Estimating this model is challenging because we need to both decompose TFP into sequences of best-practice shocks $\{\eta_{jk}\}$ for all countries and, at the same time, recover the network channels through which best-practice shocks in one country affect the best-practice shocks in other countries—that is, the coefficients $\{\psi_{jk}\}$. In practice, we suspect that there are only a few countries that generate transmissible innovation. If our hypothesis is correct, most coefficients will be zero, $\psi_{ijk} = 0$, with only a few exceptions.

For estimation purposes, we maintain that each innovation shock can be decomposed as the sum of two independent terms. The first term, called transmissible innovation shock, is a shock that can affect TFP growth in countries different from the one where it has originated. Inventions of new products that can be universally used, such as the mobile phone, the smartphone, or the computer, fall within the realm of such shocks. The second term, called nontransmissible innovation, can affect the current and future TFP growth only in the country where it originated. Examples of such shocks include innovations that are driven by opportunities or tastes that are specific to a given country but not present elsewhere. In reality it is hard to find an innovation that is entirely of one type or the other: the economic impact of an innovation depends on the consumer preferences and the structure of the economy of the country where the innovation is adopted. That is, each innovation is to some extent transmissible and to some extent nontransmissible. In what follows, we have taken the conservative econometric stance that nontransmissible innovation is innovation that is completely independent from innovation and productivity growth in other countries.

Formally:

$$\eta_{it} = \eta_{it}^{T} + \eta_{it}^{NT},$$

where η_{it}^{T} stands for a transmissible shock and η_{it}^{NT} for a nontransmissible shock.

Both the transmissible and the nontransmissible shocks are the sum of a weighted average of past shocks and an innovation shock for each period. Formally:

$$\eta_{it}^T = \sum_{k=1}^{t-1} \rho_{i,t-1-k}^T \, \eta_{ik}^T + \varepsilon_{it}^T;$$

$$\eta_{it}^{NT} = \sum_{k=1}^{t-1} \rho_{i,t-1-k}^{NT} \, \eta_{ik}^{NT} + \varepsilon_{it}^{NT}.$$

In our econometric work, we maintain several assumptions on the specified random variables. In particular, we assume that the errors ε_{it}^{NT} and ε_{it}^T are independent from each other, across countries, and over time. We also assume that the transmissible and the nontransmissible shocks are stationary stochastic processes: $\rho_{i,t-1-k}^{NT} \in (-1, 1)$ and $\rho_{i,t-1-k}^T \in (-1, 1)$ for all t and k. Thus, the specification that we take to the data is:

$$\Delta T_{it} = \sum_{j} \sum_{k=1}^{t} \psi_{ijk} \eta_{jk}^T + \sum_{k=1}^{t-1} \rho_{i,t-1-k}^{NT} \, \eta_{ik}^{NT} + \varepsilon_{it}^{NT};$$

where the first sum represents the contribution of the past and present transmissible shock in all countries different from i to the TFP growth in country i during period t and the second one represents the contribution of past and present nontransmissible shocks in country i itself on its own TFP growth during period t.

We estimate the model in two steps. In the first step, we regress TFP growth on the observable regressors X_{it}, such as employment participation and annual drift that affects all countries. Then we apply factor analysis to the residual TFP growth to extract the transmissible shocks $\{\eta_{jk}^T\}$ from the lagged and present TFP growth series for countries $j = 1, \ldots, J$. This procedure works well when TFP depends on relatively few lagged best-practice shocks and there are relatively few countries that generate the transmissible best-practice shocks. The latter condition is not particularly strong, since in history there have been only a few countries potentially at the frontier of innovation: the US, the UK, France, Germany, Japan, and so on. We experiment with various numbers of lags, from 5 to 1, and find that in the case of transmittable shocks a specification with 2 lags fits the data best. We also experiment with different specifications for the autoregressive structure of the nontransmissible shocks and find that an AR(1) process does a reasonably good job in capturing the observed dynamics.

3. Transmission Mechanism

Tables 2.5 and 2.6, in the appendix, present the estimated factor loadings for our model of TFP decomposition. The specifications include nontransmissible country-specific error processes; transmissible error processes; annual dummies; and structural breaks in 1914, 1939, and 1972. After each structural break, we allow the stochastic process that generates the indigenous innovation shocks across countries to change. Our estimates indicate that there are two statistically significant structural breaks: one in 1946 and the other in 1972. In what follows, we focus the discussion primarily on the empirical results after WWII.

For the period until 1939, we find that there are two major factors that explain approximately 31 percent of the variation in the TFP series. The eigenvalues associated with these factors are close in magnitude to around 10. The first factor loads heavily on the US, while the second factor does so on France and the UK. For the period after 1945, we find that there are three transmissible factors that account for approximately 42 percent of the variation in the TFP series and the three factors account for 35–85 percent of the variance in each variable. The eigenvalues of the first three factors are 11.52, 11.09, and 10.36. The fourth factor has an eigenvalue of around 4.00 and the rest decline quickly afterward.

The factor analysis of the transmissible components of TFP growth lends itself to an intuitive interpretation, which helps us track how innovation propagates across the world. The first factor captures shocks that are generated in the US, the UK, Japan, Belgium, Denmark, Norway, Sweden, Finland, Canada, and Ireland. The second factor loads heavily on shocks that are generated in the US, the UK, Japan, Sweden, Denmark, and Canada, while the third factor includes shocks that are generated in the US, the UK, Canada, and Norway. We obtain the transmissible shock generated by each country from the formula that links the factors already discussed and the observed series.

The results indicate that transmissible shocks that enter in the third factor have a positive and statistically significant effect on TFP growth across the globe at the 5 percent significance level. In other words, the US, the UK, and to a smaller extent Canada and Norway are countries that generate indigenous innovation shocks that are transmitted across the world. The results also reveal that the persistence in the TFP growth series is well approximated by an AR(1) process with an average coefficient of persistence around 0.12 for the period 1950–1972 and 0.23 for the period 1972–2012. Interestingly, we find a small, statistically insignificant persistence in the process that generates the indigenous innovation shocks in the years before 1945.

4. Innovation: Trends and Global Transmission

The discussion of our substantive findings starts with a review of the countries that have generated most indigenous innovation in the world since

WWII and then traces how indigenous innovation evolved over time for each specific country. Then it maps out how indigenous innovation shocks have been propagating across the world. The section concludes with a comparison of pre-WWII and post-WWII trends in indigenous innovation.

4.1. Postwar Trends in Innovation

Table 2.1 reports in its first two columns the average indigenous innovation for each country and the part of TFP growth, called imported innovation, that can be traced to transmissible shocks from abroad. The results cover the period 1950–1972. The third column is the sum of the preceding two, and the last one reports actual TFP growth. The main result is that the US, the UK, and the Scandinavian countries have higher indigenous innovation than the continental European countries and Japan. These differences in indigenous innovation, however, do not necessarily translate into observably high TFP growth, as some of the countries in continental Europe turn out to be very good at adopting indigenous innovation from abroad. Indeed, the results for continental Europe support the hypothesis that, in the 30 years after the end of WWII, war-torn Europe caught up very successfully and quickly with the technological leader at the time, the US. Our key contribution in this context is the qualification that the observed rapid TFP growth in continental Europe in the period 1945–1972 is primarily due to catching up to the world technological frontier rather than indigenous innovation.

Table 2.2 has the same structure as Table 2.1, but it covers the period 1972–2012. The associated estimates present evidence for a slowdown in TFP growth globally by almost 2 percent in the period 1972–2012 relative to the preceding period, 1950–1972. In addition, the transmission of indigenous innovation shocks has become more persistent relative to the preceding period. While the relative position of the US as a leader in indigenous innovation remains unchallenged, the magnitude of the associated indigenous innovation shocks has dropped dramatically. The ability of countries to take advantage of the best practices across countries varies: the differences are statistically significant and of approximately the same magnitude as the differences in the indigenous innovation residuals.

4.2. Propagation of US Indigenous Innovation

Next we investigate in some detail how transmissible indigenous innovation in the US propagates across the world and transforms into imported innovation. Table 2.3 reports the cumulative effect of a transmissible US

Table 2.1. Estimates of annual indigenous and annual imported innovation for 1950–1972

Country	Indigenous	Imported	$\widehat{\Delta TFP}$	ΔTFP
Australia	0.42	1.42	1.84	1.30
Canada	0.49	1.45	1.94	1.04
Finland	0.55	1.56	2.11	2.08
France	0.32	2.01	2.33	2.86
Germany	0.42	1.39	1.81	−0.66
Italy	0.40	1.85	2.25	2.47
Japan	0.34	2.47	2.81	4.58
Netherlands	0.34	1.65	1.99	1.73
Norway	0.29	1.71	2.00	1.56
Spain	0.44	2.03	2.47	3.55
Sweden	0.42	1.43	1.85	1.50
United Kingdom	0.76	0.66	1.32	0.86
United States	1.02	0.51	1.53	0.99
Average	0.42	1.66	2.19	2.19

Notes: The first column reports indigenous innovation, while the second reports the contribution of imported innovation to TFP growth. The third column presents the sum of the first two, and the last one presents the actual TFP series.

Table 2.2. Estimates of annual indigenous and annual imported innovation for 1972–2012

Country	Indigenous	Imported	$\widehat{\Delta TFP}$	ΔTFP
Australia	0.13	0.17	0.30	0.46
Canada	0.09	0.18	0.27	0.35
Finland	0.22	0.76	0.98	1.02
France	0.05	0.06	0.11	0.04
Germany	0.08	0.09	0.17	0.07
Italy	0.09	0.10	0.19	0.12
Japan	0.04	0.11	0.14	0.10
Netherlands	0.05	0.24	0.29	0.36
Norway	0.02	0.32	0.34	0.34
Spain	0.07	0.13	0.20	0.29
Sweden	0.16	0.26	0.42	0.62
United Kingdom	0.18	0.33	0.51	0.67
United States	0.22	0.37	0.59	0.73
Average	0.11	0.14	0.22	0.25

Notes: The first column reports indigenous innovation, while the second reports the contribution of imported innovation to TFP growth. The third column presents the sum of the first two, and the last one presents the actual TFP series.

indigenous innovation shock of one standard deviation on TFP growth in other countries, and it contrasts the results for the periods 1950–1972 and 1972–2012. The most important difference between the two periods is the decline in the magnitude of the transmitted shocks. In most cases, this decline is greater than the decline in indigenous innovation in the US itself. Thus, the estimates suggest that the ability to adopt innovation from abroad has declined in many countries since the early 1970s.

Figures 2.1 and 2.2 illustrate the differences in the effect of indigenous innovation shocks in the US on TFP growth in G7 countries, while Table 2.3 summarizes the cumulative effect of US indigenous shocks on other G7 economies. They reveal that the dynamics of the propagation of US indigenous innovation shocks across countries differs significantly. The results show that US innovation shocks start affecting TFP growth in other G7 countries within two years, and most of the transmission of innovation is completed within five to six years. Moreover, countries differ in the speed and degree of adoption of US indigenous innovation. For example, while Italy does not stand out as a major center of transmissible indigenous innovation across the world, it manages to quickly adopt American innovation to a much greater extent than any other G7 country. Other countries that stand out in their ability to take advantage of US-based innovation are Canada, the UK, and France. This pattern holds for the periods both before and after 1972.

Table 2.3. Cumulative contribution of a US transmissible indigenous innovation shock to TFP growth across different countries

Country	1950–1972	1972–2012
Australia	1.55	0.20
Canada	1.95	0.26
Finland	2.87	0.38
France	2.02	0.27
Germany	1.58	0.21
Italy	2.99	0.40
Japan	1.39	0.18
Netherlands	2.09	0.28
Norway	1.25	0.16
Spain	0.57	0.08
Sweden	2.29	0.30
United Kingdom	2.04	0.27
United States	2.55	0.34

Note: A US transmissible indigenous innovation shock has a magnitude of one standard deviation of the US indigenous innovation.

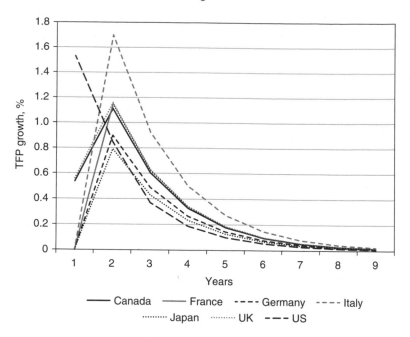

Figure 2.1. Propagation of US indigenous innovation shocks, G7, 1950–1972

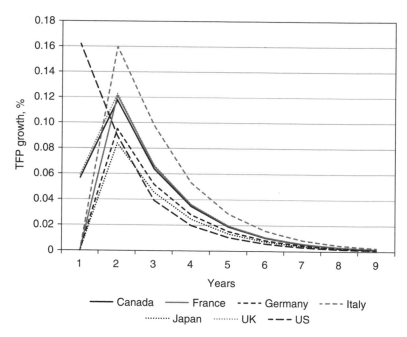

Figure 2.2. Propagation of US indigenous innovation shocks, G7, 1972–2011

4.3. Long-Term Trends

The discussion of the results concludes with an overview of long-term trends in indigenous innovation since the late 19th century, which are contrasted with the more recent developments since the end of WWII. Figure 2.3 presents the cumulative indigenous innovation in the US, the UK, Germany, France, and Italy since 1890. It reveals that the US has been consistently accumulating more indigenous innovation than any other country in the period, particularly after WWII. In fact, the estimates show that the gap between the US and the country with the second-highest cumulative indigenous innovation appears to have increased in recent decades. The figure also reveals some interesting differences in the trends of indigenous innovation in France and the UK before and after WWII. It shows that France was a major powerhouse of indigenous innovation before WWII, second only to the US. The two world wars, however, did much to destroy and slow down innovation in the country, which gradually recovered in the decades following the end of WWII only to stagnate in the 1980s and the 1990s. In contrast, cumulative indigenous innovation in the UK consistently lags behind that in France, Germany, and Italy in the years before the 1950s even though the UK did not experience the cataclysmic destruction of WWII to the same degree as the continental European countries. As the UK has

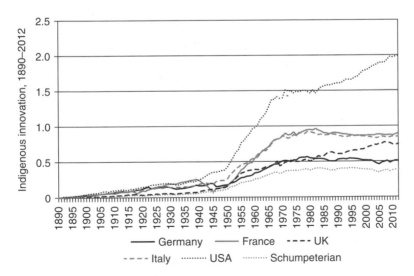

Figure 2.3. Cumulative indigenous innovation in the US, the UK, France, Germany, and Italy, 1890–2012

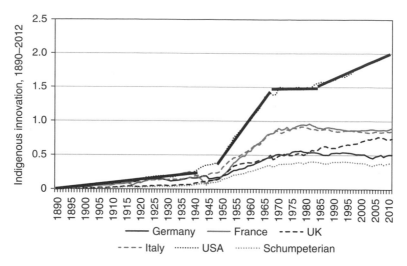

Figure 2.4. Cumulative indigenous innovation in the US, the UK, France, Germany, and Italy, 1890–2012, along with linear predictions of indigenous innovation for the US for the periods 1890–1940, 1950–1970, 1970–1985, and 1985–2010

managed to retain its rates of indigenous innovation after the early 1970s, British cumulative indigenous innovation has actually managed to overtake its counterparts for Germany and Italy and almost closed the gap with the one for France in recent years. The inclusion of linear predictions for the US series for the periods 1890–1914, 1919–1939, 1950–1970, 1970–1985, and 1985–2010 allows us to quickly investigate major changes in the rate of growth of indigenous innovation, which are captured by changes in the slope of trend.

One limitation of Figure 2.3 is that it compares indigenous innovation rates over a very long period of time that has experienced dramatic political events and major economic and technological changes. In particular, the data for continental European countries during the two world wars constitute a major challenge. In our estimation work, we have tried to address these issues by allowing for structural breaks and war-year dummies. Nevertheless, the quality of the fit of the model for the war years is low. For this reason, we believe that there is some virtue in comparing economic performance, and innovation in particular, over relatively short periods of time that were not subject to global political shocks.

An examination of the linear predictions in Figure 2.4 appears to confirm our previous conclusions based on the levels of indigenous innovation.

This representation of the results allows us to examine the hypothesis that some countries have experienced constant rates of indigenous innovation during some time periods. If that were the case for a given country in a given time period, the cumulative indigenous innovation would have been well approximated by an exponentially increasing curve. Instead, we find that a linear approximation provides a good fit. Broadly, we detect three different periods: pre-WWII, the postwar years until the early 1970s, and the decades afterward. Within each of these periods, the indigenous innovation rates varied across countries but seem to have remained quite stable from one year to the next. During the first period, both the US and the European countries, especially France, generated indigenous innovation. During the second period, the rates of indigenous innovation increased dramatically in all developed countries, while the US became the undisputed leader in innovation. The results suggest that this innovation revolution came to a halt in the early 1970s across the globe. In the years after 1990, the US appears to have managed to make some sort of a recovery: its indigenous innovation has picked up pace again, but the rates are clearly much lower than in the 1950s and the 1960s. The most significant other feature that we detect during this third period is that indigenous innovation completely dried up Europe. The only exception is the UK, for which we note a considerable increase in its average rate of indigenous innovation after WWII, relative to the period before WWII.

Table 2.4 summarizes the cumulative indigenous innovation for the US, the UK, France, Italy, and Germany during emblematic periods in modern economic history: the last two decades before WWI, the interwar years, the decades of recovery after WWII, the years of transition and economic turbulence in the 1970s and the 1980s, and the time of the IT revolution. A comparison of indigenous innovation across countries within each period allows us to identify the relative importance of each country as a center

Table 2.4. Estimates of cumulative indigenous innovation in the US, the UK, France, Italy, and Germany for the last two decades before WWI, the interwar years, and the periods 1950–1970, 1970–1990, and 1990–2010

	US	UK	France	Italy	Germany
1890–1910	0.09	0.02	0.05	0.07	0.07
1919–1939	0.08	0.03	0.16	0.06	0.06
1950–1970	0.65	0.26	0.58	0.47	0.28
1970–1990	0.09	0.10	0.02	0.00	0.01
1990–2010	0.14	0.08	−0.02	−0.01	−0.02

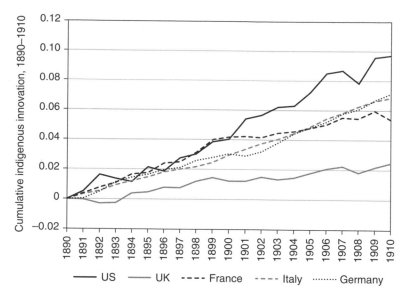

Figure 2.5. Cumulative indigenous innovation in the US, the UK, France, Germany, and Italy, 1890–1910

of innovation. The table reveals that, with the exception of the interwar years, the US has been the global engine of innovation.

Figure 2.5 confirms that in each year from 1890 to 1910, the US was the country with the highest cumulative indigenous innovation. Thus, our results support the hypothesis that one of the reasons for the transformation of the US into the world's leading economy is its capacity for innovating. Interestingly, the results also show that France was a historically very important center of innovation until the 1970s, especially during the interwar years. Indeed, Figure 2.6 shows that France experienced the highest cumulative indigenous innovation between the two world wars. The magnitude of innovation in Italy is always lower than that in France, but the dynamics is very similar. Interestingly, our estimates characterize Germany as not very innovative in each of the considered historical periods. This observation holds for both the time before and the time after WWI. The indigenous innovation in the UK follows a similar pattern to that of Germany, with the important exception of the last four decades. Unlike Germany, the UK experienced a recovery in its rate of indigenous innovation after the late 1970s. As a result, the UK is the only one of the large European economies that still generates indigenous innovation. In contrast, Table 2.4 suggests that indigenous innovation appears to have become extinct in the other large European economies.

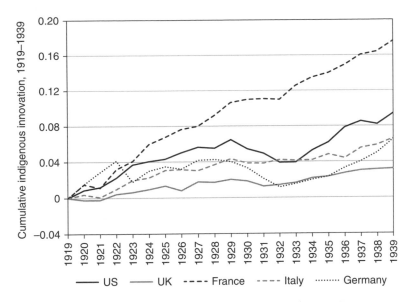

Figure 2.6. Cumulative indigenous innovation in the US, the UK, France, Germany, and Italy, 1919–1939

5. Conclusions

We have presented a generalized TFP decomposition that allows for persistence in the innovation shocks over time and transmission of such shocks across countries. Before WWII, the main generators of indigenous innovation were the US, the UK, and France. After WWII, the US and, to a smaller extent, the UK generated innovation shocks that were transmitted to the other countries. While the usual disclaimers about the use of country-level TFP data apply, we believe that our framework sheds some light on the channels through which TFP shocks propagate across the world. Moreover, our methodology is applicable to regional, industrial, firm-level, and even individual-level data.

APPENDIX

Table 2.5. Estimates of best-practice factors

Variable	Factor 1	Factor 2	Factor 3*
Australia			0.6296
Australia (t − 1)		0.6483	
Australia (t − 2)	0.6485		
Australia (t − 3)			
Canada			0.6890
Canada (t − 1)		0.6644	0.3324
Canada (t − 2)	0.6802	0.3475	
Canada (t − 3)	0.6318		
Finland			0.7623
Finland (t − 1)		0.7343	
Finland (t − 2)	0.7726		
Finland (t − 3)	0.4939	−0.4069	
France			0.7085
France (t − 1)		0.7803	
France (t − 2)	0.7130		
France (t − 3)		−0.3568	
Germany			0.5285
Germany (t − 1)		0.5453	
Germany (t − 2)	0.4436		
Germany (t − 3)		−0.4144	

Notes: The eigenvalues of the first three factors are 11.52, 11.09, and 10.36. These factors account for 42 percent in the variance, and the common variance of the three factors accounts for 45–85 percent of the variance in each variable. Asterisks indicate statistical significance at the 5 percent level.

Table 2.6. Estimates of best-practice factors

Variable	Factor 1	Factor 2	Factor 3*
Italy			0.8288
Italy (t − 1)		0.8553	
Italy (t − 2)	0.8219		
Italy (t − 3)		−0.4071	
Japan			0.4894
Japan (t − 1)		0.4960	
Japan (t − 2)	0.4295		−0.4538
Japan (t − 3)	0.3140	−0.4915	
Netherlands			0.7337
Netherlands (t − 1)		0.7793	
Netherlands (t − 2)	0.7403		
Netherlands (t − 3)		−0.4096	
Norway			0.4987
Norway (t − 1)		0.4241	0.3349
Norway (t − 2)	0.5632	0.3070	
Norway (t − 3)	0.5857		
Spain			
Spain (t − 1)		0.3066	
Spain (t − 2)	0.3114		
Spain (t − 3)			
Sweden			0.7069
Sweden (t − 1)		0.6031	
Sweden (t − 2)	0.6094	0.4275	
Sweden (t − 3)	0.4751		
UK			0.6730
UK (t − 1)		0.6625	0.3250
UK (t − 2)	0.5476	0.4402	
UK (t − 3)	0.6247		
US			0.6575
US (t − 1)		0.6047	0.3933
US (t − 2)	0.4978	0.4830	
US (t − 3)	0.6509		

Notes: The eigenvalues of the first three factors are 11.52, 11.09, and 10.36. These factors account for 42 percent in the variance, and the common variance of the three factors accounts for 45–85 percent of the variance in each variable. Asterisks indicate statistical significance at the 5 percent level.

3

Indigenous Innovation during the IT Revolution

We Never Had It So Good?

Raicho Bojilov

ABSTRACT Based on the data and methodology presented before, we discuss recent trends in indigenous and imported innovation. Our results show that indigenous innovation in the US and the resulting total factor productivity (TFP) growth since 1990 are higher than in the 1970s and the 1980s, but still lower than what they used to be in the 1950s and the 1960s. The UK followed a similar path in recent times. In contrast, indigenous innovation in continental European economies and Japan slowed down even further in the period after 1990. Even worse, these latter economies were also slow in adopting innovations developed outside their borders. We conclude with a discussion of possible alternative explanations and an overview of the questions raised by our results but left for future research.

Introduction

The extended time span of the data that we use allows us to compare trends in productivity across countries and, most importantly, across very different time periods, from the pre-WWI era, to the period between the two world wars, to the post-WWII decades, to the years of the IT revolution. Our methodological approach enables us to recover the network through which indigenous innovation shocks propagate across the world and how the associated network structure changed from one era to the next. In this chapter, we focus on indigenous innovation and, in turn, productivity growth during the IT revolution. First, we compare the average growth rate of indigenous innovation for the period across countries and then examine the country-specific dynamics for the US, the UK, France, Germany, and Japan.

Our results show that there has been no structural change in the transmission network for the period after 1990 relative to the preceding post-WWII decades. Moreover, we see that the annual rates of indigenous innovation in the US and the UK have made only a partial recovery during the IT revolution: while higher than the rates for the period 1970–1990, they are still lower relative to the rates witnessed in the postwar years until the late 1960s. Also, our estimates show that the continental European economies and Japan have not experienced even such a moderate recovery. Interestingly, we find that unlike in the glorious 30 years after WWII, these economies have been rather slow in adopting the (IT) innovations originating in the US and the UK. We conclude the chapter with a discussion of the possible causes of the observed statistical patterns. In particular, we consider what may be the industry-level dynamics that stand behind the observed aggregate rates of indigenous innovation in the US.

1. Cumulative Indigenous Innovation after WWII

We start with an overview of the cumulative indigenous innovation in the US and the leading European economies after WWII. Figure 3.1 presents the cumulative indigenous innovation in the US, the UK, Germany, France, and Italy between 1946 and 2012. It points out a few noticeable facts. First, the US generated more cumulative indigenous innovation than any other major economy in the world during the period.

Second, Figure 3.2, which is the companion representation of the same data with linear predictions for the US indigenous innovation for the periods 1950–1970, 1970–1985, and 1985–2010, indicates the presence of a structural break in the indigenous innovation series for all countries around 1970. Third, the results show that the US witnessed a recovery in its rate of indigenous innovation in the mid-1980s. However, the new rate of accumulation appears smaller than its counterpart for the 1950s and the 1960s. The same figure shows that the main economies on the mainland of Europe also fell victim to a dramatic slowdown in the 1970s. Unfortunately for them, the estimates reveal that these economies never managed to experience a recovery of the type that the US enjoyed during the 1980s and the 1990s.

In fact, our point estimates for the cumulative growth of indigenous innovation in these economies are sometimes negative, but these somewhat

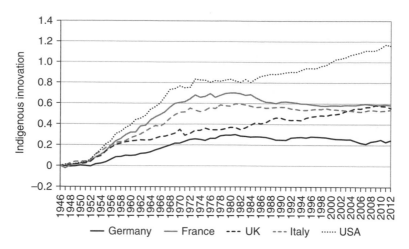

Figure 3.1. Cumulative indigenous innovation in the US, the UK, France, Germany, and Italy, 1946–2012

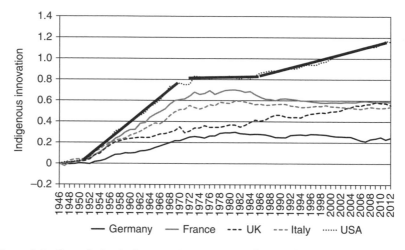

Figure 3.2. Cumulative indigenous innovation in the US, the UK, France, Germany, and Italy, 1946–2012, along with linear predictions for US indigenous innovation for the periods 1950–1970, 1970–1985, and 1985–2010

puzzling negative rates are never statistically significant from zero. We are particularly cautious in our interpretation of the series for Germany because of the reunification of the country during the 1990s. Finally, the figure reveals that indigenous innovation in the UK followed a rather idiosyncratic path after WWII. The data suggest that the UK accumulated a lot of indig-

Table 3.1. Estimated cumulative indigenous innovation (%) in the G7 economies and Sweden for the 1950s, 1960s, 1970s, 1980s, 1990s, and 2000s

	Canada	France	Germany	Italy	Japan	UK	US	Sweden
1950–1960	16.09	32.84	13.88	23.49	29.50	19.96	37.14	20.28
1960–1970	5.00	21.64	12.54	17.60	16.51	7.25	25.93	11.04
1970–1980	−0.69	4.94	2.69	2.64	−0.25	2.97	2.80	9.58
1980–1990	0.72	−2.42	−1.30	−2.80	8.49	6.84	5.58	14.22
1990–2000	−1.11	−1.92	−0.92	−0.82	−0.39	4.60	6.76	19.72
2000–2010	0.36	0.27	−1.00	0.11	7.58	3.29	6.43	20.44

enous innovation during the 1950s but the process slowed down in the 1960s. Interestingly, since then its indigenous innovation appears to have grown at a more or less constant rate that is in the same ballpark as the US rate after the mid-1980s.

Table 3.1 offers another cut of the data by comparing decade by decade the cumulative innovation of the world's largest economies since the end of WWII. The results confirm the preceding observations. The US was the global innovation leader in the 1950s and the 1960s. During the same 20 years, France, Japan, and Italy were also generating a lot of indigenous innovation themselves. At the same time, the three major economies with the lowest rates of indigenous innovation were Canada, Germany, and the UK. The 1960s witnessed slightly lower rates of accumulation of indigenous innovation than during the preceding decade. Still, the US maintained its lead.

Figure 3.3 illustrates year by year this observation by plotting the accumulation of indigenous innovation in the US, the UK, France, Germany, and Italy from 1950 to 1970. Table 3.1 also shows that the generation of indigenous innovation dramatically slowed down in the early 1970s. In fact, during this turbulent period, France, Italy, Germany, and the UK managed to accumulate slightly more indigenous innovation than the US itself.

While the differences between the rate for the US and the rates for these countries are not statistically significant, this finding highlights the dramatic decline of indigenous innovation in the US during the 1970s. As Figure 3.4 shows, the US managed to regain its global leadership in the generation of innovation during the 1990s and the 2000s. However, the impressive relative performance of the US is due to both its own recovery and the dismal performance of the other major developed economies during the last two decades. The most intriguing aspect of our results is the stellar performance of Nordic economies since the 1970s, which is exemplified by the case of Sweden. As in all other economies, indigenous innovation in Sweden slowed down in the 1970s. However, it has steadily increased since then. In fact,

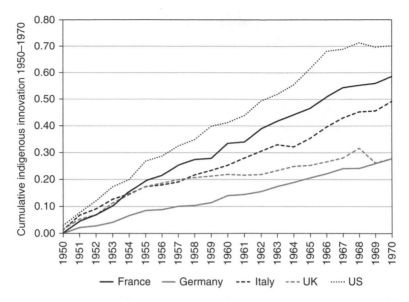

Figure 3.3. Cumulative indigenous innovation in the US, the UK, France, Germany, and Italy, 1950–1970

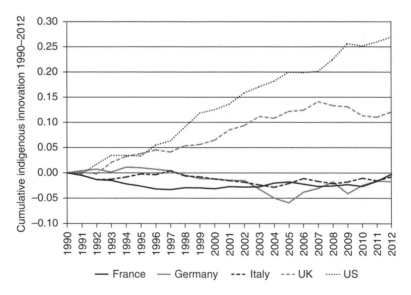

Figure 3.4. Cumulative indigenous innovation in the US, the UK, France, Germany, and Italy, 1990–2012

cumulative indigenous innovation in Sweden increased by 20 percent during the 1990s, compared with only about 7 percent in the US, and by another 20 percent between 2000 and 2012, compared with only 6.4 percent in the US. Sweden is by no means an exception: we record a similar pattern for Finland, Denmark, and Iceland, too.

2. Comparison of Annual Rates of Indigenous Innovation during the IT Revolution

We continue by comparing recent trends in indigenous innovation and imported innovation across the developed world from 1990 to 2012. Table 3.2 reports the average annual indigenous innovation and imported innovation for the set of developed economies in our sample. It reveals that the average rate of indigenous innovation for the sample is higher for the period 1990–2012 than for the preceding period, 1970–1990. At the same time, we also find that the average rate of imported innovation for the sample is actually lower in the considered period than in the preceding two decades. Furthermore, we reject the hypothesis that there has been a structural change in the transmission network that allows innovation to propagate

Table 3.2. Estimates of cumulative indigenous innovation and imported innovation (%) for 1990–2012

Country	Indigenous	Imported	$\widehat{\Delta TFP}$	ΔTFP
Australia	0.42	0.16	0.58	0.57
Canada	0.11	0.12	0.23	0.34
Finland	0.32	0.39	0.71	0.87
France	0.03	0.03	0.06	0.02
Germany	0.08	0.03	0.11	0.03
Italy	0.00	0.00	0.00	0.05
Japan	0.08	0.02	0.10	0.03
Netherlands	0.23	0.24	0.47	0.41
Norway	0.07	0.24	0.31	0.16
Spain	0.09	0.11	0.20	0.09
Sweden	0.67	0.34	1.01	1.04
United Kingdom	0.35	0.26	0.62	0.66
United States	0.58	0.29	0.87	0.98
Average	0.26	0.17	0.43	0.37
Schumpeterian		0.02		

Notes: The first column reports indigenous innovation, while the second reports the contribution of imported innovation to TFP growth. The third column presents the sum of the first two, and the last one presents the actual TFP series.

across the globe. Next, we discuss our estimates for the largest developed economies.

Comparing the raw numbers, we find that the annual TFP growth rate between 1990 and 2012 is not higher than but very similar to the annual TFP growth rate for the first two post-WWII decades. Furthermore, accounting for short-term fluctuations and factors actually implies that the TFP growth rate in the earlier period was higher than the growth rate during the IT revolution. We explore these issues further by comparing indigenous and imported innovation during the IT revolution to their counterparts for the preceding decades. The average annual indigenous innovation in the US between 1990 and 2012 has been about three times higher than the average annual indigenous innovation between 1970 and 1990. At the same time, it is only about 60 percent of the average annual indigenous innovation for the period 1950–1970. We also find that the average annual imported innovation in the US for the period 1990–2012 is very similar to its counterpart for the period 1970–1990. Thus, imported innovation contributes about a third to the average annual growth in TFP during the IT revolution compared with about one-half for the preceding two decades.

The results for the UK are very similar. Comparing the average annual rates of TFP growth, we find that TFP growth in the immediate postwar decades is still a bit higher than in the years of the IT revolution. In more detail, we find that the average annual indigenous innovation in the UK increased more than two times after 1990 compared with the 1970s and even compared with the 1980s. Nevertheless, the British rate of about 0.36 percent, in the 1990s and the 2000s, is still less than half of what it was in the first decades after WWII. We find that, similar to the US, the average annual imported innovation in the UK since 1990 is lower than what it used to be for the period 1970–1990. As a result, indigenous innovation now accounts for about half of TFP growth in the UK. The only consolation for the UK is that the slowdown in its innovation after 1970s is relatively smaller than the slowdown in other European nations. Indeed, a comparison between the UK and France is quite revealing.

In the three decades after WWII, France experienced a spectacular TFP growth rate of more than 2.5 percent. Most of it, however, seems to have been associated with a rapid catching up to the best practices in the world, as witnessed by the high rate of imported innovation. In fact, the French annual rate of indigenous innovation between 1950 and 1970 was lower than those in the US and the UK. Our estimates show that both indigenous and imported innovation in France failed to recover in the 1990s and the 2000s from the slowdown of the 1970s. In fact, all sorts of innovation appear to have stagnated at rates that are indistinguishable from zero. The situation is very similar in Italy and Japan, which also experienced rapid productivity expansions in the first post-WWII decades. The case of Germany also appears very similar, but we are somewhat cautious in our interpretation because of the changing borders of the country and the associated adjustments in the growth accounting that were required to control for the effect of former East Germany.

The only other countries that have experienced a recovery in their indigenous innovation relative to the 1970s and the 1980s are the Scandinavian countries. In particular, Sweden and Finland have achieved very high rates of average annual TFP growth of around 1 percent since 1990. This performance compared favorably to the growth rates for the 1970s and the 1980s. In the case of Sweden, we record an increase in the average annual indigenous innovation from 0.46 percent for 1950–1970 to 0.69 percent during the years of the IT revolution. Both of these averages are much higher than the corresponding rate for 1970–1990. Interestingly, Sweden also improved in its ability to adopt innovations from abroad relative to the period 1970–1990. The evolution of innovation and productivity in Finland followed a similar path. On the basis of these findings, we make several conclusions.

Under the existing methodology for the estimation of TFP, there is no dramatic increase in productivity during the IT revolution despite all the anecdotal evidence that comes from industry- and microlevel studies. If anything, the average annual rates of indigenous innovation after 1990 are for the most part still lower than what they used to be during the first post-WWII decades, even for the US. While the US rate of indigenous innovation in the last two decades is higher than in the 1970s and the 1980s, it is still lower than its counterpart for the period before 1970. Similarly, the UK and the Scandinavian countries experienced a partial recovery in their rate of indigenous innovation. Our estimates also reveal that, in relative terms, the US is still the country with the highest rate of indigenous innovation, along with the Scandinavian countries and the UK. At the same time, the rates of indigenous and imported innovation in continental Europe ground to a complete halt in the years following 1990. In contrast, the Scandinavian countries continue to have much higher rates of indigenous and imported innovation than the rest of Europe, which has contributed substantially to their high productivity gains.

3. Dynamics of Indigenous Innovation in the Major Economies

One of the advantages of our empirical approach is that we allow each country to generate indigenous innovation, which at least in principle could be transmissible to all other countries. In the following paragraphs we review the post-WWII dynamics of indigenous innovation rates in the major developed economies with a focus on the last 30 years. We use the US as a benchmark in order to evaluate the evolution of indigenous innovation in other countries.

Figure 3.5 plots indigenous innovations in the US and the UK from 1950 to 2012. It illustrates that the 1950s are the decade with the highest indigenous innovation in the US, followed by the 1960s, usually in the range of 2 to 4 percent. The dynamics of indigenous innovation change in the early 1970s: the magnitude of the shocks declines sharply, while the persistence of the effect of the shocks increases significantly. In particular, the 1970s witnessed dismal indigenous innovation in the US that fluctuated between 0 and 0.5 percent on an annual basis. In turn, the US experienced only partial recovery in the 1980s as indigenous innovation lifted up a bit to the range of 0 to 1 percent.

One of the big surprises of our results is that during the so-called IT revolution, we do not detect any peaks either in the raw data of productivity or in our decomposed series of indigenous innovation. In fact, it seems that the higher average rate of indigenous innovation in the 1990s and the early 2000s for the US is driven by higher realized minima rather than by some unprecedented positive innovation shocks. Furthermore, both the raw series themselves and our results show that the volatility in the innovation

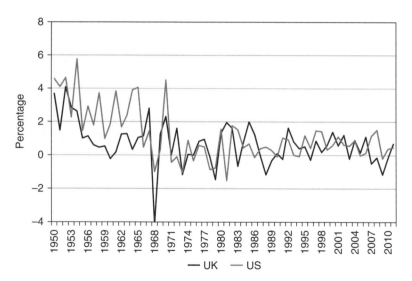

Figure 3.5. Comparison between indigenous innovation in the US and in the UK after WWII

and productivity series declined over time until the onset of the Great Recession. Notably, these changes have been accompanied by an increase in the persistence of the effect of innovation shocks on US productivity. Consequently, the decline in the magnitude of the innovation shocks is somewhat offset by the duration of their positive impact on TFP growth. During the last years for which we have data, 2005–2013, we witness a dramatic slowdown in TFP growth to a range that has not been witnessed since the early 1980s. These findings run against the popular narrative that the US is in the midst of an unprecedented flowering of innovation.

In comparison, the UK experienced consistently lower rates of indigenous innovation in the 1950s and the 1960s. Interestingly, in the following decades, the differences between the indigenous innovation in the two countries decrease significantly, largely as a result of the slowdown in US indigenous innovation. In other words, the relative standing of the UK improved after the 1980s and the country retained a small but positive rate of indigenous innovation throughout the postwar era. Still, the UK also witnessed a dramatic slowdown in productivity just before the onset of the Great Recession. The extent of this decline seems to be even more severe than the one in the US.

The dynamics of indigenous innovation in France is very different, as illustrated in Figure 3.6. France experienced high but declining rates of indigenous innovation in the 1950s and the 1960, which were only slightly lower than the US ones. In the 1970s, France and the US actually had very

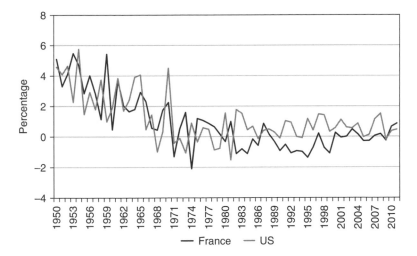

Figure 3.6. Comparison between indigenous innovation in the US and in France after WWII

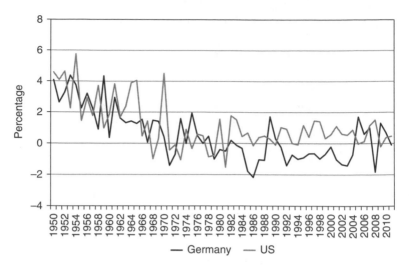

Figure 3.7. Comparison between indigenous innovation in the US and in Germany after WWII

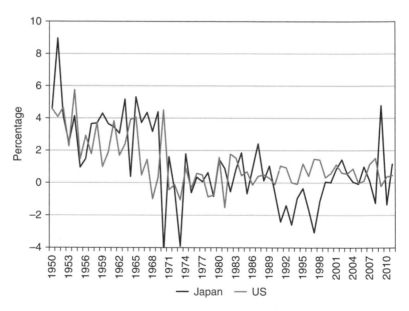

Figure 3.8. Comparison between indigenous innovation in the US and in Japan after WWII

similar rates of indigenous innovation. However, while in the 1980s and the 1990s the US experienced a partial recovery, French indigenous innovation continued to decline until it virtually reached zero in the 1990s and the 2000s. Figure 3.7 shows that the dynamics of indigenous innovation in Germany is very similar to that of France. The big difference between the two countries is that France appears to have consistently higher rates of indigenous innovation than Germany. Finally, Figure 3.8 reveals that indigenous innovation in Japan followed a very similar path to indigenous innovation in Germany, with the only difference being that Japan actually had higher rates of indigenous innovation than the US for a short time in the 1980s.

4. Discussion: Choice of Measure and Possible Bias

There is no universally accepted measure of innovation, and all existing candidates have their pros and cons, depending on the investigated context. We have advanced so far a research agenda that aims at exploring the dynamics and spatial dependence of TFP, one of the existing measures, across countries and time to investigate how the dynamics of innovation has changed on a national level as a result of the IT revolution.

The main shortcoming of TFP as a measure of productivity is that it represents the disturbance term in a growth regression and, as such, it is a shadowy upper-bound estimate of innovation. At the same time, it incorporates innovation in all of its guises. Also, our data cover countries over long time horizons. The same, however, cannot be said about any of the other existing measures of innovation. At the same time, actual data on concrete measures of innovations have a number of advantages. One of them is that such measures refer to concrete economic phenomena, whose definition is unequivocal. In contrast, TFP measures offer at best a theater of shadows.

Another very important concern that needs to be addressed is the possibility that TFP growth understates productivity growth as a result of the specific nature of IT innovation. Existing measures of economic activity and the associated growth accounting were developed at a time when both production and consumption were not as dispersed in time and space as today. For this reason, the existing measures, the argument goes, likely understate the gains in efficiency and in individual utility.

We are sympathetic to such concerns about the relevancy of the existing methodology and practices in growth accounting. As the jury is still out, we consider our foregoing findings as one additional piece of evidence that will hopefully contribute to a better understanding of innovation during the IT revolution. Our view is that our findings at the very least provide a cautionary warning against the widespread euphoria about the great strides in productivity made during the IT revolution.

Moreover, a few observations make us discount the concerns that our results may suffer from a downward bias. Previous research based on microlevel data has indicated unequivocally that the US is the global leader in IT innovation. Thus, if the existing methodology in growth accounting were prone to underreport productivity and welfare gains, then one would expect that the raw TFP series for the US to be more affected than the TFP series in other developed economies. In other words, the presence of such a bias is likely to understate the differences in productivity growth between the US and, say, continental Europe. To the extent to which innovation in the IT sector is largely responsible for efficiency and welfare gains in the US over the last 30 years, this line of thinking implies that the gap between the US and economies that are less affected by IT innovation should be shrinking. The data do not appear to lend much support to such an argument.

5. A Possible Explanation

Understanding the sources of innovation and how it propagates across economies is of primary importance to understanding the economic forces that have shaped the trends in indigenous innovation that we have discussed here. The patterns that we have uncovered may appear at first sight puzzling and in contradiction to a plethora of microlevel and anecdotal evidence. We believe that an understanding of indigenous innovation in the IT industry and how it relates to innovation and productivity in the other industries is of primary importance. In what follows, we provide some evidence to support this claim, which also motivates much of the work reported in the following chapters.

Indisputably, the US economy defined the technological frontier in the first years after the end of WWII. Most European countries and Japan, however, managed to catch up with the US by adopting the best practices defined in the US. Moreover, these economies also successfully generated their own innovation that propagated across the globe. Thus, by the early 1970s, the technological differences between the US and the rest of the developed economies had shrunk considerably. Following the structural shocks of the 1970s, the aggregate productivity growth in the US recovered somewhat.

Nevertheless, the productivity growth since 1990 has been lower than the productivity growth for the period 1950–1970.

A cursory review of cumulative productivity growth rates across major industries in the US since the mid-1980s reveals that productivity gains have been very unequally distributed across industries (see Figure 3.9 and Figure 3.10). The IT industry has been the undisputed innovation leader in the US since the mid-1980s, and that is reflected in its high productivity growth. Figure 3.9 shows clearly that the productivity in the IT sector during the IT revolution has increased more than twelvefold. Such gains dwarf the productivity growth in any other US industry.

Thus, it may seem at first sight that Figure 3.9 conforms to the accepted wisdom about the economic impact of the IT revolution. This is not the case. If innovations and the resulting productivity gains in the IT industry had such a profound and transformative effect on the economy, then one would expect to see the productivity gains in the IT industry spill over to the other industries of the economy. Yet Figure 3.9 casts a shadow on the story about the revolutionary and transformative nature of IT innovations: neither manufacturing nor services experienced productivity gains of nearly the same magnitude as the IT industry. Moreover, Figure 3.10 shows that productivity in the US manufacturing industries has been growing faster than productivity in service industries, in particular retail trade.

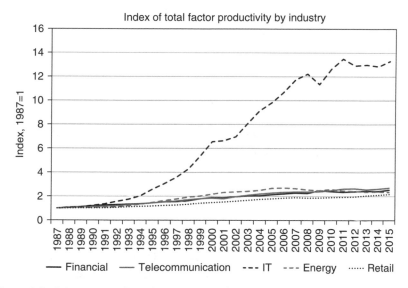

Figure 3.9. Divergence of productivity growth rates across industries in the US since the mid-1980s. *Data source:* Bureau of Labor Statistics.

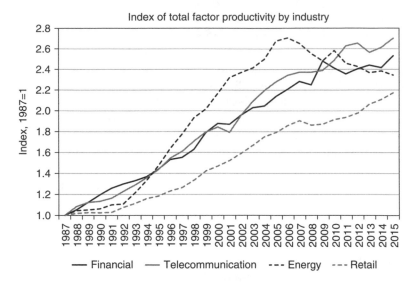

Figure 3.10. Heterogeneity in productivity growth rates across major industries, excluding the IT industry. *Data source:* Banque de France.

Somewhat surprisingly, we do not witness, even with a lag, a major pickup in the productivity growth in other industries that are directly and indirectly connected to the IT industry. One would expect that if the IT industry were the engine of the US economy that generates the products, technologies, and techniques of the future, then the other industries would eventually experience a jump in productivity rates to levels comparable to those of the IT industry. Thus, one may wonder why aggregate productivity in the US has not grown much more in accordance with the innovations and major productivity gains that have been achieved in the IT industry.

These observations raise the possibility that the observed dynamics is due to the equilibrium interaction between innovation in the IT industry and the rest of the economy. To fix ideas, let us consider an economy with two sectors. The first is a traditional, mature sector. It is characterized by industries with high levels of market concentration, low rates of innovation, and, in turn, low rates of productivity growth. The second sector, called the "IT sector," captures the features of emerging young and innovative industries. This sector is characterized by very high levels of innovation and productivity growth, as well as a high degree of competition. As usual, there are two factors of production, capital and labor, and we consider different scenarios for the intensity of the production process in each of the sectors. This setting reflects salient features of the US economy, for example. The setting that we explore follows in the footsteps of several recent advances in the endogenous growth literature, which tries to incorporate innovation and automation.

The ultimate objective is to characterize the steady states of such an economy and the transitional dynamics that results from a large innovation shock in the IT sector, such as the internet boom of the late 1990s and the early 2000s. The key dynamics that is captured in such a model involves the interaction between innovation and relative prices. An innovation shock in the competitive sector has two effects on the economy: one direct and one indirect. The direct effect is to boost productivity, increase wages, and attract more labor in the affected sector. The indirect effect operates through prices. In our setting, the companies that dominate the traditional sector may be able, under certain conditions, to maintain the relative high prices of their products by abusing market power in the form of high price markups. As a result, innovation can drive down the price of goods in the young, emerging sector relative to the goods in the established, mature sector. The implication is that the innovative companies face a declining revenue stream while their real labor costs are on the rise. As a result, labor compensation is depressed and workers move from the high-productivity sector to the low-productivity sector. Meanwhile, the dampened profits in the innovative sector tend to discourage the realization of innovation that under the old prices would have been marginally profitable.

The resulting dynamics is of paramount importance to the prospects of the economy. In the worst possible case, the vicious cycle of falling relative prices and falling innovation would end when the rates of innovation in the investment and manufacturing goods sector go down to the same low level as in the mature sector. Within our model framework, the initial effect of a strong innovation shock would undoubtedly be to immediately depress labor compensation. In the real world, frictions could smooth the effect of the shock, leading to a prolonged period of stable or declining labor compensation. What the resulting new steady state of the economy would be is hard to tell without formally solving the model. For this reason, we postpone further discussion until Chapter 10.

6. Conclusions

The empirical evidence presented in this chapter shows that in terms of aggregate productivity gains, the IT revolution hardly qualifies as a time with an unprecedented peak in innovation.

Our results show that the transmission network through which innovation shocks propagate across countries has not changed. While indigenous
innovation in the US, the UK, and the Scandinavian countries has picked
up some steam since 1990 relative to the 1970s and the 1980s, it is still
either lower or just below what it used to be in the 1950s and the 1960s.
Another key finding is that continental European countries failed to experience even such a moderate recovery of indigenous innovation. These results, particularly in the context of the US and the UK, run against the accepted common wisdom.

We also explored possible explanations for the observed data pattern.
One simple explanation is that the growth-accounting methodology that is
used to come up with the TFP series is outdated. To be sure, we recognize
the limitations of national-level TFP data. Still, such an explanation cannot
account for the differences in innovation in the US and, say, the continental
European economies. Moreover, it also does not square with the fact that
much of the productivity gains in the US that led to the observed diver-
gences in relative productivity can be traced back to IT innovations. In combination with our macrolevel findings, the huge divergence in the productivity gains across US industries suggests that one possible explanation for
the observed data patterns may be related to the interplay between prices
and IT innovation in equilibrium. The following chapters investigate this
hypothesis in some detail, along with some alternative explanations for the
results reported so far.

II

THE ROOTS AND BENEFITS
OF INNOVATION

4

A Case Study of Iceland's Successful Innovators

Gylfi Zoega

ABSTRACT In this chapter we establish a common set of values and resulting attitudes that characterize the founders of four successful, innovating companies. Each company is founded on the basis of an indigenous innovation, not merely the application of new technology. Some of the values detected and determined will then be used in subsequent studies on the relationship between values and innovation at the national level.

Introduction

In previous chapters, it was found that indigenous innovation in the 1990s was higher in the US, the UK, and Scandinavia than in the continental European economies and Japan after 1990 and picked up from its pace in the 1970s and the 1980s while it slowed down further on the continent and in Japan. The objectives of the four chapters in this part of the book are, first, to establish a set of values and beliefs that can explain this pattern and, second, to study the consequences for labor force participation and job satisfaction when such values are lacking.

The objective of this chapter is to determine a common set of values and resulting attitudes that characterize innovators by interviewing the founders of four companies. The results of these interviews will then be used to guide the empirical work conducted in the subsequent chapters using aggregate data on values and beliefs. The companies include two software companies, Solfar Studios[1] and Plain Vanilla;[2] one producer of prosthetic limbs, Össur;[3] and one company that developed software to maximize airlines' seat utilization rates, Calidris, now a part of Sabre Airline Solutions.[4] Of the four, Solfar and Össur are still independent companies, Calidris became part of Sabre Airline Solutions, and Plain Vanilla folded its operations and fired its staff in 2016.

1. Interviews

The interviews took place in September and October 2015 at the University of Iceland and Plain Vanilla's headquarters. Each innovator was invited for an interview, and minutes were taken. The purpose of the interviews was to understand the founding ideas behind each company and, most importantly, to identify a common set of values and resulting attitudes among the founders.

1.1. Solfar Studios

We interviewed Thor Gunnarsson, founder of Solfar Studios. He has a long history and experience in the software business dating back to the early 1990s.

1.1.1. History. Most software companies existing in Iceland today trace their origins to a company called OZ, founded in the 1990s.[5] The formation of that company was the beginning of innovation in the software sector. When OZ was dissolved at the end of the decade, the main players went on to create other companies. One of these companies was CCP Games, which creates computer games that allow people all over the world to play together.[6] A third-generation company, Solfar, was founded in 2014 by three senior executives of CCP Games and OZ. These individuals, who can be characterized as "serial entrepreneurs," had previously worked in the UK and the US. Our interviewee, Gunnarsson, was one of these three people. He said that when Solfar was founded, they had the notion that they could set up a creative studio in the entertainment software sector in Reykjavík, given the experienced talent base that had accumulated there over the previous 20 years.

The individuals who came from OZ had an interest in computer graphics; at OZ they combined real-time graphics with the social environment on the internet in a three-dimensional, multiuser setting. Hence, when they founded CCP, it was their personal interests and background that led them to establish an online computer game company. CCP had very limited competition until Solfar produced a new technology platform: the virtual reality headset.

These companies catered to new markets where their skillset—computer graphics, video games, and immersive three-dimensional environments—could be used. These Icelandic companies were propelled by the initial interests of the founders and their accumulated expertise dating back to OZ. The success of these software companies attracted overseas talent, which then set in motion a new set of start-ups. Creative destruction is common in the industry. Companies fail, and people move or start new companies.

The innovation that took place in Iceland was made possible by new technologies that do not penalize long distances. Software does not require inputs that must be imported, since anyone with the required skills can develop the software anywhere in the world. The cost of production in the software business is also limited, because the business is knowledge based. In effect, the cost of distribution was made trivial with the introduction of the internet, making it possible for distant countries to access the market. Other factors favoring Iceland include early and rapid adoption of the internet and cultural receptivity to innovation.

1.1.2. Values and infrastructure. The foundation for the creation of the new software companies was a pool of people who were trained in software programming, had studied abroad, and had a solid educational background. Iceland has good schools and universities, and many people go overseas for postgraduate studies. (One cofounder of Solfar studied physics abroad.) These students then take their academic learning back to Iceland, where a variety of people who have studied in different countries come together to pool their ideas and experience. In this sense, Iceland is not homogeneous but rather a melting pot of people with different educational backgrounds who bring together traditions and approaches from a diverse set of countries.

The culture of the country was another foundation on which the success of these companies was based. Iceland's tradition of storytelling, literary history, fine arts, poetry, and music, when combined with programming skills, creates an environment ripe for innovation in this sector. Furthermore, Iceland is forgiving of failure and appreciative of risk-taking, whereas in the UK, for instance, failure is frowned upon. Risk-taking is a part of Icelandic culture. Hence risk-taking, good education, and creative individuals in Iceland helped the software industry to develop.

In terms of the institutional setup, the regulatory framework and easy access to financing made Iceland a good place to start a company, although it is more difficult to expand an already successful start-up without moving elsewhere. The country provides a good environment for families, with inexpensive kindergartens, free schooling, and subsidized healthcare. As a result, innovators with families do not have to risk their children's schooling or their family's healthcare when they set up a company. This provides further incentive to take risks.

Experience indicates that it is better to fail early and restart rather than spend substantial time forecasting and planning. Because the market is fast-moving, developing prototypes and testing the market is more useful than extensive planning. However, Gunnarsson started OZ with a detailed business plan because a business plan is a useful thought exercise and also required by creditors. A good combination of people and a good plan go together.

1.1.3. Financing and the macroeconomic environment. The financing environment in Iceland is mixed. Early-stage financing is reasonably accessible and includes friends and family, angels, and seed financing. In contrast, there is a gap in expansion capital—just over a million dollars—which has hampered growth. Larger-scale financing through banks and pension funds is also available, and more recently launched venture capitalist funds, such as Brunnur, support start-ups.

The capital controls imposed in 2008 and in effect until early 2017 hampered foreign investors wishing to invest in Iceland. Under the capital controls, bureaucracy was a significant impediment to capital inflows, and there was some friction involved in dealing with the Central Bank. In this sense, Iceland differed from other Western countries and more closely resembled a developing country like China. But abolishing capital controls does not solve all problems associated with being located in a tiny country with the world's smallest independent currency. Before capital controls, there were exchange-rate fluctuations that nearly made CCP move abroad.

1.1.4. Trust. CCP decided to stay in Iceland despite the exchange-rate volatility and subsequent capital controls (from which CCP was exempt, but the country's reputation among investors was nevertheless affected) because its executives were familiar with the environment and knew the rules. There are fewer frictions, laxer regulation, and more rapid decision-making in Iceland than in neighboring countries such as Sweden and the UK.

Icelandic companies have a less hierarchical structure; they are flatter organizations with less veneration for senior executives. This is part of the culture, due perhaps to small company size. At CCP, with 650 employees spread across many countries, one could see that the hierarchy in Iceland was flat compared with the other countries.

Moreover, there tends to be more trust in business relationships in Iceland. People trust each other until a lack of trustworthiness is proved. This is a function of how small Iceland is—most people in a particular industry know each other. Personal and business reputations come with individuals who are given the benefit of the doubt. In contrast, in the US or in China, one has no frame of reference for the people one meets; therefore, skepticism is greater. In the US, the default operating procedure is not to trust others until trust is earned.

Trust is one of the reasons for the rapid formation of companies in Iceland. There is also a large element of trust in employer-employee relationships, one's relationship with one's bank, with lawyers, and so forth.

1.1.5. Export orientation due to small size of country. Not having a home market has also helped Icelandic start-ups. The companies have to start out thinking about the international market; thus they immediately face competition from companies abroad. This also helped Nokia in Finland. Conversely, in China there are very large game developers that operate only in China and have no success in exporting because of a lack of competition from abroad.

1.1.6. Desirable qualities of employees and the values of founders. Employees should be independently minded, think outside the box, and be able to make decisions for themselves or the small team they are working with. Communication skills are important, as is education, but work experience can substitute. As the company grows, the need for more specialization sets in. Rapid decision-making and communication skills are important in the smallest firms (<30 people). The founders' personalities will affect the kind of people who are hired, but as the company grows, a more diverse group of people is recruited.

Founders like the rewarding nature of working in a highly creative industry. They are attracted by financial independence and the prospect of becoming rich, although money is not the principal motivator. People who are attracted to innovation have an appetite for uncertainty and risk-taking, which often leads to successful start-ups. An appetite for challenge, the willingness to take risks, the ability to work in an uncertain situation, personal temperament, and background are key factors. Finally, innovators should be able to accept failure and not take it too much to heart. Societal attitudes toward failure may help or hurt, as the case might be. In Iceland, failure tends to be forgiven, which helps would-be innovators.

1.2. Plain Vanilla

At Plain Vanilla, we interviewed Arni Jonsson, chief technology officer, and Thorsteinn Fridriksson, the CEO.

1.2.1. History. Plain Vanilla is the company that launched the unexpected hit *Quiz Up,* a trivia game that became very popular with more than 40 million users. Plain Vanilla employed 90 people full time in 2016. The company was founded by Fridriksson in 2010, soon after he graduated from Oxford University.

Before founding Plain Vanilla, Fridriksson had worked mainly for other start-ups. He was generally interested in the start-up concept and idolized innovators like Steve Jobs and Elon Musk. A turning point in Fridriksson's life occurred during his time at Oxford when he participated in the program Silicon Valley Comes to Oxford. Some of the biggest names in Silicon Valley—including Tesla founder Elon Musk and LinkedIn founder Reid Hoffman—visited MBA students and spent a full week with them. Fridriksson found the program very inspiring, but when he came back to Iceland in 2009, the country was in the midst of an economic crisis. While working in start-ups for other innovators, he realized that he wanted to establish his own business.

Plain Vanilla comprises several divisions. One is in charge of sending survey questions to users. The company does not compose the survey questions; rather, it fields questions from experts, which it then edits. It also responds to users' demand for new features in the game.

Most of Plain Vanilla's staff members are programmers or engineers who create the *Quiz Up* apps for iOS and Android, run the websites, and perform data analytics. While the users are using the apps, the company tracks their moves. The analysts are notified, for example, if a majority of users use one feature instead of another, which helps the company gauge product performance. Company staff includes quality assurance and user support personnel, a product manager, graphic designers, a financial department, and a human resources department.

1.2.2. Funding. Securing funding for Plain Vanilla was not easy. One of the cofounders put all of his savings into the company, and collectively, the founders did several side projects for other companies to raise revenue. Plain Vanilla developed the Icelandic Dominos Pizza app, for example, which generated substantial revenue. However, what they raised was just enough to launch the game *The Moogies.*

"We basically had to make it or break it, and it broke," said Jonsson. In spite of this setback, the founders managed to keep the company afloat by focusing on what had previously been side projects. These were gloomy times. They did not give up because they were able to raise minimum revenue by working as contractors for others, and they believed in what they were doing; they figured that as long as they could pay the bills, there was no point in giving up.

They managed to raise some capital from an Icelandic investor on the premise that they had an idea and were going to work with a foreign incubator. This investor gave them a few million Icelandic krónur in return for partnership in the company, but this was only enough to keep them afloat for a few months. They had exhausted the financial resources available in Iceland.

After the financial crisis of 2008, investors were skeptical, and even though OZ and CCP had been successful, Plain Vanilla was often denied funding because those companies belonged to the past and many others had failed since. Investors doubted that Plain Vanilla would be any different. Even though they carried on and contacted a start-up incubator in San Francisco through the friend of a cofounder, when the founders arrived in San Francisco, they were once again in a make-it-or-break-it situation.

When Plain Vanilla presented the idea to the US incubator, the response was lukewarm. In the incubator's opinion, trivia games were some of the most boring imaginable. But they didn't turn Plain Vanilla away. At first glance they thought Plain Vanilla was up to something good. The people at the incubator were experienced, but Plain Vanilla's founders gradually came to realize that the people at the incubator had no idea what Plain Vanilla was doing.

The incubator helped found Plain Vanilla Corporation in Delaware, which is the parent company of Plain Vanilla in Iceland, and handled all the legal matters. All that remained was to sign the papers to transfer ownership to the Delaware company. Then, all of a sudden, the owner of the US incubator disappeared; the person, who turned out to be a chronic alcoholic, was drinking heavily and nowhere to be found. At this point, Plain Vanilla's founders realized that they had to break away from the incubator. They hadn't signed any binding agreement with the incubator, so they backed out. The incubator had gotten them working facilities with IGN enterprises, and Plain Vanilla's founders negotiated with IGN to keep the facilities even though they had left the incubator.

There were limited funds to work with during the time in the US, so it was crucial for Plain Vanilla to find its first investor abroad as soon as possible. Its founders contacted another Icelander, the CEO of Unity 3-D, and presented their work to him. They had no previous relationship with him, but as they said, "You know Icelanders tend to help each other out in foreign countries, so he agreed to meet with us." He became their first foreign investor. Unity 3-D is a very successful company that produces the game-development platform on which most mobile games run; therefore, the CEO has a huge network of contacts in this sector. The contact that proved to be most fruitful was Sequoia Capital, a venture capital firm specializing in start-up stage investments in private companies. The story of how they got a meeting with Sequoia garnered fairly extensive news coverage for a while and has become something of a legend.

The Icelandic investor had set up a meeting with the head of Sequoia Capital and the stakes were high. "So the Sequoia guy shows up and the Icelandic investor tells him that he is finishing a meeting with the CEO of PV [Plain Vanilla] and will be with him ASAP, but he should maybe join them for the last minutes, for he might be interested in this idea PV is working with. The Sequoia guy got a little irritated because the investor had tricked him into meeting with the CEO." Within five minutes, the CEO managed to sell the *Quiz Up* concept to one of the most influential investors in Silicon Valley. Sequoia invested in Plain Vanilla, and that attracted other investors as well, so when Plain Vanilla's founders headed back to Iceland, they had over US$1.1 million in equity—a huge victory.

1.2.3. Product development. The US incubator connected Plain Vanilla to a wide network in the US while providing financial support for the development of the founders' new idea: creating a trivia game for mobile devices. The idea came about when they reviewed their earlier failed experiment of *The Moogies. The Moogies* relied heavily on videos, which made the content-creating process extremely slow. Plain Vanilla's group of graphic designers and illustrators worked for over a year creating the video content for that game. "If you want to make it in the app store, you have to be quick to adapt. You have to constantly update your product in order to remind the consumer of it," said Fridriksson. So the founders discussed among themselves what kind of games they could create and update every month. They saw a new opportunity in trivia games.

No one had really entered that market, and they decided to seize the moment. Trivia is a well-known concept in board games, and they had seen other developers use board game ideas as a springboard, including an app based on Pictionary and the Scrabble-based *Words with Friends* app. At this time, there was no trivia-focused app that could be considered successful.

What separated the Plain Vanilla trivia game from the existing competition was quality. It is very easy to create a trivia game for use in single-player mode by a solo player, but Plain Vanilla's founders thought that playing online would be a more pleasant experience. So the company took its trivia games to the next level. Previous developers had focused on copying Trivial Pursuit instead of incorporating creative thinking into the process. This, of course, is a limiting factor. There are a limited number of topics and possibilities. But Plain Vanilla's line of thinking was this: the user has a device that is connected to the internet; let's take advantage of that and create an interactive trivia game with endless possibilities. In this sense, it was the first company to fully utilize mobile technology in this category of games. It planned to launch multiple apps, one for each trivia question topic.

1.2.4. *On making plans.* According to Jonsson, plans are all well and good, but an innovator must be willing to change them as the wind shifts. The world of technology is so fast-moving that it is not realistic to make long-term plans. Plain Vanilla started out with some plans but has made many changes over time. The original plan was to create a large number of small-scale apps, or satellites. It created *Quiz Up Eurovision,* which attracted 2,000 users; next came *Quiz Up Batman,* in cooperation with IGN, which had 200,000 users. Then it designed the official *Twilight* app, which was promoted by the producers of the *Twilight Saga.* The *Quiz Up Twilight* app had around 1 million users.

Next, Plain Vanilla was going to release what it called the "mother app," with a vast number of categories to choose from. The plan was to direct users to the mother app through the satellite apps and to keep releasing new satellites every month. The mother app, *Quiz Up 1.0,* was released on November 7, 2013. It was an instant success. During the first week, over 1 million people downloaded it. Plain Vanilla's founders had dared to hope for a million downloads over the first two months but considered that to be optimistic. *Quiz Up 1.0* was the most downloaded app in the app store for several weeks.

By this time, Plain Vanilla realized that it should focus on *Quiz Up 1.0,* which meant no more satellite apps; the company had to change course. It had established a user base large enough to be its number one priority, so there was no need to do anything else. This is an example of plans changing virtually in the blink of an eye. *Quiz Up 2.0* was released on May 21, 2015. The update introduced more social features. Each topic has its own front page where users can post pictures or links to a website related to the topic and have discussions. Users who like *Game of Thrones,* for instance, probably like both the TV show and the books; they are also likely interested in videos or pictures of actors who appear in the show, and so on. Plain Vanilla staff is constantly working on improvements for *Quiz Up 2.0.* Around the time this interview began, the company sent out a press release about a new game show on NBC, to be called *Quiz Up America.*

1.2.5. What makes innovating attractive? Innovating gives a level of freedom, including not having to be somewhere from nine to five. Then there is the need to create something. Jonsson thinks this line of work requires dogged determination. Sometimes the work requires 14-hour days for several months on end, leaving no time for anything else. But there are rewards, too. It is the combination of creativity, freedom, and the need for doggedness that is so appealing.

Jonsson has stock options and golden handcuffs, but that is not why he is doing this. He feels passionate about creating, but success requires having the ambition to generate a remarkable product. He wanted to create the best app in the world and spent a week perfecting the scrolling feature within the app alone. He wanted it to feel just right for the user.

Good taste matters as well; if a developer doesn't have good taste, people will not like the product. Creativity and persistence are of little use without good taste, and the creator must set high standards.

1.2.6. Necessary qualities in staff. Jonsson values experience more than education. He said, "If someone didn't go to university but had created his own app, I would hire him rather than some guy with a degree who has only done some school projects." He looks for smart people, but the most crucial thing is the ability to communicate well. If they can't communicate, then they might have great ideas but no one will hear about them. "Our employees have to function in a group and communicate with their peers," he said. "Some members of our staff are musicians, but I think that is just a coincidence; at least, it's not intentional. The hiring process is really tough. They interview you, and if you might be something they are looking for, they get you working for four to five hours on real projects, follow your every move, ask you to describe what you are doing, the reasons behind it, and so on."

What the CEO values in his senior staff members is some element that comes with people who possess impetus. People don't change very much from their teens onward, so he values what they've done in the past. If someone has set up his own business and failed, that is the best recommendation that person can get. Whether the person was active in her school's social scene says a lot. "I think most of my senior staff was at some time the head of the student union in their college. Some people say that this title is meaningless, but there are some characteristics that come with it. They have initiative and they have impetus."

1.2.7. On networking. Networking can be extremely valuable if one is presentable and willing to use people skills, which is just being good at networking. Ideally, networking should be methodical; upon meeting a person, one has to realize what it is one wants from them. This might sound a little bit cold and unemotional, but if an innovator is looking for investors, for example, and meets someone he or she realizes is unlikely to invest in the idea, the innovator must consider who that person's contacts are. The goal with every meeting should be either collaboration or an introduction that leads somewhere else. The social structure of Silicon Valley is layered, perhaps not unlike the caste system in India. Those at the bottom have an idea but no funding. At the next level are innovators with funding, then those with established businesses, followed by those who have become investors, and so on. Participants must start at the bottom and tackle each level as it comes, just as in a video game where players gain experience points in order to reach the next level. As a player, one meets higher-ranked players who can make horizontal or vertical introductions. This is, without a doubt, a small world. The key is to get to the top of it.

Even when dealing with the large US businesses, it all boils down to interpersonal communications. Jonsson said, "If you are afraid to go in there and ask for an appointment with the CEO, you are making a mistake. You won't always succeed, but you've nothing to lose and should definitely not be afraid. They are just people like you and me who sometimes have trouble at home and experience good and bad days. If you manage to establish a bond with them, that can be influential for your business. So in short, the most surprising thing is how *human* communications are when you are doing business at this level."

1.3. Calidris

Calidris was formed by Magnus Oskarsson and Kolbeinn Arinbjarnarson in 2002. The company provides revenue integrity and business intelligence solutions for the global airline industry. Calidris offers several advantages: first, an entry-level revenue integrity service, the Calidris Booking Integrity solution, which finds problems in airline bookings and supports the processes to eliminate them; second, the Calidris Total Revenue Integrity solution, which monitors bookings, reservations, tickets, and departure control to ensure that no revenue leakage occurs; and finally, the Calidris Empowerment solution, an integrated passenger and flight data store and process management engine.

There was a turning point when Sabre made contact in September 2009. Sabre and Amadeus are the two dominant providers of IT services to airlines and the travel industry. Sabre, originally founded by American Airlines and IBM, developed the world's first e-commerce system. Sabre has

9,000 employees and is headquartered in Dallas, Texas. It offers a multitude of passenger marketing and optimization services to airlines and wanted to acquire Calidris because it needed a world-class revenue integrity system. The acquisition was completed on March 29, 2010.

A manager from Sabre moved to Iceland to integrate Calidris within Sabre. The founders continued for three years as product evangelists. The Sabre manager studied Iceland's business culture and promoted the Iceland branch in Dallas, which was key to successful integration. The local office continues within Sabre and now has 55 staff members, up from 35 at the time of the acquisition. Calidris was the first Icelandic IT start-up to maintain a healthy operation in Iceland after being taken over by a foreign firm.

1.3.1. The background of the innovator. Oskarsson started his university studies in engineering but soon shifted to computer science, which was just starting at the University of Iceland. He earned a bachelor's degree in computer science and began working at the National University Hospital of Iceland. He then finished a master's degree in computer science in the US and an MBA in Switzerland.

1.3.2. Product background. After finishing his MBA, Oskarsson worked for Icelandair for six years and became quite familiar with airline operations. He created the frequent flyer program still in use and implemented a modern revenue management system. The objective is to maximize profits by balancing prices and seat utilization. The system forecasts demand for seats at different prices and optimizes revenue by limiting availability to lower-priced seats if purchased in advance and higher-priced seats if purchased closer to departure, thus taking advantage of the differences in price sensitivity and buying behavior of different market segments. This was a change from the practice of the 1960s, when all seats were sold at the same price. Prices are lower if you buy well in advance.

This idea for revenue integrity came up at Icelandair. To maximize load factor, the common airline practice was to forecast the number of no-shows and overbook to compensate for the expected no-shows. One peak-season day in July when all of the flights were fully booked, a flight from New York had 10 vacant seats despite significant overbooking. Looking for an explanation, Oskarsson then asked for a printout of the no-show bookings. A woman told him that she could have told him in February that these people would not show up. The reason was that passengers who book through a travel agent do not have to buy the ticket at booking time, and Icelandair did not monitor whether the bookings had actually been paid and tickets issued. Oskarsson realized that they were addressing this problem on the wrong level of detail: they should have been monitoring bookings and ensuring they were genuine and really paid for, instead of forecasting no-shows at the flight level. But it was not possible to implement these new processes in the 30-year-old IT systems that airline used. Two ideas emerged: first, to replicate the bookings from the old systems to a database that made it possible to do the work, and second, to use the data to find problem bookings and eliminate them if they were not paid for and ticketed at the prescribed time, freeing up capacity that could be sold to real paying passengers. No solutions seemed to be available on the market.

After leaving Icelandair for a stint as managing director of OZ, Oskarsson founded Stonewater International with an American partner and started to develop a system based on those two ideas. The system monitored the airline bookings, looking for fake names like Mr. Test and Mr. Donald Duck, passengers who had double bookings, and bookings that were not ticketed and paid when they should have been. Icelandair was the pilot customer and paid for the development work. This system reduced the number of no-shows by 60 percent in the first year of operation.

The American partner quit in 2002 and Oskarsson and his cofounder, Arinbjarnarson, an ex-colleague at Icelandair, founded Calidris, which took over the operations of Stonewater. At this time, the concept of revenue integrity was being established in the airline world, and Calidris was quickly able to establish itself as a leader in the field, initially by having the best technical solution and subsequently by creating the most value for the airline customers.

1.3.3. Expansion. Calidris started its international expansion with a contract with Finnair in 2001. While the terrorist attacks on September 11, 2001, reduced demand for the company's services, work for Finnair kept it alive.

At this time, Finnair began to use a newly developed reservation system from Amadeus, and Calidris integrated its system with Amadeus, which proved to be a key to later success. The company continued to expand by adding leading airlines such as Emirates in 2004 and British Airways (which signed a large contract for the data replication and process management solution without the revenue integrity system) in 2006.

Mr. Test dropped from the bookings, as did Mr. Donald Duck. Passengers booked on two flights to the same destination could be dropped from one flight since they could not be in two places at the same time. The company found that travel agents were able to gobble up low-price seats and thus cheat airlines by booking dummy bookings to fill all available seats, then, when a real customer arrived, canceling one of the bookings and quickly rebooking to get access to low-cost seats when they should not be available. Calidris prevents such schemes. With the Calidris solution, Emirates increased its profits by $8 million in the first six months and seat utilization on high-demand flights rose from 92 percent to 97 percent.

Later, the company added Austrian Airlines, Avianca in Colombia, Virgin Atlantic, Czech Airlines, and a number of smaller airlines. The company also entered into a large contract with Cathay Pacific in Hong Kong for the data store and process management solution.

By 2018, the revenue integrity solution was in use at 50 airlines and Sabre had implemented the Calidris data store and process management solution at some of the world's largest airlines, such as Southwest Airlines.

1.3.4. On operations and financing. For the first 10 years, Calidris relied on financing from operations for its development and did not look for outside financing. The revenue from the first customers paid for the first versions, and the founders initially did consulting jobs on the side, so there was less need for start-up capital. Good planning was essential in those years, although the plans never materialized quite as expected. All profit was used for expansion, such as more staff to develop better products.

The company was lucky to attract outstanding talent from the start. The first employees were computer science students who worked summer and part-time jobs, and later Oskarsson added a core team of old colleagues from OZ. The focus was always on hiring the best talent possible. In 2003, Calidris hired an external managing director, freeing the founders to focus on product management and sales.

The strengthening of the Icelandic krona by 20 percent in 2005 nearly killed the company, and to mitigate the risk, the company outsourced part of its development to India. However, the overhead of managing teams across cultures and time zones did not make this worthwhile.

Problems emerged in 2007 after a rapid expansion when sales plans did not materialize. At that time customers paid only an initial license fee but not for ongoing services. There were layoffs, but the company survived with half the headcount. New shareholders that joined the company owned 45 percent, the two founders 45 percent, and staff 10 percent. Oskarsson took over as managing director again and continued in that position until the sale to Sabre.

1.3.5. On values and keys to success. The company uses its three values, mutual success, enjoyment, and knowledge, as its guiding light. The main value, mutual success, is analogous to trust. It means that if the company creates value for its customers, the company benefits, and if the company does well, the employees benefit. All employees became shareholders in the company, earning the right to shares over five years. The company pursues a no-secrets policy and shares all financial information with employees.

Enjoyment is the other key value; working with interesting people on interesting problems for interesting customers is really enjoyable. And if the customers' staff finds it more enjoyable to work with the company than with any competitor, they will continue to do business. The company emphasizes cooperation and teamwork and uses extracurricular activities to promote that, such as winning the cycle-to-work competition among companies year after year. The position of the office is unique. It is the only office building on top of Öskjuhlíð, a hill and a nature park in the middle of Reykjavík, a very central and yet very quiet location between a graveyard and a school for deaf children. The company hired a chef to serve high-quality lunches every day, encouraging the staff to sit and chat during lunchtime. Family values are important: spouses are invited to all parties and extracurricular activities, and kids have their own playroom in the office.

Other keys to innovation in Iceland include various cultural attitudes toward and beliefs about work. Knowledge, for example, is vital. Calidris is a knowledge company by definition. Other valuable attitudes include appreciation for the ability to create something out of nothing—for example, digital technology—the opportunity to engage in challenging tasks and rewarding work, and the ability to deal with uncertainty and ambiguity. Icelandic society also provides a well-developed social safety net with free education and healthcare, which, combined with a limited liability company status, eases the risk for employees at start-ups. Sometimes there are high rates of return; sometimes there are not. OZ was a great school in innovation and the group from OZ made a big difference to Calidris because they had been through similar experiences.

Taking into consideration the difference in cultures can also aid in success. In India, the social structure is hierarchical, and obedience is important. In the Baltics, this is not the case. Power distance differs from one country to another. In Korea, Belgium, and France, there is a high level of power distance, while in the Netherlands it is lower, and in Iceland it is very low, making it easy for Icelanders to work with anyone at any rank.

The global nature of the airline industry was also a key to success; airlines are used to working with vendors from around the world, so coming from a small, obscure corner of the world did not prove to be a problem as long as the company delivered superior value.

1.4. Össur

Finally, we can briefly describe a company in an entirely different business. Össur was founded in 1971 by Össur Kristinsson and currently employs 2,300 workers in 18 countries. Össur is an innovative company that produces prosthetic limbs. It started as a firm that repaired prosthetic limbs but branched out into production. We interviewed Jon Sigurdsson, its CEO.

The company was first listed on the Iceland Stock Exchange in 1999 and expanded rapidly through a series of strategic acquisitions. It has been listed on the NASDAQ OMX Copenhagen Stock Exchange since 2009. Össur is currently a global company, recognized as a "technology pioneer" by the World Economic Forum, with operations in the US, Europe, and Asia. Its main innovation was the development of a breakthrough silicone interface for prosthetic sockets. The company has added numerous life-changing products to its portfolio, such as dynamic braces that relieve the pain of knee osteoarthritis and the world's first complete bionic leg incorporating bionic technology.

1.4.1. Financing and management. Retained earnings financed the company's initial innovations. The founder relinquished control and left the company when operations expanded. The new management decided to issue shares in order to facilitate further expansion of its product line and a distribution system. The company also issued corporate bonds with the help of a commercial bank, which were bought by some of the country's pension funds. Capital from the stock market and from bond issues, as well as assistance from the investment firm Kaupthing, allowed the company to take over an American firm in 2000. This was the largest takeover by an Icelandic company until then. The acquired firm had a distribution system in the United States, and the innovations introduced by Össur were new and not close substitutes for any existing products on the market.

Soon after the company began to grow, the capital flowing into Iceland created a stock market bubble. This drew the stock market's attention away from a manufacturing firm like Össur as investors began investing in the financial sector. Össur management then went on a road show in other countries in order to attract capital. As a result, Fidelity Fund invested in Össur's shares in the Icelandic stock market. A Swedish fund followed suit, as did a Danish fund and many others. The ownership of the company became non-Icelandic as a result.

With more capital, Össur could take over more businesses abroad; the foreign owners expressed the desire to relocate the company to a larger country. Despite the foreign owners' recommendation of moving to a foreign bank, the Icelandic bank Kaupthing continued supporting Össur's operations. This was because Kaupthing offered better terms on its loans to Össur. When Kaupthing collapsed in 2008, the company turned to foreign banks.

1.4.2. Planning and macroeconomic development. No business plans were made at the very beginning when innovative activity commenced, but they were gradually developed. The planning was made more difficult by the volatile business environment, which featured exchange-rate fluctuations and volatile wage growth. Because of the foreign funding and a lack of takeovers before 2008, the company was well financed when the financial crisis hit in 2008. Össur was the only company on the Icelandic stock market that did not need debt restructuring, while some of the shareholders were hurt by the collapse of the exchange rate because they had borrowed in foreign currencies in order to buy shares in the company.

From 2002 onward, the company's accounts were in foreign currencies. The company requested that the shares on the Icelandic stock exchange be listed in foreign currencies, but this request was turned down by the Central Bank and the tax authorities. This is why shareholders who were leveraged in foreign currencies suffered when both the currency and share prices collapsed in autumn 2008. The introduction of capital controls in Iceland made the shares worthless to foreign investors. The company responded by listing its shares on the stock market in Copenhagen, in effect becoming a foreign company.

2. Conclusions

We have interviewed these innovators in order to establish a set of personal and cultural traits that are conducive to innovation. We can summarize them as follows.

- Innovators like the rewarding nature of the work, have an interest in working in a creative industry, and value financial independence.
- Innovators tend to like uncertainty and have an appetite for risk.
- They are also able to accept failure.
- The following factors support innovation:
  - simple laws and regulations—the absence of red tape, easy access to financing and funds

- a flat organizational structure where employees are not afraid of saying what they think to their bosses
- trust in business relationships
- innovation for the world market and not starting with the home market
- a culture that is forgiving of failure and appreciative of risk-taking
- a welfare state—free education and healthcare

5

The Force of Values

Gylfi Zoega

ABSTRACT   We study measures of values, institutions, and innovation for 20 OECD countries. Our choice of variables is partly based on the survey of Icelandic innovators in Chapter 4. We find a strong relationship between a latent variable that captures both values and institutions, on the one hand, and a latent variable measuring economic performance on the other hand. In particular, we find that trust, the willingness to take the initiative, the desire to achieve on the job, teaching children to be independent, and the acceptance of competition contribute positively to economic performance. Teaching children to be obedient may, in contrast, reduce economic performance. Economic performance is measured by indigenous total factor productivity (TFP) growth, imported TFP growth, job satisfaction, male labor force participation, and employment. Fertility is also included in this variable as a measure of optimism about the future.

Introduction

In Chapter 2 we found that indigenous innovation in the 1990s was higher in the US, the UK, and Scandinavia than in the continental European economies and Japan after 1990. The objective of this chapter is to establish a set of values and beliefs that can explain this pattern using aggregate data on values as well as describing the consequences when such values are lacking.

The performance of the economy, its growth rate, its employment rate, and its level of output determine our standards of living and our level of job satisfaction. The main driving force behind the performance of the economy is the rate of innovations made by talented individuals. The late William Baumol made the point that every nation has its share of talented individuals, but how they spend their time and which goals they have depends on the values of society and its institutions.[1] This chapter is about innovation and values. We explore which values and resulting attitudes are most conducive to innovation. We ask whether differences in observed values and resulting attitudes help explain differences in the rate of indigenous innovation across countries. We try to answer whether some countries are endowed with values and resulting attitudes more conducive to innovation and which cultural attributes are most conducive to innovation.

1. Innovation and Economic Performance

The concept at the heart of our study is innovation, which is the driver of growth. We define an indigenous innovation to be an invention made in the home country that has been significantly adopted by businesses or consumers in the economy. In contrast, imported innovations are innovations made in other countries and adopted by businesses in the home country. An indigenous innovation consists, in our framework, of a genuinely new idea born in the mind of a businessperson that no one has thought of before, which is then put into practice. Examples include the foundation of the 24-hour news channel CNN, the smartphone, or the iPad.

Indigenous innovations are not adaptations to the changing business environment, such as that performed by the Hayekian entrepreneur, who acts to bring the economy toward its potential output level. According to Hayek, shifting conditions—for example, population increases or discoveries made by engineers and scientists—open the way for commercial applications by entrepreneurs, which brought the economy closer to the efficiency frontier.[2] In his view, creativity is not found among the entrepreneurs; instead it is the scientists who come up with the new ideas. Examples include the commercial jet aircraft, which owes its existence to the work of engineers during WWII; automobiles, which owe their existence to the technological discovery of the internal combustion engine; and elevators, which owe their existence to the discovery by Elisha Otis in 1852 of the so-called safety brake that prevents elevators from falling down the elevator shaft. Neither are indigenous innovations the Schumpeterian entrepreneur's commercial application of technological discoveries made by scientists.

Instead, in our framework, which is used in this chapter, indigenous innovations are new business ideas that expand the production frontier. An economy of indigenous innovation is one that continuously expands its production possibility through a stream of new ideas—about new products and new production methods—by businesspeople that are gradually diffused over the rest of the economy.

The source of new ideas is the creativity of businesspeople who use their imagination to conceive of new products or methods and who use their ingenuity in implementing those products or methods. The indigenous innovation in a country derives from the creativity of the nation and its ability to utilize these innovations, while the ability of an economy to innovate depends on the economic system in place. In particular, the capitalist system can enable innovation in several ways. First, it can provide support through helpful institutions—such as the patent system—and through the willingness of authorities to help new businesses prosper, accept the forces of creative destruction, and so on. It can also do so by discouraging attempts to protect vested interests, which characterize corporatist economies. The nation must also include a large number of talented individuals who have the interest and insightfulness to innovate. These people have some intuition about business that makes them capable of thinking about new products and new ways to produce them; they are also willing to take risks and accept the possibility of failure. Finally, values and beliefs matter, including the values and resulting attitudes instilled in children and the society's attitudes toward innovators, which dictate whether they are admired or envied, and whether the creative individuals receive support from their communities or attempts are made at repressing them, to name a few examples.

Phelps (2017) describes how the origins of the prevailing values and resulting attitudes toward innovative activity may be found in a nation's ethic, which Max Weber traced to the influence of religion.[3] In the book *Mass Flourishing* (2013), Phelps describes how the spirit of dynamism varies between countries and changes over time. He describes how these attitudes grew more prevalent in parts of the West from the beginning of the 16th century well into the 1800s—in particular in Britain, the US, Germany, and France.[4] While Weber traced the changed values and resulting attitudes to the Protestant Reformation, Phelps traces it to the emergence of what he calls the modern ethic in the late Renaissance and the baroque era.

This modern ethic values individualism and the desire to create the new. These values replaced the "traditional values" (or communitarian values) that oppose change and new entrants, as well as "family values" that prevent members of the family from breaking away and taking risks. According to Phelps, modern values gradually created the modern economy, which is capable of generating and sustaining dynamism (the continuous creation of new ideas, what we call indigenous innovations). This resulted in an explosion of innovation, which generated rapid productivity growth from the beginning of the 19th century to the end of the 1960s. Labor productivity growth was unprecedented at around 3 percent per annum, making productivity double every 20 years or so. As a result, wages and living standards rose at an unprecedented rate, and the workplace gradually became more rewarding.

Since the mid-1970s, low levels of productivity growth have been observed in the Western world, especially in Europe. The end of the golden age of growth in Europe coincided with the collapse of the Bretton Woods system and the beginning of the floating exchange rate regime. The increased volatility of exchange rates and the massive capital flows that were unleashed may have affected growth rates. Other factors that were unleashed include the rise of corporatism and its set of stifling regulations that make it more costly to operate businesses, consumer protections, licensing requirements, and the protection of long-lived patents.[5] Some of these regulations serve special interests in addition to their stated goal of protecting one group, such as consumers, from the harmful effects of another, such as businesses and banks. There has also been a visible change in the business culture. Short-termism that aims at maximizing bonuses and seeking rent within companies reduces the incentive to innovate.

Underlying this corruption of government and corporations is a change of values in which protection of the vested interests is prioritized over innovation and risk-taking. The corporatists do not approve of uncertainty and disorder, something that is ingrained in a dynamic innovative economy. Instead, what is valued is a steady rise in consumption and leisure brought about by gradual gains in efficiency.

Here we will explore the relationship between innovations and cultural values. We also take institutions into account, since these may have impeded innovations and growth in recent decades.

2. Review of the Literature

We study values at the aggregate level using survey data, but these are only the sum of the values of individuals. The question is whether the prevailing attitudes include those conducive to innovation. While Joseph Schumpeter's definition of the entrepreneur differs from our definition of the innovator, as discussed earlier, the personality traits may not be entirely dissimilar. Schumpeter (1911/12) describes the entrepreneur as having the dream and the will to found a private kingdom, usually, though not necessarily, also a dynasty; having the will to conquer and the impulse to fight, to prove oneself superior to others, and to succeed not for the fruits of success but for success itself. In other words, the financial result is a secondary consideration valued mainly as an index of success and as a symptom of victory.[6] Moreover, according to Schumpeter, entrepreneurs enjoy building things, getting things done, or simply exercising their energy and ingenuity; they like to seek out difficulties and change in order to change.

In his seminal study, McClelland (1961) found that entrepreneurial behavior can be associated with personality characteristics, such as the desire for achievement, moderate risk aversion, a preference for novel activities, and the tendency to assume personal responsibility for successes or failure.[7] Brockhaus (1982) associates three attributes with entrepreneurial behavior: the need for achievement, an internal locus of control, and risk-taking propensities.[8] According to Sexton and Bowman (1985), entrepreneurs need autonomy, independence, and dominance.[9] According to Licht and Siegel (2006), wealth attainment is less important for entrepreneurs than power, vision, leadership, and independence.[10] Cromie (2000) summarizes the literature by writing that entrepreneurs have seven distinguishing characteristics: a need for achievement, a need for control over events, a propensity for risk-taking, creativity, autonomy, a tolerance for ambiguity, and self-confidence.[11]

The prevailing values in society also matter. There have been many studies relating economic performance to prevailing values and resulting attitudes, which may affect innovation. Lynn (1991) found that differences in attitudes toward competitiveness can help explain differences in economic growth in a sample of 41 countries.[12] Countries where the population is more accepting of competition can be expected to grow more rapidly. Shane (1993) examined the effect of such cultural values as individualism, uncertainty avoidance, and masculinity on national rates of innovation in 33 countries in 1975 and 1980; he found that high rates of innovation were most closely related to cultural values that promote the acceptance of uncertainty, but he acknowledged that individualism is also an influence.[13] These authors concluded that nations may differ in their rates of innovation because of the cultural values of their citizens.

A number of studies have documented the importance of trust. Economists have been aware of this aspect for some time. In an early contribution, Banfield (1958) studied the economy of a poor village in southern Italy and attributed poverty to a set of values that were detrimental to economic performance.[14] People tended to trust other family members but put less trust in other members of the community. Those findings are related and similar to those of Putnam (1993), who argued that the northern regions of Italy were performing better than those in the South because the northerners, on average, belonged to more associations.[15] Knack and Keefer (1997) stress the importance of trust in incomplete contracts because it decreases the level of uncertainty.[16] Tabellini (2010) discusses the economic importance of trust from the angle of the prisoner's dilemma.[17] He found that trust increases the efficiency of anonymous market exchanges and reduces the need for external enforcement of contracts. Thus, trust helps an innovative economy by making it easier to enforce incomplete contracts with suppliers and buyers of new products and services, and by reducing principal agent problems within newly established firms, thus reducing the risk associated with new investments.[18] Many studies have documented a relationship between trust among citizens as reported in surveys and national output and income per capita.[19]

Among those studies close to ours, there are also studies of how values and resulting attitudes in general in the workplace affect performance. Phelps (2006) explores the relationship between economic performance and values and resulting attitudes.[20] He found that economies exhibited better performance where more people regard work as important to them, want to show initiative at work, find jobs that are interesting, accept competition in markets, and prefer new ideas to old ones.

Tabellini (2010) used cultural variables to explain the variation in output per capita and the growth of output in European regions.[21] He used questions from the World Values Survey to describe the positive aspects of culture: one measured trust of other people, another measured tolerance and respect for other people, and the third measured the degree to which people feel they have control of their own lives. There was one negative cultural trait, the extent to which parents try to teach their children to be obedient. He found that these value variables could help explain differences in output and growth across European regions.

In another study, Phelps and Zoega (2009) found that the possession of a good work ethic, the ability to take initiative, and the ability to place trust in others raise job satisfaction and also affect the rate of unemployment and labor force participation.[22] In related work by Bojilov and Phelps (2012), the authors found that job satisfaction is higher in nations where more people think it is fair to pay more to the more productive, agree that the direction of firms is best left to the owners, and feel that new ideas may be worth developing and testing.[23] In particular, the study found that economic performance is worse in nations where "traditional" attitudes are strong.

In *Mass Flourishing* (2013), Phelps discusses the factors that make nations flourish on a wide scale and the possible reasons why such flourishing is under threat today.[24] He traces the innovations and prosperity in many nations—from the 19th century to the 1960s—to modern values such as the desire to create, explore, and meet challenges. He argues that it was these values that fueled the dynamism that was necessary for the widespread, indigenous innovation that created "mass flourishing"—meaningful work, self-expression, and personal growth.

Arnorsson and Zoega (2016) measure values and beliefs by region in Europe and relate them to youth unemployment and youth labor force participation.[25] Social capital is measured by the level of trust in fellow citizens, as well as by the set of shared values that have to do with behavior in the labor market. The results show a clear relationship between values and youth unemployment and participation, including when differences in institutions and the state of the business cycle between countries are taken into account. Thus, teaching children to be independent, imaginative, and tolerant contributes positively to values, as does a higher level of trust toward fellow citizens. The differences can account for differences in unemployment, male labor force participation, and the average hours of work across regions.

3. Exploring the Data and Empirical Relationships

We start by describing the data briefly, then explain the empirical method that we employ (the method of canonical correlations proposed by Harold Hotelling in the 1930s and widely used in other social sciences), and then show the results in table form and graphs.[26]

3.1. The Data

In our context, cultural values and institutional variables make up one latent variable and economic performance another. We use our statistical method to generate a single cultural variable based on answers to questions in the World Values Survey. In our choice of variables, we are guided by the values found in our interviews of the successful Icelandic innovators, described in Chapter 4. These include the extent to which people trust their fellow citizens; the extent to which they desire job security; the ability to take the initiative on the job or to achieve on the job; the values instilled in children, which include obedience and independence; and attitudes toward competition. The institutional variable measuring economic freedom is taken from the Heritage Foundation. The latent economic performance variable is calculated as a weighted average of the rate of indigenous innovation, the rate of imported (or adapted) innovation taken from Chapter 2, job satisfaction, the employment rate $(1 - u)$, the fertility rate, and the rate of male labor force participation. We include the fertility rate as an indicator of the optimism parents have concerning the future. The numbers for each country are shown in Table 5.1.

We note several patterns in the data. Parents in southern Europe are keener to teach their children to be obedient than parents in northern Europe and the United States, while the latter value independence more. We also observe that the UK and the US are more accepting of competition than the rest of the countries (apart from Norway). Northern Europe and the US are also higher on the list when it comes to economic freedom. The US and Sweden have the highest rates of indigenous innovation.

3.2. Canonical Correlations

We employ the method of canonical correlations to map the relationship between values and innovation.[27] The method makes sense of the cross-covariance matrices of two multidimensional variables. To perform the canonical correlation, we gather together some observed measures into two different variable sets, X and Y, which represent the two multidimensional components of the latent variables, henceforth known as the canonical variables X and Y. The variable X is our measure of values, and the variable Y is our measure of innovation. Next, we assign weights to the variables within X and Y—see Table 5.2—in order to create two linear combinations, X^* and Y^*, one for each variable set, which maximize the bivariate correlation between the canonical variables. The set of linear combinations, called canonical functions, are chosen to maximize the canonical correlation between the two latent canonical variables X^* and Y^*. Several uncorrelated components or functions can be determined, as in principal components analysis.

The first function creates the linear combination, so the two latent variables are as strongly correlated as possible. However, there will probably be some residual variance left over which cannot be explained by the first canonical function. That means we can find another linear combination that maximizes the correlation between X^* and Y^* given the residual variance subject to the constraint that the new function has to be perfectly uncorrelated with the previous one. This gives us another set of X^* and Y^*. The

Table 5.1. Variables used in analysis

	X										Y			
	Values							Institutions	Innovation		Economic performance			
		Job			Children							Other variables		
	Trust	Job security	Job Initiative	Achieve	Obedience	Independence	Accepting competition	Economic freedom	Indigenous	Imported	Job satisf.	Empl. rate	Fert. rate	Lab. f. part.
Australia	46.2	71.4	64.3	57.1	0.4	0.6	28.6	82.2	0.4	0.2	12.5	93.2	1.8	72.6
Austria	36.8	71.7	45.6	56.7	0.1	0.7	17.5	71.4	0.3	0.3	24.0	95.3	1.4	68.2
Belgium	34.6	32.0	35.2	38.5	0.4	0.3	8.1	71.7	0.1	0.1	9.1	92.1	1.7	60.7
Canada	99.9	50.0	50.0	50.0	1.0	0.0	0.0	80.2	0.4	0.1	0.0	91.9	1.6	72.5
Denmark	76.0	44.3	50.8	57.4	0.1	0.8	12.4	79.2	0.3	0.2	22.5	93.9	1.8	71.0
Finland	64.7	69.4	46.4	61.5	0.2	0.5	7.0	74.6	0.3	0.4	7.2	89.3	1.8	66.8
France	27.2	29.4	35.2	46.9	0.3	0.3	8.5	64.7	0.1	0.0	11.0	89.8	1.9	62.9
Germany	38.8	78.5	44.5	53.1	0.1	0.7	13.6	70.6	0.1	0.0	13.0	91.9	1.3	67.3
Greece	21.3	55.2	34.2	46.7	0.2	0.4	14.2	60.6	0.0	0.1	11.4	88.6	1.3	63.9
Ireland	38.9	80.6	57.6	70.4	0.6	0.6	19.2	82.5	0.2	0.4	26.1	90.5	2.0	70.0
Italy	30.8	73.9	51.7	67.4	0.3	0.4	17.0	62.6	0.0	0.0	15.8	90.4	1.3	61.6
Japan	39.1	0.0	0.0	0.0	1.0	0.8	0.0	73.0	0.0	0.0	0.0	96.0	1.4	74.9
Netherlands	61.7	46.1	79.1	63.8	0.3	0.5	5.4	77.4	0.3	0.2	7.4	95.2	1.7	71.9
Norway	75.1	25.0	50.0	25.0	0.2	0.9	25.0	68.6	0.1	0.2	0.0	95.9	1.9	75.8
Portugal	17.2	88.7	61.0	74.4	0.3	0.4	9.1	63.9	0.2	0.0	13.5	92.6	1.4	68.8
Spain	34.3	100.0	33.3	66.7	0.3	0.4	7.9	69.1	0.1	0.1	9.6	83.3	1.3	66.2
Sweden	70.7	100.0	100.0	100.0	0.2	0.6	16.4	70.8	0.6	0.3	14.9	92.7	1.8	69.5
Switzerland	55.4	51.7	65.5	64.3	0.1	0.6	12.1	79.5	0.3	0.1	16.9	96.4	1.5	77.3
UK	40.3	28.6	42.9	28.6	0.4	0.5	20.5	79.4	0.3	0.2	14.9	93.1	1.8	70.3
US	39.4	67.7	47.3	67.1	0.3	0.5	27.3	81.0	0.65	0.28	22.2	93.4	2.0	73.6

Notes: The innovation variables, employment rate, fertility rate, and male labor force participation are averages from 1993 to 2013; the measures of people values are taken from the European Values Study conducted in 2008 and 2009; the measure of economic freedom is from the Heritage Foundation index for 2008.

first function is the most important; the second has another linear combination that maximizes the correlation between X^* and Y^* given the residual variance subject to the constraint that the new function has to be perfectly uncorrelated with the previous one and so on. This process can be repeated as many times as there are variables in the smaller variable set, or until there is no residual variance left. The researcher may begin to interpret the results when all the canonical functions have been retrieved.[28] Appendix I has the definitions of important concepts for the interpretation of the results following an example described by Sherry and Henson (2005).[29]

In Table 5.2 we report the results of the canonical correlation analysis for a set of 20 countries.[30] The results consist of a function generating a canonical correlation.[31] The first column in the function has a standardized coefficient: the weight attached to the variables to generate the linear combination X^* or Y^* so as to maximize the correlation between the two.[32] The second column has the structure coefficient: the bivariate correlation between each observed variable and the latent variable, X^* or Y^*. The higher the value of the structure coefficient, the more correlated the variable is with the relevant latent variable. The sign of the correlation is also important. In most cases the sign of the standardized and the structure coefficients are the same. In the few cases that they are not the same, we find that the sign of the structure coefficient is more informative.[33] The third column lists the squared value of the structure coefficient: the proportion of the variance that an observed variable shares linearly with a latent variable. Finally, the last column is the communality coefficient: it sums up the squared value of the structure coefficients and hence gives an assessment of the importance of each observed variable for all the significant functions.

The first canonical correlation has a coefficient of 0.951, and the hypothesis that it is nonexistent can be rejected at the 5 percent level. The table shows that X^*—the latent variable that measures innovation-inducing values—consists of trust, the willingness to take initiative, the desire to achieve on the job, teaching children to be independent, acceptance of competition, and economic freedom, all of which contribute positively to innovation, and teaching children to be obedient, which has a negative effect.[34]

The findings are that Y^* consists positively of indigenous innovation, imported innovation job satisfaction—justified by assuming that innovative industries bring more job satisfaction—employment, and male labor force participation.[35] We also included the fertility rate in the Y variable, which we justify by the fact that high fertility is indicative of optimism about the future. Of these, the employment rate is the least significant and the rate of indigenous innovation the most significant.

Table 5.2. Canonical correlation analysis, 1993–2013

Variable	Std. coef.	Str. coef.	Str. coef^2	Com. coef. (%)
Input—values conducive or detrimental to innovation				
Trust	−0.103	0.066	0.004	93
Job security	−0.727	0.426	0.181	90
Job initiative	−0.635	0.499	0.249	91
Job achievement	1.656	0.593	0.351	96
Children obedience	0.045	−0.292	0.085	99
Children independence	0.101	0.187	0.035	97
Acceptance of competition	0.513	0.593	0.352	61
Economic freedom	0.567	0.602	0.362	84
Output—consequences—benefits				
Indigenous innovation	0.307	0.725	0.525	100
Imported innovation	−0.102	0.580	0.336	100
Job satisfaction	0.711	0.810	0.656	100
Employment	−0.245	0.103	0.011	100
Fertility rate	0.372	0.594	0.353	100
Male labor participation	0.267	0.245	0.060	100

Canonical correlation coefficient		Squared canonical coefficient	
0.951		0.904	
F-statistics	1.8219		
Prob. >F	0.0351		

3.3. Graphs

Figure 5.1 shows the relationship between the estimated latent variable for values and institutions X^* and the latent variable for innovation Y^*. The fit of the relationship is quite striking from the least innovative economy, which is, surprisingly, Japan, to the most innovative one, which is the United States.

In the upper right-hand corner, we have countries that have the most innovation-inducing values, as well as the most innovative economies. These are the United States, Ireland, Denmark, Sweden, Australia, and Switzerland. In the bottom left-hand corner, we have the worst-performing economies both in terms of values and in terms of the level of innovation. These are Japan, Norway, Greece, Belgium, and Canada.

A similar pattern emerges in Figure 5.2, where we plot both indigenous and imported innovation against the latent values variable X^*. The fit is now worse than in Figure 5.1, but the pattern of countries is similar. When it comes to imported innovation, we find that Ireland, Finland, and Sweden

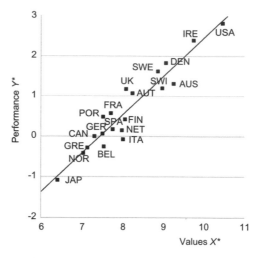

Figure 5.1. Values and innovation. *Notes:* The figure plots the canonical correlation from Table 5.2. Abbreviations: Australia (AUS), Austria (AUT), Belgium (BEL), Canada (CAN), Denmark (DEN), Finland (FIN), France (FRA), Germany (GER), Greece (GRE), Ireland (IRE), Italy (ITA), Japan (JAP), Netherlands (NET), Norway (NOR), Portugal (POR), Spain (SPA), Sweden (SWE), Switzerland (SWI), the United Kingdom (UK), and the United States (USA).

are at the top of the list, and Japan, Portugal, Italy, Germany, and France are at the bottom of the list. The most and the least innovative countries thus remain the same with a few exceptions. The United States is no longer at the top of the list when it comes to adopting innovation; instead it is Finland and Ireland. Finland does better than its values would lead us to predict, and Switzerland, Australia, and the United States do worse.

These results give support to the thesis in Phelps (2006) and Bojilov and Phelps (2012) that dynamism derives from modern values.[36] The results are also consistent with the results of the study of the pattern of indigenous innovation in Chapter 2. There it is shown that the rate of indigenous innovation was higher in the US, the UK, and Scandinavia after 1990 than in the continental European countries and Japan. The country with the values most conducive to innovation is the US, followed by Ireland, Australia, Denmark, Sweden, and Switzerland. Thereafter, we have the UK, Finland, and Austria. Of these, Sweden seems to do better than its values would suggest and Ireland somewhat worse. In contrast, Germany, France, Italy, and Japan are lacking in such values and have lower rates of indigenous innovation. These finding thus help explain the pattern of indigenous innovation found in Chapter 2.

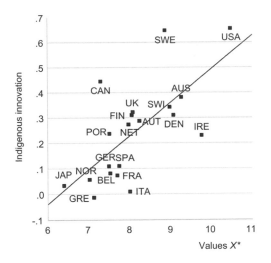

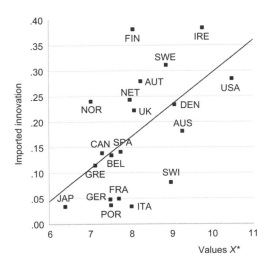

Figure 5.2. Values, indigenous innovation and imported innovation.
Note: Abbreviations: Australia (AUS), Austria (AUT), Belgium (BEL), Canada (CAN), Denmark (DEN), Finland (FIN), France (FRA), Germany (GER), Greece (GRE), Ireland (IRE), Italy (ITA), Japan (JAP), Netherlands (NET), Norway (NOR), Portugal (POR), Spain (SPA), Sweden (SWE), Switzerland (SWI), the United Kingdom (UK), and the United States (USA).

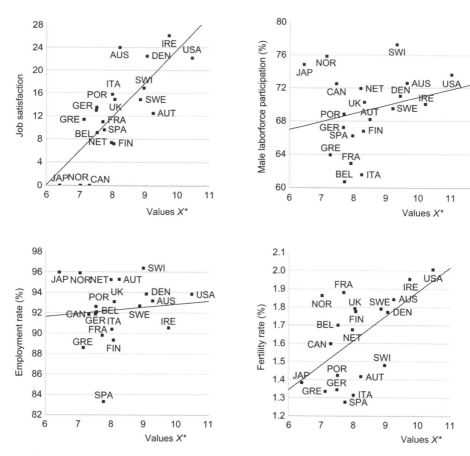

Figure 5.3. Job satisfaction, male labor force participation, employment rate, and fertility rate. *Note:* Abbreviations: Australia (AUS), Austria (AUT), Belgium (BEL), Canada (CAN), Denmark (DEN), Finland (FIN), France (FRA), Germany (GER), Greece (GRE), Ireland (IRE), Italy (ITA), Japan (JAP), Netherlands (NET), Norway (NOR), Portugal (POR), Spain (SPA), Sweden (SWE), Switzerland (SWI), the United Kingdom (UK), and the United States (USA).

We next plot the four remaining economic performance variables against the latent values variable in Figure 5.3

Again, there is a strong upward-sloping relationship, and the alignment of the countries is similar to before. The United States does well in all four graphs, as do the English-speaking and the Nordic countries, while the southern European countries and Japan do a lot worse. Japan has high employment and male labor force participation, while job satisfaction and fertility are very low.

4. Conclusions

We have studied measures of values and resulting attitudes and various measures of innovation for 20 OECD countries. Several variables contribute positively to the innovation-inducing values variable, such as trust, the willingness to take initiative, the desire to achieve on the job, teaching children to be independent, and the acceptance of competition. In addition, economic freedom is important. One variable—an emphasis on teaching children to be obedient—has a negative impact on the latent values variable; hence, it may reduce innovation. The economic performance variable depends positively on indigenous innovation, imported innovation, job satisfaction, employment, fertility, and male labor force participation.

APPENDIX I

Canonical Correlation: Main Concepts

- *Canonical correlation coefficient:* The correlation between the two latent variables X^* and Y^* in a given canonical function.
- *Squared canonical correlation:* Represents the proportion of variance shared by the two latent variables. It indicates the amount of shared variance between the variable sets.
- *Canonical function:* Set of standardized coefficients from the observed variable sets.
- *Standardized coefficient:* The weights attached to observed variables in the two variable sets to yield the linear combinations that maximize the correlation between the two latent variables—that is, the canonical correlation. They are standardized because of the constraint that the variance of the pair of canonical variables in a canonical function is equal, $var(X_i^*) = var(Y_i^*) = 1 \ \forall \ i,$ where i represents the number of canonical functions. This is vital for obtaining unique values for the coefficients.
- *Structure coefficient:* The bivariate correlation between an observed variable and a latent variable, X or Y. They help to define the structure of the latent variable by estimating which observed variables contribute to the creation of the latent variable.
- *Squared structure coefficient:* The proportion of variance an observed variable linearly shares with a latent variable.
- *Communality coefficient:* The proportion of variance in each variable that is explained by all the canonical functions that are interpreted. It informs the researcher about the usefulness of the observed variable for the whole model.

APPENDIX II
Variable Descriptions

Variable	Measure	Details	Identifier	Source
Trust	Row percentage	Those who replied that most people can be trusted after being asked, "Generally speaking, would you say that most people can be trusted or that you can't be too careful in dealing with people?"	Q7	EVS (2011)
Job security	Row percentage	The percentage of people who mentioned job security as an important aspect of a job	Q14	EVS (2011)
Job initiative	Row percentage	The percentage of people who mentioned the opportunity to use initiative as an important aspect of a job	Q14	EVS (2011)
Job achieve	Row percentage	The percentage of people who mentioned the feeling that they can achieve something as an important aspect of a job	Q14	EVS (2011)
Children obedience	Row percentage	Those who listed obedience as a quality to teach children at home	Q52	EVS (2011)
Children independence	Row percentage	Those who listed independence as a quality to teach children at home	Q52	EVS (2011)
Children imagination	Row percentage	Those who listed imagination as a quality to teach children at home	Q52	EVS (2011)
Children tolerance	Row percentage	Those who listed tolerance and respect as qualities to teach children at home	Q52	EVS (2011)
Acceptance of competition	Row percentage	Those who fully agreed that competition stimulates people to work hard and develop new ideas		
Economic freedom		The 2008 value of the Heritage Foundation index for economic freedom		
Indigenous innovation	Percentage	Taken from Chapter 2		
Imported innovation	Percentage	Taken from Chapter 2		

(*continued*)

Variable	Measure	Details	Identifier	Source
Job satisfaction	Row percentage	Those who said they were overall satisfied (10) with their job on the scale 1 (dissatisfied) to 10 (satisfied)		EVS (2011)
Male employment rate		Average from 1991 to 2013		World Bank (2017)
Fertility rate		Average from 1991 to 2013		World Bank (2017)
Male labor force participation rate		Average from 1991 to 2013		World Bank (2017)

Note: EVS = European Values Study.

6

Individual Values, Entrepreneurship, and Innovation

Raicho Bojilov

ABSTRACT This chapter investigates the causal link between economic culture and economic performance. Using data from the World Values Survey (WVS) for 1990–1993, we design an index of modernism and an index of traditionalism, which summarize in a simple way most of the beliefs, attitudes, and social norms about economic life in a society. Our results show that the index of modernism is positively correlated with total factor productivity (TFP) growth and indigenous and imported innovation, while the index of traditionalism is not. To address concerns about endogeneity and reversed causation, we consider a proxy for our index of modernism. Using data from the General Social Survey (GSS), we uncover the impact of the country of origin of one's ancestors on the probability that a first-, second-, third-, or fourth-generation American becomes a successful entrepreneur. We treat the estimated country effects as our proxy for inherited modernism. The results show that the country effects are positively related to both the index of modernism and our measures of economic performance, TFP growth, indigenous innovation, and imported innovation.

Introduction

Recent research in economics has found a strong causal relation between aggregate levels of social trust and gross domestic product growth (see, for example, Algan and Cahuc, 2010).[1] Butler, Giuliano, and Guiso (2016) also provide evidence that moderate levels of social trust on the individual level have a positive effect on individual economic performance.[2] While there is a broad consensus that social trust is crucial to economic growth, it still remains an open question whether other beliefs, attitudes, and social norms about economic life have a causal impact on economic performance.[3] This chapter investigates this issue on both individual and nation-wide levels.

Figure 6.1 plots the annual average growth rates of TFP for the period 1993–2013 for a set of developed economies against an index of modernism that we design in the course of our work. It shows that there is a strong positive correlation between our measure of modernism and economic performance, TFP. Naturally, Figure 6.1 hardly constitutes a proof of causality. This chapter investigates to what extent the observed patterns survive the implementation of our empirical strategy, which is designed to address some of the obvious concerns about endogeneity and reversed causality.

As a first step, we consider individual-level data from a set of developed economies on beliefs, attitudes, and social norms about economic life, which come from the second wave of the WVS. Using these data, we design in Section 2 a very simple index of modernism and an index of traditionalism. Next, we relate the indexes of modernism and traditionalism to the annual average TFP growth rates and indigenous and imported innovation for our set of developed economies. The results confirm the observed pattern in Figure 6.1: we document a strong positive association between our index of modernism and our measures of productivity growth and innovation.

To address some of the obvious econometric concerns, we study how the country of origin of one's ancestors affects the individual economic performance of first-, second-, third-, and fourth-generation Americans. In particular, we study how the country of origin affects the probability of becoming a successful entrepreneur, where a successful entrepreneur is defined as someone who has created a business that employs more than 10 individuals. Then, we use the estimated country effects as proxies for the index of modernism. The results show a positive correlation between the country effects and the index of modernism, as well as a positive relationship between the country effects and TFP growth, indigenous innovation, and imported innovation. To the extent to which we have addressed the most acute issues of reversed causality and endogeneity, we believe that our results provide the first evidence for a causal relation between economic performance, in particular economic innovation, and a broader set of beliefs, attitudes, and norms that reflect the economic culture of a country.

1. Literature Review

This chapter contributes to the related literature in two aspects. First, we attempt to relate the characteristics of an economy to individual attitudes and beliefs. Second, we focus on the conditions for innovation and the proclivity to innovate at the individual level. The difference was previously discussed in Chapter 2.

In the analysis of individual-level data, our work also relates closely to recent methodological advances in establishing a causal relation between social trust and individual outcomes. Since the path-breaking work of Banfield (1958), Coleman (1974), and Putnam (2000), trust, broadly defined as a cooperative attitude outside the family circle, has been considered by social scientists to be a key element of many economic and social outcomes.[4] Studies of how immigrants' attitudes evolve as a function of their country of origin and country of arrival shed an interesting light on the malleability of trust. They show that the beliefs and behaviors of immigrants are influenced by their countries of origin (Miguel and Jean, 2011).[5]

Individual beliefs and attitudes are not set in stone. The environment can modify them. But they are systematically characterized by the kind of inertia that can leave its mark on at least one and perhaps more generations. One of the most common strategies for establishing a causal relation between trust and culture more generally, on one hand, and economic performance, on the other, is to search for historical events that cause exogenous variations in trust that could be used as instruments. To rationalize the use of historical events, the literature draws on the theory of the transmission of values. Studies by Bisin and Verdier (2001); Guiso, Sapienza, and Zingales (2016); and Tabellini (2010) stress the role of two main forces.[6] A portion of current values is shaped by the contemporaneous environment (horizontal transmission of values), and another portion is shaped by beliefs inherited from earlier generations (vertical transmission of values).

Algan and Cahuc (2010) propose to use this time variation in inherited trust in a standard growth equation.[7] Since it is already well established that the parents' social capital is a good predictor of the social capital of children, they use the trust that US descendants have inherited from their forebears who immigrated from different countries at different dates to detect changes in inherited trust in the countries of origin. They can get time-varying measures of trust inherited from the origin country and the destination country by running the same exercise for forebears who immigrated in other periods—for instance, between 1920 and 1950. With time-varying measures of inherited trust, they can estimate the impact of changes in inherited trust on changes in income per capita in the countries of origin. By providing a time-varying measure of trust over long periods, they can control for both omitted time-invariant factors and other observed time-varying factors, such as changes in the economic, political, cultural, and social environments.

2. Indexes of Modernism and Traditionalism

In this section, we describe our indexes of traditionalism and modernism, which have been discussed at greater length in Bojilov and Phelps (2013).[8] Then, we briefly review the levels of traditionalism and modernism in different countries according to our two indexes. We construct an index of traditionalism for a set of developed OECD countries based on the second wave of the WVS, conducted between 1990 and 1993.[9] The index is simply equal to the average of the proportion of people who respond in the affirmative to a set of questions. We give equal weight to each question because the limited size of the data does not allow us to derive factors and because assigning equal weight appears to us as good as any other arbitrary assignment of relative importance.

The first question that we include in the index is, "Do you think that service and help to others is important in life?" (a007). With it, we hope to determine the presence of a sense of duty and commitment to the larger community in which one lives. It is consistent with the teachings of all major religions and traditional philosophical schools. It also reflects a key feature in classical conservatism: individuals and the meaning of life within the web of bonds that a society represents.

We also incorporate the questions, "Should children respect and love their parents?" (a025) and, "Should parents be responsible for their children?" (a026). These two questions reflect the degree to which one individual is defined in the context of her or his relation with the rest of society. We like these questions because they call attention to fundamental issues about what modernity is in an unexpected context. Since the time of the late Roman Empire, social relations have often been explained to laymen through an easy-to-appreciate analogy: the monarch relates to his subjects as the head of the family relates to his children. What makes the analogy very powerful is the combination of a logical fallacy with the universal cultural preeminence of the paterfamilias from the Iron Age until the birth of modernity. The arrival of modernity, with its industrialization, wars, and changes in family and society, put all of these traditional roles and percep tions in question. Doubts about traditional roles in society and the family, as well as relativism and the conditionality of one's relation to others, even within the family, are captured, we believe, through the negative response to questions a025 and a026.

Another way to interpret these questions is to explore the extent to which changes in the understanding of social order have affected the understanding of family relations and roles. Within a social context, the US Declaration of Independence was the first document to provide a very powerful rationale for overthrowing the old order: a government that has violated its obligations to its people has also forfeited any claim to the respect and the obedience of its people. This principle has been evoked innumerable times since. But to what extent has the same concept of contractual relations also entered the private sphere, family relations in particular? We hope that the responses to questions a025 and a026 shed some light on this question.

Finally, we also consider the question, "Is unselfishness an important child quality?" (a041). This question reflects the same concerns expressed earlier but in a more abstract context. Consciously or not, the importance of one's own good has been a central feature of modernity. Individualism is central to classical liberalism, to the understanding of society in terms of contractual relations, and, we believe, to the meaning of modernity. The question, as stated, is provocative and may be misunderstood by the respondents. Yet we believe that the respondents had to confront the question of whether they would, as parents, ultimately prefer that their children give precedence in their actions to their communal duties or to their self-interest.

Is traditionalism good or bad? We do not perceive traditional values and concerns as obsolete or degenerate. A sense of community, social trust, and consideration for others are not necessarily bad things, and in many contexts, they may be crucial to economic development and prosperity, as noted already by many. One hypothesis is that if they are very strong, that may hamper individual initiative, the implementation of new technologies, or the adoption of new products. Alternatively, traditional values may create a sense of shared destiny when people undertake an economic venture, or they may build social capital. For a currently relevant example, many people have suggested that the traditional values of Confucianism are responsible for the strong work ethic of modern Chinese. We take no stand on the role of traditionalism: We are simply interested in statistically controlling for the effect of traditional values on economic development.

We also construct an index of modernism. This index, like the index of traditionalism, is equal to the average of the proportion of people who have answered in the affirmative to some questions contained in the second wave of the WVS. As in the case of traditionalism, the sample size does not allow us to extract factors, so from all arbitrary rules, we assume that each question has the same contribution to the index. We include a set of questions intended to capture the attitude of the respondents to change and its consequences. We hope that the response to the question, "Are you worried about new things?" (e045) reflects attitudes toward the process that generates new products, technologies, techniques, morals, and so on. That is, we hope that it reflects the respondent's degree of self-confidence when facing the rapidly changing world of modernity. The question, "Do you accept new ideas?" (e046) is supposed to shed light on another aspect of the same phenomenon: respondents may be worried about new things but regard them as necessary evils or as unpleasant phenomena that one must nevertheless accept as an inevitable part of modern life. Finally, the question, "Do you think that changes bring new opportunities?" (e047) reflects the extent to which respondents associate new developments with new opportunities to be explored and exploited. An individual may dislike the uncertainty associated with the lottery that modern life is, may accept it as inevitable but believe that the lottery itself provides an exciting set of opportunities, or may regard it as an inevitable evil.

In addition, we also include some questions that are designed to determine respondents' views on the consequence of change in a modern world. We hope that attitudes toward inequality and fairness are central to respondents' answers to the question, "Two secretaries differ in their productivity. Is it fair to pay more to the more productive one?" (c059). That is, the question is whether fairness is to be understood as identical titles implying identical pay or different productivities implying different pay. Phenomena associated with modernity have continuously challenged traditional institutions, and this has led to a corporatist reaction against some of the evils of modern life. The question of the governance of businesses has been central to the ensuing debate: Should owners have control over the management of their firms, or should they consult with other parties involved in the production process, such as workers and government regulators? We hope to capture at least some of these issues with the question, "Do you agree that the owners ought to manage their firms?" (c060). Finally, we also include in our index the question, "Do you agree that competition is good?" (e039), which exposes individual attitudes toward another defining feature of modern economic life. Respondents with a more corporatist or traditionalist view would exhibit skepticism about the virtues of competition. Indeed, related schools of thought point out that competition often may undercut social welfare as a result of the displacement of people and the destruction of long-standing social contexts and communities. There are alternative views

Table 6.1. Indexes of modernism and traditionalism

Country	Modernism	Traditionalism
Austria	0.60	0.57
Belgium	0.54	0.40
Canada	0.66	0.50
Denmark	0.62	0.50
Finland	0.61	0.52
France	0.52	0.51
Germany	0.59	0.56
Ireland	0.63	0.61
Italy	0.58	0.53
Japan	0.47	0.61
Netherlands	0.62	0.57
Norway	0.57	0.55
Portugal	0.56	0.86
Spain	0.52	0.70
Sweden	0.58	0.65
UK	0.58	0.47
US	0.62	0.37

Data source: Bojilov and Phelps (2013).

as well: competition may destroy the old but simultaneously free people to achieve their true potential and ensure that they do good by doing well, through the action of the proverbial invisible hand.

We report the two indexes by country in Table 6.1. The average across countries on the index of modernism is 0.58. The countries with the highest values are the US, Denmark, Ireland, and Canada, at 0.62, 0.62, 0.63, and 0.66, respectively, while the countries with the lowest values are Japan, Spain, and France, at 0.47, 0.52, and 0.52, respectively. Eyeballing the numbers reported in the table, one notices that the Scandinavian and Anglo-Saxon, or more generally northern European countries, have high levels of modernism according to the index. The picture in the South of Europe is, however, much more complex. Their average level of modernism is low relative to the North, but Italy's level is equal to that of the UK and almost the same as that in Germany and Denmark. How can one, then, possibly try to explain the divergence in the economic performance of Italy and the North? Perhaps, the index of traditionalism can suggest a possible explanation.

The average level of traditionalism according to the index is 0.51. The three countries with the highest levels of traditionalism are Portugal, Spain, and Sweden, at 0.86, 0.70, and 0.65, respectively. The three countries with the lowest levels of traditionalism are the US, Belgium, and the UK, at 0.37,

0.40, and 0.47, respectively. The level of the US is just below that of Denmark and Canada. As is the case for modernism, there seems to be a tentative division in Europe between a less traditionalist North and a more traditionalist South. Going back to the case of Italy, we see that traditionalism is relatively high at 0.53.

We find a strong negative correlation of 0.58 between the index of modernism and the index of traditionalism. This finding conforms to our expectation that an increase in modernism is associated with a decrease in traditionalism. However, we have not imposed such a relation on the data through some theoretical restriction when designing the indexes. Thus, the negative correlation is reassuring in the sense that it coincides with our preconceptions based on previous studies in economics and in other social sciences.

3. TFP, Indigenous Innovation, and Imported Innovation

To obtain our aggregate measures of innovation in this chapter, we reestimate our model from Chapter 2 but using only TFP data from the Penn World Tables covering the period from 1950 to 2013. The results that we obtain in this new specification are consistent with those reported in Chapter 2 on the post-WWII period. The reason why we do this exercise is that we can extend the set of countries that we study to the following 17 developed countries: Austria, Belgium, Canada, Denmark, Finland, France, Germany, Ireland, Italy, Japan, the Netherlands, Norway, Portugal, Spain, Sweden, the United Kingdom, and the United States.

The methodology that we use to decompose the TFP growth series into indigenous and imported innovation is discussed at length in Chapter 2. Here, we briefly review the average annual rates of the raw TFP series and indigenous and imported innovation for the period 1993–2013, the two decades after the second wave of the WVS.

Table 6.2 focuses on recent trends in indigenous and imported innovation. It reveals that the US, along with Sweden, is still the country with the highest rate of indigenous innovation, followed by Canada and the UK. Interestingly, while the rate of US indigenous innovation in the last two decades is higher than it was in the 1970s and the 1980s, it is still lower than its counterpart for the period before 1972. Similarly, the UK experienced a partial recovery in its rate of indigenous innovation. At the same time, the rates of indigenous and imported innovation in continental Europe ground to a complete halt in the years following 1990.

Table 6.2. Estimates of cumulative indigenous and cumulative imported innovation for 1993–2013

Country	Indigenous	Imported	$\widehat{\Delta TFP}$	ΔTFP
Austria	0.29	0.28	0.57	0.42
Belgium	0.06	0.11	0.17	0.04
Canada	0.44	0.14	0.58	0.36
Denmark	0.31	0.23	0.54	0.61
Finland	0.31	0.38	0.69	0.86
France	0.07	0.05	0.12	0.03
Germany	0.11	0.05	0.16	0.03
Ireland	0.23	0.38	0.61	0.61
Italy	0.01	0.03	0.04	0.05
Japan	0.03	0.03	0.07	0.03
Netherlands	0.27	0.24	0.51	0.41
Norway	0.06	0.24	0.3	0.17
Portugal	0.26	0.03	0.29	0.2
Spain	0.11	0.14	0.25	0.08
Sweden	0.65	0.31	0.96	0.97
UK	0.32	0.22	0.55	0.63
US	0.65	0.28	0.94	0.97

Notes: The first column reports predicted indigenous innovation, while the second reports the contribution of predicted imported innovation to TFP growth. The third column presents the sum of the first two, and the last one presents the actual TFP series.

4. Innovation and Inherited Beliefs

We postulate that indigenous innovation Y_{ct} in a country c for generation t (25 years) is a function of the index of modernism M_{ct}, controls X_{ct}, and fixed effects for time and country:

$$Y_{ct} = \alpha_0 + \alpha_1 M_{ct} + X_{ct}\alpha + F_c + F_t + \varepsilon_{ct}$$

The index of modernism itself is a function of inherited modernism, controls, and fixed effects:

$$M_{ct} = \beta_0 + \beta_1 M_{ct-1} + Z_{ct}\beta + \Phi_c + \Phi_t + \varepsilon_{ct}$$

There are two major econometric concerns in this context. The first one is that M_{ct-1} is not observed before 1980s. Thus, we use as a proxy for inherited modernism the time-invariant effect of the country of origin of one's ancestors that is obtained in a panel data probit model of the likelihood of

Table 6.3. Estimated country effects on the probability of becoming an entrepreneur and on having high income

Country	Entrepreneur, large		High income	
	Coef.	z	Coef.	z
Austria	0.019	0.09	0.115	0.98
Canada	0.360	2.25	0.009	0.08
China	0.055	0.15	0.139	0.64
Denmark	0.633	2.37	0.044	0.46
Finland	0.190	3.73	0.087	0.72
France	0.187	1.92	0.014	0.22
Germany	0.153	2.31	0.042	1.61
Ireland	0.081	−1.41	0.097	3.32
Italy	0.050	0.64	0.046	1.11
Japan	0.490	1.91	0.512	2.86
Mexico	0.024	0.19	0.002	0.04
Norway	0.537	1.45	0.143	2.30
Spain	0.103	−3.49	0.057	0.58
Sweden	0.795	2.70	0.193	3.04
UK	0.312	2.60	0.158	5.51
US (4th gen)	0.682	2.01	0.274	15.34

Note: The data come from the estimates reported in this chapter.

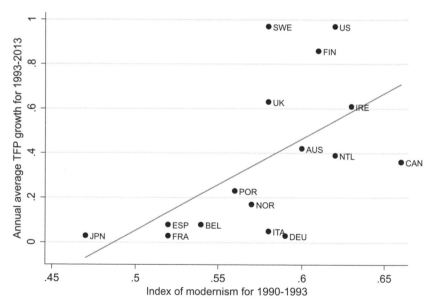

Figure 6.1. Relation between the index of modernism, 1990–1993, and the annual average TFP growth for 1993–2013. *Notes:* The data come from the estimates reported in this chapter. The sample includes the following countries: Austria (AUS), Belgium (BEL), Canada (CAN), Denmark (DEN), Finland (FIN), France (FRA), Germany (DEU), Ireland (IRE), Italy (ITA), Japan (JPN), the Netherlands (NTL), Norway (NOR), Portugal (POR), Spain (ESP), Sweden (SWE), the United Kingdom (UK), and the United States (US). The observations for Denmark and Ireland are very similar, so the observation for Denmark is omitted from the plot for presentational clarity.

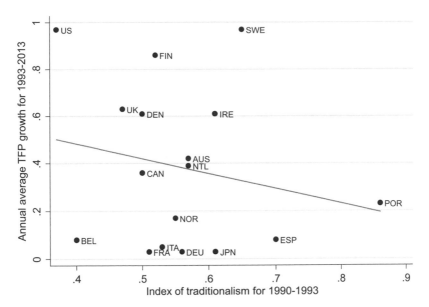

Figure 6.2. Relation between the index of traditionalism, 1990–1993, and the annual average TFP growth for 1993–2013. *Notes:* The data come from the estimates reported in this chapter. The sample includes the following countries: Austria (AUS), Belgium (BEL), Canada (CAN), Denmark (DEN), Finland (FIN), France (FRA), Germany (DEU), Ireland (IRE), Italy (ITA), Japan (JPN), the Netherlands (NTL), Norway (NOR), Portugal (POR), Spain (ESP), Sweden (SWE), the United Kingdom (UK), and the United States (US).

becoming an entrepreneur in the US. The second concern is that inherited modernism and economic performance may be codetermined by a common factor. For this reason, we consider second-, third-, and fourth-generation Americans born between 1945 and 1970 and focus on economic performance after 1990. The ancestors of these Americans moved to the US in the interwar years, before WWI, or in the 19th century. Thus, it is less likely that there is a common factor that affects both innovation at the time of the IT revolution and the inherited beliefs that were formed more than 70 years ago.

This strategy can address some of the identification issues discussed. First, by using the beliefs of US immigrants inherited from the home country instead of the average trust of the current residents of the country, we can exclude reverse causality. We believe that it is very plausible that beliefs in the country of origin of one's ancestors have evolved according to what happened in that country rather than what happened in the US. Similarly, the

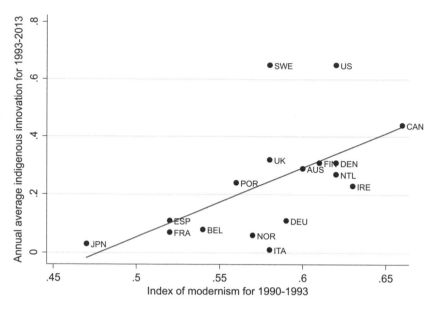

Figure 6.3. Relation between the index of modernism, 1990–1993, and the annual indigenous innovation for 1993–2013. *Notes:* The data come from the estimates reported in this chapter. The sample includes the following countries: Austria (AUS), Belgium (BEL), Canada (CAN), Denmark (DEN), Finland (FIN), France (FRA), Germany (DEU), Ireland (IRE), Italy (ITA), Japan (JPN), the Netherlands (NTL), Norway (NOR), Portugal (POR), Spain (ESP), Sweden (SWE), the United Kingdom (UK), and the United States (US).

evolution of beliefs and attitudes of the descendants of US immigrants is only affected by shocks to the US economy. Moreover, this framework implies that our direct measure of inherited beliefs may play the role of an instrument for culture.

We estimate the inherited beliefs by US immigrants from their home countries by using data from the GSS. Inherited beliefs are measured as the country of origin fixed effect in an individual-level probit regression for the likelihood of creating a company that employs more than 10 workers and the probability of having a high income at the time of the GSS interview, controlling for individual characteristics at the time of birth. We focus on inherited trust from before 1945 for the generation born between 1945 and 1970. Our analysis considers two individual outcomes at the time of the GSS interview: the probability of being a self-employed manager of a company that employs at least 10 individuals and the probability of having a high income. To limit any concerns about reversed causality or endogeneity,

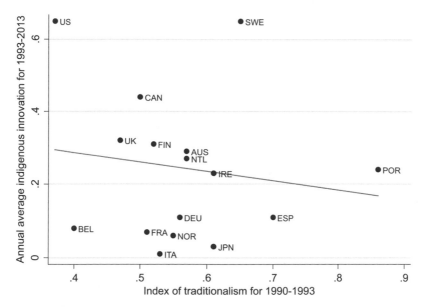

Figure 6.4. Relation between the index of traditionalism, 1990–1993, and the annual indigenous innovation for 1993–2013. *Notes:* The data come from the estimates reported in this chapter. The sample includes the following countries: Austria (AUS), Belgium (BEL), Canada (CAN), Denmark (DEN), Finland (FIN), France (FRA), Germany (DEU), Ireland (IRE), Italy (ITA), Japan (JPN), the Netherlands (NTL), Norway (NOR), Portugal (POR), Spain (ESP), Sweden (SWE), the United Kingdom (UK), and the United States (US). The observations for Denmark and Finland are very similar, so the observation for Denmark is omitted from the plot for presentational clarity.

we include as explanatory variables only characteristics available at the time of birth of the interviewee, such as educational attainment of parents, their occupations, their religion, the number of siblings one has, and the country of origin of one's ancestors.

The results are reported in Table 6.3. The following discussion of the empirical results focuses on the object of interest in our analysis: the country effects in the regression. The reference category in our regressions is country of origin in Eastern Europe or Poland. We find that relative to Eastern Europe and Poland, having ancestors from Austria, China, and Mexico has a very similar impact on the probability of being an entrepreneur who hires more than 10 workers. The only country of origin that has greater negative impact on the entrepreneurial activity of future generations of Americans is Spain. The three countries of origin with the highest positive impact on the entrepreneurial activity of future American generations are the UK, Denmark, and Sweden. The coefficients for Japan and Norway are also highly

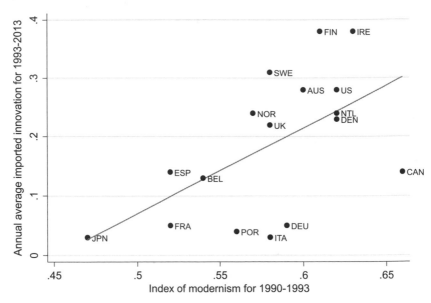

Figure 6.5. Relation between the index of modernism, 1990–1993, and the annual imported innovation for 1993–2013. *Notes:* The data come from the estimates reported in this chapter. The sample includes the following countries: Austria (AUS), Belgium (BEL), Canada (CAN), Denmark (DEN), Finland (FIN), France (FRA), Germany (DEU), Ireland (IRE), Italy (ITA), Japan (JPN), the Netherlands (NTL), Norway (NOR), Portugal (POR), Spain (ESP), Sweden (SWE), the United Kingdom (UK), and the United States (US).

positive, but they are not estimated precisely, possibly because of the small number of descendants from these countries. In our regressions, we also include a US dummy that stands for individuals whose ancestors have lived for at least four generations in the US. It is positive and highly significant.

Our second specification involves the estimation of the probability of having a high income at the time of GSS interview, conditional, again, on information available at the time of birth. As before, we consider a probit estimation framework. The results show that individuals with ancestors from Austria, Canada, China, Denmark, Finland, France, and Mexico are as likely to have a high income as individuals with Eastern European ancestors. The coefficients for Germany and Italy are positive, but not significant. The only countries that stand out as having a positive impact on the income prospects of future Americans are the US itself, the UK, Sweden, and Japan.

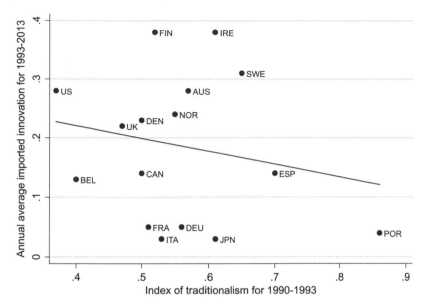

Figure 6.6. Relation between the index of traditionalism, 1990–1993, and the annual imported innovation for 1993–2013. *Notes:* The data come from the estimates reported in this chapter. The sample includes the following countries: Austria (AUS), Belgium (BEL), Canada (CAN), Denmark (DEN), Finland (FIN), France (FRA), Germany (DEU), Ireland (IRE), Italy (ITA), Japan (JPN), the Netherlands (NTL), Norway (NOR), Portugal (POR), Spain (ESP), Sweden (SWE), the United Kingdom (UK), and the United States (US). The observations for the Netherlands and Norway are very similar, so the observation for the Netherlands is omitted from the plot for presentational clarity.

5. Innovation and Modernism

We are finally ready to address the key question about the relation between innovation and modernism. Figure 6.1 plots our index of modernism, based on the second wave of the WVS, 1990–1993, against the average annual TFP growth for the period 1993–2013. As discussed in this chapter's introduction, we find a strong positive relation with a goodness of *t* equal to 0.33.

Next, Figure 6.2 investigates the relation between the index of traditionalism, based on the same data from the second wave of the WVS, and the average annual TFP growth from 1993 to 2013. The slope of the linear prediction is negative, but not significant. Indeed, a casual

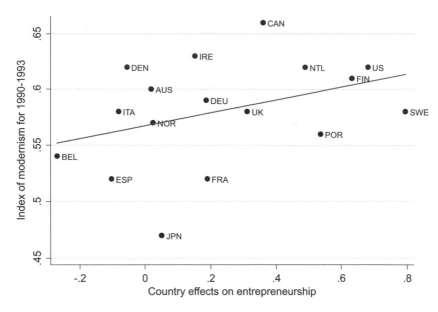

Figure 6.7. Relation between the index of modernism, 1990–1993, and the estimated country effects. *Notes:* The data come from the estimates reported in this chapter. The sample includes the following countries: Austria (AUS), Belgium (BEL), Canada (CAN), Denmark (DEN), Finland (FIN), France (FRA), Germany (DEU), Ireland (IRE), Italy (ITA), Japan (JPN), the Netherlands (NTL), Norway (NOR), Portugal (POR), Spain (ESP), Sweden (SWE), the United Kingdom (UK), and the United States (US).

examination of the scatter plot confirms the absence of any recognizable pattern in the data.

To investigate the relation between innovation and the values of modernism, we plot in Figure 6.3 the index of modernism against our estimates of the average annual indigenous innovation for the period 1993–2013. The results reveal the existence of a tight positive relationship between indigenous innovation and the index of modernism. Figure 6.5 shows that a similar positive relation exists between the index of modernism and imported innovation. At the same time, Figures 6.4 and 6.6 indicate that the index of traditionalism is related neither to indigenous nor to imported innovation. Thus, the impact of modernism and traditionalism on indigenous innovation appears to be very similar to what we previously found to be the relation between modernism, traditionalism, and TFP growth.

We find again a positive relation between modernism and the adoption of innovation from abroad, but this time it is estimated a bit less precisely. As before, the results do not provide any evidence of a significant

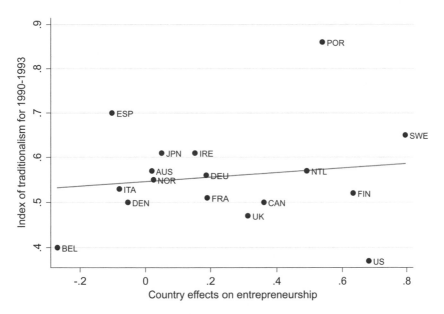

Figure 6.8. Relation between the index of traditionalism, 1990–1993, and the estimated country effects. *Notes:* The data come from the estimates reported in this chapter. The sample includes the following countries: Austria (AUS), Belgium (BEL), Canada (CAN), Denmark (DEN), Finland (FIN), France (FRA), Germany (DEU), Ireland (IRE), Italy (ITA), Japan (JPN), the Netherlands (NTL), Norway (NOR), Portugal (POR), Spain (ESP), Sweden (SWE), the United Kingdom (UK), and the United States (US).

impact, positive or negative, of traditionalism. Together, the plots suggest that modernism is strongly related to both the ability to generate indigenous innovation and the ability to adopt existing innovation from abroad.

Figure 6.3 revealed the presence of a strong positive correlation between aggregate outcomes, such as TFP and imported or indigenous innovation, on the one hand, and the spread and strength of values associated with modernism, on the other hand. However, such a correlation does not indicate causation because of the endogeneity and reverse causality concerns discussed at some length in the preceding section.

For this reason, we use the estimated effects from Table 6.3 as a proxy for the index of modernism. The identifying assumption here is that the country effects reflect the cumulative effect of the inherited beliefs from one's ancestors on entrepreneurial activity. As such, they are at least partially correlated with the index of modernism in each of the countries from which the ancestors of the GSS interviewees came.

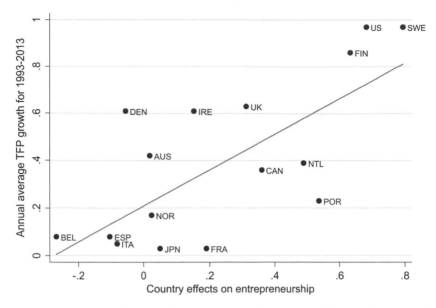

Figure 6.9. Relation between the average annual TFP growth for 1993–2013 and the estimated country effects. *Notes:* The data come from the estimates reported in this chapter. The sample includes the following countries: Austria (AUS), Belgium (BEL), Canada (CAN), Denmark (DEN), Finland (FIN), France (FRA), Germany (DEU), Ireland (IRE), Italy (ITA), Japan (JPN), the Netherlands (NTL), Norway (NOR), Portugal (POR), Spain (ESP), Sweden (SWE), the United Kingdom (UK), and the United States (US). The observations for France and Germany are very similar, so the observation for Germany is omitted from the plot for presentational clarity.

Figure 6.7 investigates the relationship between the index of modernism and the estimated country effects from the preceding section. It shows that there is a significant positive relation between the two.

At the same time, Figure 6.8 reveals that there is no significant correlation between the country effects and the index of traditionalism. In addition, we note that it is unlikely that the beliefs Americans have inherited from their ancestors have a direct impact on productivity or innovation in the country of origin of the ancestors. Thus, we conclude that the estimated country effects meet the basic requirements for being a proxy for the index of modernism.

Finally, we are ready to investigate the relationship between the estimated country effects as a proxy for modernism and the average annual TFP growth rate for the period 1993 to 2013. Figure 6.9 shows that there is a strong positive relation. The point estimate for the country effects in the

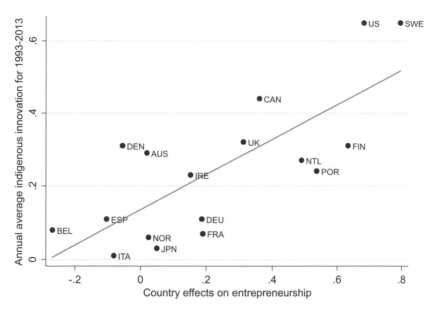

Figure 6.10. Relation between the average annual indigenous innovation for 1993–2013 and the estimated country effects. *Notes:* The data come from the estimates reported in this chapter. The sample includes the following countries: Austria (AUS), Belgium (BEL), Canada (CAN), Denmark (DEN), Finland (FIN), France (FRA), Germany (DEU), Ireland (IRE), Italy (ITA), Japan (JPN), the Netherlands (NTL), Norway (NOR), Portugal (POR), Spain (ESP), Sweden (SWE), the United Kingdom (UK), and the United States (US).

linear regression is 0.76, and it is statistically significant at the 5 percent significance level with an overall goodness of fit of around 0.48. To the extent to which our empirical strategy addresses basic endogeneity concerns and issues of reverse causality, we conclude that these results lend support to the hypothesis of a causal impact of modernist cultural values, such as individualism, drive to achieve, and a desire to explore, on aggregate innovation, measured by TFP.

We conclude by investigating the relationship between the estimated country effects and our own measures of indigenous innovation and imported innovation. Figure 6.10 plots the country effects against the average annual indigenous innovation for the period 1993–2013. We find again a strong positive relation between the two. The slope coefficient in the linear regression of the average annual indigenous innovation on the country effects is estimated at 0.48. It is statistically significant at the 5 percent significance level and the overall goodness of fit is approximately 0.58.

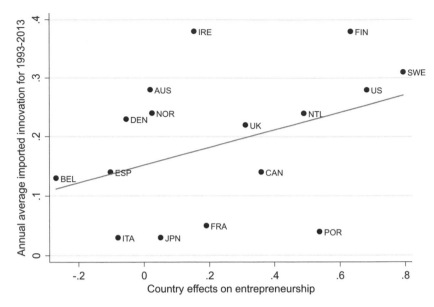

Figure 6.11. Relation between the average annual imported innovation for 1993–2013 and the estimated country effects. *Notes:* The data come from the estimates reported in this chapter. The sample includes the following countries: Austria (AUS), Belgium (BEL), Canada (CAN), Denmark (DEN), Finland (FIN), France (FRA), Germany (DEU), Ireland (IRE), Italy (ITA), Japan (JPN), the Netherlands (NTL), Norway (NOR), Portugal (POR), Spain (ESP), Sweden (SWE), the United Kingdom (UK), and the United States (US). The observations for France and Germany are very similar, so the observation for Germany is omitted from the plot for presentational clarity.

Figure 6.11 shows that there exists also a positive relationship between imported innovation and the estimated country effects. In fact, we can reject the hypothesis that the slope coefficient in the associated regression is zero at the 10 percent significance level but not at the 5 percent significance level.

6. Conclusion

In this chapter, we investigated the relationship between beliefs and attitudes about economic life and economic performance on both aggregate and individual levels. In particular, we focused on the crucial issues of productivity growth and innovation. As preliminary steps in our work, we designed two simple indexes that summarized some basic beliefs and attitudes about economic life, which we called indexes of modernism and of traditionalism. Then, we established that there is a positive correlation between the index of modernism and the previously estimated indigenous and imported innovation, as well as the raw TFP data. To address obvious endogeneity concerns and possible reverse causality, we apply an empirical strategy similar to the one in Algan and Cahuc (2010).[10] Our results show that the country of origin of one's ancestors continues to have a significant effect on the likelihood of becoming an entrepreneur and having a high income long after the time of the immigration of one's ancestors. We show that this effect of the country of origin is positively correlated with the current values of the index of modernism in the respective countries.

Moreover, the associated country effects are related positively to TFP and to both our measure of indigenous innovation and our measure of imported innovation. Thus, we conclude that our results lend some support to the hypothesis that there is a positive causal effect of broad economic culture on economic performance, in particular innovation.

7

Innovation, Job Satisfaction, and Performance in Western European Countries

Gylfi Zoega

ABSTRACT   We study the consequences of low rates of innovation in a sample of 16 European countries. In particular, we study the relationship of these low rates to job satisfaction and the labor market participation of men. Job satisfaction has fallen in the EU over this period, as has the labor force participation of men. We conclude that low levels of innovation may be adversely affecting the levels of job satisfaction and happiness in many European countries.

Introduction

In previous chapters of this volume, we have documented the fall in indigenous innovation throughout the West. Moreover, bad economic performance in general—such as slow growth, low job satisfaction, or low rates of male labor force participation—was shown to be related to values and resulting attitudes such as a lack of trust in society, teaching children to be obedient instead of independent and tolerant, not wanting to achieve on the job, not accepting competition, and not enjoying economic freedom. In this chapter, we will explore the consequences of bad economic performance in a sample of 16 Western European countries. Economic performance is measured by innovation, job satisfaction, and male labor force participation.

1. Job Satisfaction and Labor Force Participation, 1981–2008

The ultimate goal of economic activity must be to make people satisfied at work and happy in the sense of flourishing in their professional and private lives. In earlier chapters, we have measured the rate of indigenous innovation and shown the relationship between institutions and indigenous innovation. These results show a slowdown of innovation in the 1970s and the effect of values on the rate of innovation, both indigenous and transmitted, in a cross section of OECD countries. Here, we investigate which European countries are doing best when it comes to job satisfaction—the fulfillment people get at work—labor force participation, and overall life happiness.

Table 7.1 shows the proportion of responders in the European Values Study who claim to be satisfied at work when asked to rate their satisfaction on a scale from 1 to 10, where 1 means "dissatisfied," 10 means "satisfied," and the numbers in between indicate intermediate levels of satisfaction. The first four columns show the proportion who chose 10 (that is, are "satisfied"), and the next four columns show the proportion who chose 8 or above. The last three columns show our estimated rate of innovation, average value from 1991 to 2013, from Chapter 2. These are the rate of indigenous innovation, the rate of transmitted innovation, and actual total factor productivity (TFP) growth.

Several observations can be made about the patterns found in the table. First, job satisfaction has fallen in many of the countries since 1981, as shown in Figure 7.1, which includes the level of job satisfaction from 1981 to 2008. Second, the level of job satisfaction is higher in the Nordic countries, Ireland, Switzerland, and the UK than in many Continental economies, such as Belgium, the Netherlands, and Spain. Third, there appears to be some convergence of job satisfaction between 1981 and 2008; the countries where workers were most satisfied in 1981 are the countries where job satisfaction has decreased the most since then.

When the sum of those who chose 8 or above is used in columns 5–8, the results change so that the same decline in job satisfaction is not observed. It follows that it is mainly in the proportion who claim to be perfectly satisfied (that is, who chose 10) that the differences across countries emerge.

We next turn to labor force participation for men. Figure 7.2 shows the values from 1984 to 2014. Note that the participation rate for men has fallen in all countries except the Netherlands and Germany. We also put

Table 7.1. Job satisfaction and innovation

	Job satisfaction, proportion "satisfied" (10)				Job satisfaction, proportion choosing 8-10				Innovation, 1991–2013		
	1981	1990	1999	2008	1981	1990	1999	2008	Indigenous	Transmission	Actual TFP
Belgium	15.2	19.3	12.4	9.0	59.7	64.2	53.0	65.5	0.08	0.13	0.08
Denmark	36.5	26.1	20.6	23.0	74.9	75.5	69.5	72.4	0.31	0.23	0.61
Finland	—	12.0	7.1	7.5	—	61.0	57.4	63.0	0.31	0.38	0.86
France	9.5	8.2	7.4	11.0	42.1	40.1	43.0	53.1	0.07	0.05	0.03
Germany	9.4	7.2	12.5	12.5	48.9	46.9	55.5	59.4	0.11	0.05	0.03
Ireland	24.0	25.0	26.5	24.9	68.2	64.2	59.0	70.5	0.23	0.38	0.61
Italy	21.6	14.6	14.1	15.9	55.3	53.0	49.8	52.3	0.01	0.03	0.05
Netherlands	16.9	9.6	4.4	7.1	65.0	68.0	58.9	65.6	0.27	0.24	0.39
Norway	31.6	21.2	—	18.8	75.3	66.5	—	69.5	0.06	0.24	0.17
Spain	16.6	12.7	12.0	9.7	46.2	45.2	48.9	49.5	0.11	0.14	0.08
Sweden	20.7	21.0	7.5	14.4	69.9	71.6	52.2	62.6	0.65	0.31	0.97
Switzerland	—	—	—	16.9	—	—	—	76.2	0.34	0.08	0.20
UK	22.8	18.4	10.3	15.9	63.6	55.9	48.3	59.9	0.32	0.22	0.63

Data source: European Values Study (https://europeanvaluesstudy.eu/).

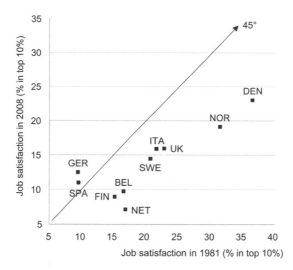

Figure 7.1. The fall of job satisfaction. *Notes:* The figure shows the share of responders in the European Values Study who claimed to be satisfied at work as a function of the proportion satisfied in 1981 and in 2008. The upward-sloping line is the 45° line. The country labels are Belgium (BEL), Denmark (DEN), Finland (FIN), Germany (GER), Italy (ITA), Netherlands (NET), Norway (NOR), Spain (SPA), Sweden (SWE), and the United Kingdom (UK). *Data source:* European Values Study.

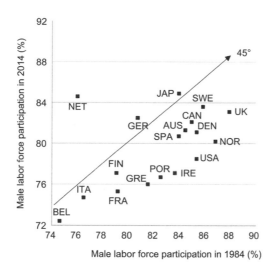

Figure 7.2. The fall of male labor force participation rates. *Notes:* The upward-sloping line is the 45° line. The country labels are Belgium (BEL), Denmark (DEN), Finland (FIN), France (FRA), Germany (GER), Greece (GRE), Ireland (IRE), Italy (ITA), the Netherlands (NET), Norway (NOR), Portugal (POR), Spain (SPA), Sweden (SWE), the United Kingdom (UK), and the United States (USA).

the US in the figure for comparison. Note that its performance is no better than that of the European countries.

2. Innovation and Measured Happiness

The rate of innovation may be affecting both job satisfaction and male labor force participation. In Figure 7.3, we show, using data from the World Values Survey, that the share of the population who find themselves to be very happy, measured between 2005 and 2008, is positively related to the rate of indigenous innovation as estimated in Chapter 2. Note that we have added some non-European countries—Australia, Canada, the US, and Japan—to the group of European countries where we have observations on job satisfaction.

In Table 7.2, we take the principal components of a 14*4 vector that has measures of the proportion of responders who claim to be "very happy," indigenous innovation, the transmission of innovations from abroad, and

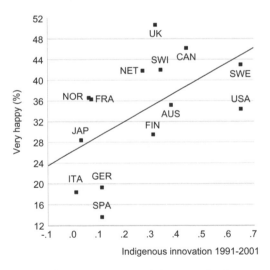

Figure 7.3. Proportion of "very happy" and the rate of indigenous innovation.
Notes: The figure shows the share claiming to be "very happy" in the 2005–2008 wave of the World Values Survey and the average rate of indigenous innovation between 1991 and 2013. The country labels are Australia (AUS), Canada (CAN), Finland (FIN), France (FRA), Germany (GER), Italy (ITA), Japan (JAP), the Netherlands (NET), Norway (NOR), Spain (SPA), Sweden (SWE), Switzerland (SWI), the United Kingdom (UK), and the United States (USA). *Source:* World Values Survey.

Table 7.2. Principal components

Number	Value	Difference	Proportion	Cumulative value	Cumulative proportion
1	2.91	2.20	0.73	2.91	0.73
2	0.72	0.39	0.18	3.63	0.91
3	0.33	0.28	0.08	3.96	0.99
4	0.04	—	0.01	4.00	1.00
Eigenvectors (loadings)					
Variable	PC 1	PC 2	PC 3	PC 4	
Indigenous	0.53	0.05	−0.70	0.47	
Transmission	0.50	−0.42	0.63	0.41	
TFP	0.56	−0.27	−0.11	−0.78	
Very happy	0.38	0.87	0.31	−0.06	

Notes: Included observations total 14 after adjustments. Balanced sample (listwise missing value deletion). Computed using ordinary correlations.

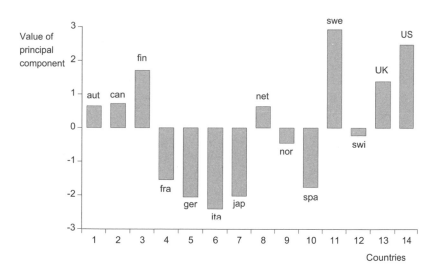

Figure 7.4. **Innovation and job satisfaction measured by a principal component.** *Note:* The country labels are Australia (aus), Canada (can), Finland (fin), France (fra), Germany (ger), Italy (ita), Japan (jap), the Netherlands (net), Norway (nor), Spain (spa), Sweden (swe), Switzerland (swi), the United Kingdom (UK), and the United States (US).

TFP growth.[1] The first principal component explains 73 percent of the variation in the matrix, and its eigenvector has a positive weight on each of the four variables. The second principal component explains 18 percent of the variation and has a positive weight on indigenous innovation and happiness but a negative weight on transmitted innovation.

We can take the principal component as a measure of economic performance. A high value indicates high rates of innovation and productivity growth, as well as a large fraction of the population feeling "very happy." See Figure 7.4.

There is a clear difference between the English-speaking countries (Australia, Canada, the UK, and the US), Finland, Sweden, and the Netherlands, on the one hand, and the rest of the continental European economies, on the other hand, in that the former group outperforms the latter.

3. Conclusions

We have found that low levels of indigenous innovation are accompanied by low and falling levels of job satisfaction, falling male labor force participation, and less measured happiness. In a sample that also includes some non-European countries, we find that performance—measured by the rate of indigenous and transmitted innovation, TFP, and the proportion declaring themselves to be very happy—is lower in the continental European countries than in the United States, the UK, Sweden, the Netherlands, Australia, Canada, and Finland.

III

TWO APPLICATIONS OF ROBOTS

8

Growth Effects of Additive and Multiplicative Robots alongside Conventional Machines

Hian Teck Hoon

ABSTRACT We study the effects of introducing two different types of robots (additive and multiplicative) in an infinitely lived one-sector aggregative model with malleable capital on wages. The wage effects of these two polar cases are dramatically different. Given malleable capital that can be retrofitted for use either as conventional machines or as robots, we show that when it is profitable for firms to adopt additive robots in the production process, the real wage drops on impact and remains permanently at the lower level even as total malleable capital accumulates. However, when multiplicative robots are adopted, we show that while the immediate impact on the real wage is ambiguous, the real wage enjoys a positive trend growth even in the absence of steady technological progress.

Introduction

The introductory chapter quoted Alfred Marshall, who notes that workers with an enterprising attitude to the workplace had shifted more and more from work that was routine or dull to work that engaged the mind. Nevertheless, in chapter 3 of his *Elements of Economics of Industry*, titled "The Scope of Economics," he notes that "the *steadiest* motive to business work is the desire for the pay which is the material reward of work."[1]

In this chapter and Chapters 9 and 10, we take up the question of how the arrival of robots, enabled by artificial intelligence (AI) and machine learning, affects the pay of workers in standard growth models. We start by deriving a stark result in this chapter (with malleable capital), that the adoption of additive robots leads to a permanent decline of real wages and a diminishing labor share of national income. This stark case where a robot is a perfect substitute for a worker is also considered in Samuelson (1988) but in the context of a classical model with circulating capital, where he states, "Now let there be invention of a robot machine that lasts one period and can do exactly the work of one man."[2] Our further analysis (in this chapter and Chapters 9 and 10) using a standard growth model, however, shows that there are at least three other channels that deliver more positive results on wage growth as a consequence of adopting robots. The first channel, examined in this chapter, is via the introduction of multiplicative robots that augment the productivity of human labor. We show that the adoption of multiplicative robots imparts a positive trend to wage growth even in the absence of technological progress. The second channel, examined in Chapter 9, is via the stimulation of investment in slow-adjusting, nonmalleable capital (such as factory buildings and physical structures) that complements total human and robotic labor. Such complementary investment, we show, exerts an upward pull on wage levels. The third channel, examined in Chapter 10, is via stimulation of innovation in the consumption goods sector as the adoption of additive robots in the capital goods sector reduces the relative price of the capital good. We show that by causing some workers in the economy to shift from participating in production to participating in innovative activity, the new wage path must be ultimately rising.

According to forecasts in 2016 by the International Federation of Robotics, more than 1.4 million new industrial robots will be installed in factories around the world by 2019.[3] This is the result of a projected 290,000-unit increase in the number of newly installed industrial robots by the end of 2016 and average annual growth of at least 13 percent from 2017 to 2019.[4] Given these forecasts, what is the likely impact of the widespread adoption of robotics on real wages and what are its effects in the long run?

The wave of research on economic growth beginning with Solow (1956) and Swan (1956) in the 1950s, and continuing into the 1960s with work by Phelps on the Golden Rules of economic growth (1966) and on two-sector growth models by Uzawa (1964), brought forth workhorse models to understand the growth of national income and wages well before the so-called Second Machine Age (see Brynjolfsson and McAfee, 2014).[5] Thus, that earlier research left unanswered a key question: What happens to the growth of income, productivity, and wages if robots are acquired and deployed that effectively add their "labor" or "work" to the labor of the employed?

Existing research on the impact of automation, robotics, and AI on jobs and wages has mainly aimed at empirically determining whether the net impact has been positive or negative from a task-based perspective. This task-based framework is fully developed in Acemoglu and Restrepo (2018).[6] The empirical results are mixed. Graetz and Michaels (2015; updated 2017) analyze panel data on robot adoption within industries in 17 countries from 1993 to 2007.[7] They find that increased robot use contributed approximately 0.37 percentage points to annual labor productivity growth while at the same time raising total factor productivity and wages. Acemoglu and Restrepo (2017) study the impact of the increase in industrial robot usage between 1990 and 2007 on US local labor markets.[8] They estimate that one more robot per 1,000 workers reduces the employment-to-population ratio by about 0.18–0.34 percentage points and wages by 0.25–0.5 percent.

The mixed empirical results suggest that opposing effects are at work, and our theoretical investigations seek to clarify the different channels through which robotization has effects within the workhorse models of economic growth. While existing research on the impact of automation and robotics has adopted a task-based approach, and we agree that this approach yields useful insights, such as shedding light on the job polarization highlighted by Goos, Manning, and Salomons (2014), we believe that it is necessary also to conduct the analysis in the standard, and more familiar, one-sector aggregative growth model.[9] Our confidence in understanding how robotization affects wages will be bolstered by such a thorough analysis.

The invention of the steam engine, electricity, and the microprocessor produced growth opportunities through their pervasive use across vast swaths of the economy. The development of robotics—the design, construction, and operation of robots enabled by AI—holds the promise of spurring growth even as it appears to cause wage declines. Since the First Industrial Revolution, fixed capital has played a central role in the production of output. In the formal neoclassical one-sector model of Solow (1956) and Swan (1956), fixed capital is modeled as conventional machines that appear along with technology and labor to generate physical output.[10] Expressed as $Y = F(K, AL)$, aggregate output (Y) is a homogeneous function of degree one in conventional machine (K) and "augmented labor" (AL). With this specification, the marginal physical productivity of labor is *increasing* in the ratio capital per augmented worker ($K/(AL)$). An issue that arises is how to model the arrival of robots in the context of the neoclassical growth model. How are AI-enabled robots different from conventional machines? Once introduced, what are their economic effects, particularly on growth, consumption, and wages?

Our approach in this chapter is to model capital as malleable and flexible in its use either as conventional machines—that is, as traditional capital—or as robots. Given its malleability, the current stock of machines can be retrofitted to function as robots once the robotic technology is available. Implicitly, the "technology" behind the construction of robots is treated as exogenously given. It is the result of technical advances made by research scientists in the AI and robotics community that we do not model explicitly. (Later, in Chapter 10, we do model endogenous innovation undertaken by the labor force to improve the quality of intermediate inputs that is driven by economic incentives.) In this chapter, we model two types of robots: additive and multiplicative. Additive robots can perform the same functions as a human worker and thus are perfectly substitutable for a human worker. This is, perhaps, the type of robot that most closely represents the layman's image of the arrival of robots in the economy. Denoting the quantity of additive robots by R_A and human labor by H, the total labor force (both robotic and human) is equal to $R_A + H$. The development of AI and machine learning has also produced a second kind of robot, which we call multiplicative, that can be described as augmenting labor power. These are robots that can plow through huge databases to provide information within minutes, helping medical personnel to do their jobs more effectively, and robots that enable older workers to carry heavy objects with little effort exerted by the human workers. Such AI-enabled robots, or "multiplicative robots," are denoted by R_M. With the introduction of multiplicative robots, total (robotic and human) labor is given by $(1 + R_M)H$.

If robots are additive, we write the production function as $Y = F(K, R_A + H)$ with degree of homogeneity equal to one in the two arguments in the production function. If robots are multiplicative, the production function is written as $Y = F(K, (1 + R_M)H)$ with degree of homogeneity equal to one in the two arguments in the production function. We also analyze the wage effects of introducing both types of robots when there are two types of jobs that human workers perform: routine jobs (H_1) that additive robots can also perform and nonroutine jobs (H_2) whose productivity multiplicative robots augment.[11] We assume that routine jobs performed by human and robotic labor, $R_A + H_1$, substitute imperfectly for nonroutine jobs enabled by multiplicative robots, $(1 + R_M)H_2$, with a constant-elasticity-of-substitution subproduction function: $[(R_A + H_1)^\rho + ((1 + R_M)H_2)^\rho]^{1/\rho}; \rho < 1.$[12]

With a linear homogeneous aggregate production function in its two arguments, we write $F(K, [(R_A + H_1)^\rho + ((1 + R_M)H_2)^\rho]^{1/\rho})$, where K represents the stock of conventional machines.

To analyze the economic effects of introducing AI-enabled robots, it is convenient to suppose that before the arrival of robots, the economy is in a stationary equilibrium with a zero rate of technological progress and zero population growth. In a convenient Ramsey infinitely lived economy, the production function, with suitable normalization, is given by $Y = F(K, H)$. The real interest rate is equal to the rate of time preference, the real wage is constant, and per capita consumption is also constant in such an economy.

A key assumption we make in this chapter is that capital is malleable, so that when the technology to produce additive robots becomes available, a piece of conventional machine can be *instantaneously* retrofitted to function as a robot and vice versa. (In Chapter 9, we will deviate from this assumption to take account of the fact that some types of fixed capital, such as factory buildings and physical structures, are not malleable and take time to install. So there is a high adjustment cost to install such capital.) With malleable capital that can be used to construct robots or conventional machines, a crucial economic principle that must hold is that the rate of return to owning a piece of conventional machine is equal to the rate of return to owning a robot—an equality of rate of return principle.[13] With the introduction of additive robots, the total nonhuman wealth (W_n) is now equal to $K + R_A$. While W_n evolves gradually over time, the division between R_A and K is endogenously determined to satisfy the equality of rate of return principle at each point in time. We note also that, given W_n, the ratio $K/(R_A + H)$ adjusts instantaneously with changes in the division between R_A and K to satisfy the equality of rate of return principle.

What are some key results of the introduction of additive robots? We show that with the arrival of additive robots, if it is profitable for firms to immediately retrofit some of the existing conventional machines to be used as robots, there is an immediate drop of the real wage. However, the real rate of interest, which is initially equal to the subjective rate of time preference, immediately jumps up to a *permanently* higher level. The rate of growth of consumption, which is initially equal to zero, also jumps up to a positive number. Along this path, the consumption per capita is growing, fueled by a more rapid pace of capital accumulation that is more than sufficient to cover physical capital depreciation. Along a balanced-growth path, total nonhuman wealth is growing at the same rate as consumption per capita, with constant shares in the form of conventional machines and additive robots. The real wage, which drops on impact when additive robots arrive, remains at a depressed level despite growth in nonhuman wealth. The reason for this is that while nonhuman wealth increases, the ratio $K/(R_A + H)$ remains invariant as capital is malleable, so the division of nonhuman wealth between K and R_A is adjusted instantaneously to satisfy the equality of rate of return principle.

What happens if the robots introduced are multiplicative in nature? We show that with the arrival of multiplicative robots, while the immediate impact is to cause the stock of conventional machines to fall when it is profitable to adopt robots (tending, by itself, to depress wages), the real wage *need not fall* because of an offsetting labor-augmenting effect coming from the multiplicative nature of the robot. As in the case of additive robots, the real rate of interest, which is initially equal to the subjective rate of time preference, immediately jumps up to a *permanently* higher level. The rate of growth of consumption, which is initially equal to zero, also jumps up to a positive number. Along this path, the consumption per capita is growing, fueled by a more rapid pace of capital accumulation that is more than sufficient to cover physical capital depreciation. The real wage, even if it drops initially (though it may actually increase, as just noted), continues to steadily increase along a balanced-growth path as nonhuman wealth grows even in the *absence of steady technological progress.*

The wage effects of introducing both types of robots are analytically similar to the polar case of introducing only multiplicative robots. More specifically, while the real wage for workers whose productivity is augmented by multiplicative robots might drop on impact, it enjoys a positive trend growth as in the pure multiplicative case. The real wage for workers in routine jobs that additive robots can also perform enjoys a productivity boost from the joint adoption of multiplicative robots if there are relatively abundant routine jobs performed by human workers compared with the number of nonroutine jobs in the economy and the elasticity of substitution between routine and nonroutine jobs is greater than one.

The rest of the chapter is organized as follows. We study the effects of introducing only additive robots in Section 1, and the effects of introducing only multiplicative robots in Section 2. The case in which both additive and multiplicative robots are adopted is examined in Section 3. Section 4 concludes.

1. Robots Perfectly *Substitute* for Human Labor: Case of Additive Robots, $H + R_A$

The size of the population, which is made up of many identical families and set equal to total human labor force, is constant and normalized to one. The number of hours worked per human worker is fixed at $\bar{H}$, so total human labor is equal to $\bar{H}$, which is allocated between overhead labor (H_f) and variable labor (H). Agents derive utility from consumption with a subjective rate of time preference, have infinite lives, face an instantaneous real interest rate $r(t)$, and receive an hourly real wage $v(t)$. Let $c(t)$ denote consumption at time t, $w_n(t)$ nonhuman wealth, and $w_h(t)$ human wealth.

The agent maximizes

$$\int_t^\infty \log c(\kappa) \exp^{-\theta(\kappa-t)} d\kappa,$$

subject to

$$\frac{dw_n(t)}{dt} = r(t)w_n(t) + v(t)\bar{H} - c(t),$$

and a transversality condition that prevents agents from going indefinitely into debt. The solution to the agent's problem is given by

$$c(t) = \theta[w_h(t) + w_n(t)],$$

where human wealth is given by

$$w_h(t) = \int_t^\infty v(\kappa)\bar{H} \exp^{\int_t^\kappa -r(v)dv} d\kappa.$$

Denoting per capita aggregate variables by capital letters, we obtain

$$C(t) = \theta[W_h(t) + W_n(t)], \tag{1}$$

$$\dot{W}_h(t) = r(t)W_h(t) - v(t)\bar{H}, \tag{2}$$

$$\dot{W}_n(t) = r(t)W_n(t) + v(t)\bar{H} - C(t), \tag{3}$$

where a dot over a variable denotes its time derivative. Taking the time derivative of (1), and using (2) and (3), we obtain, after rearrangement of terms,

$$\frac{\dot{C}(t)}{C(t)} = r(t) - \theta. \tag{4}$$

Turning to the production side of the model, we first consider a situation *before* robots are introduced. With firms having to incur overhead labor costs before actual production (leading to declining average cost), imperfectly competitive firms produce and sell a single good with a markup of price over marginal cost denoted by $m > 1$, pay wages for human labor input, and make rental payments for capital inputs, which consist entirely of conventional machines. Before the introduction of robots, each firm has access to the following production technology:

$$Y(t) = F(K(t), \bar{H}),$$

where Y is the flow of output, K is the stock of conventional machines, and H is human variable labor input. The function $F(K, H)$ exhibits constant returns to scale, and, for positive quantities of K and H, it exhibits positive and diminishing marginal products with respect to each input; it also satisfies the Inada conditions. We can write

$$y \equiv \frac{Y}{H} = f(k),$$

where $k \equiv K/H$. Capital depreciates at the rate δ. So, when letting $r^K(t)$ denote the rental rate on machines, the net rate of return to an agent who owns a unit of machine is $r^K(t) - \delta$. With machines and loans as perfect substitutes, we have $r(t) = r^K(t) - \delta$. Maximizing profits under imperfect competition leads to

$$r^K(t) = m^{-1} f'(k(t)), \tag{5}$$

$$v(t) = m^{-1}[f(k(t)) - k(t) f'(k(t))]. \tag{6}$$

Noting that $W_n(t) \equiv K(t)$ and $r^K(t)k(t)H + v(t)\bar{H} = Hf(k(t))$, we can use (5) and (6) together with (3) and (4) to obtain

$$\frac{\dot{C}(t)}{C(t)} = m^{-1} f'(k(t)) - \delta - \theta, \tag{7}$$

$$\dot{k}(t) = f(k(t)) - \frac{C(t)}{H} - \delta k(t). \tag{8}$$

With free entry and exit of firms, the condition that total revenue covers total cost pins down the markup of price over marginal cost, m. Equations (7) and (8) give a system of two dynamic equations in C and k with familiar properties given an initial value of capital stock per variable hour worked, k. In a steady state, the consumption level (C_{ss}) and the steady-state real interest rate (r_{ss}) are determined by the following pair of equations:

$$C_{ss} = H[f(k_{ss}) - \delta k_{ss}],\qquad(9)$$

$$r_{ss} = \theta,\qquad(10)$$

where $r_{ss} = m^{-1} f'(k_{ss}) - \delta$.

Consider now the effects of introducing additive robots that perfectly substitute for human labor into this familiar framework. For simplicity, we measure units of robots such that one robot can now perfectly substitute for one unit of human labor input. With the adoption of robots, the production function is now given by

$$Y(t) = F(K(t), R_A(t) + H),$$

where $R_A(t)$ is the number of additive robots. In intensive form, we can write

$$Y(t) = [R_A(t) + H] f\left(\frac{K(t)}{R_A(t) + H}\right).$$

Profit maximization under imperfect competition gives the following first-order conditions:

$$r^K(t) = m^{-1} f'\left(\frac{K(t)}{R_A(t) + H}\right),\qquad(11)$$

$$r^{R_A}(t) = m^{-1}\left[f\left(\frac{K(t)}{R_A(t) + H}\right) - \left(\frac{K(t)}{R_A(t) + H}\right) f'\left(\frac{K(t)}{R_A(t) + H}\right)\right],\qquad(12)$$

$$v(t) = m^{-1}\left[f\left(\frac{K(t)}{R_A(t) + H}\right) - \left(\frac{K(t)}{R_A(t) + H}\right) f'\left(\frac{K(t)}{R_A(t) + H}\right)\right],\qquad(13)$$

where $r^K(t)$ is the rental rate on a unit of conventional machine and $r^{R_A}(t)$ is the rental rate on an additive robot.

If capital is malleable and perfectly mobile across its two functions, we require

$$r = r^K - \delta = r^{R_A} - \delta,\qquad(14)$$

assuming the same rate of depreciation when capital is employed as a piece of conventional machine or as a robot that perfectly substitutes for human labor. Consequently, the "effective capital intensity" is a constant that satisfies

$$\frac{f\left(\dfrac{K(t)}{R_A(t)+H}\right) - \left(\dfrac{K(t)}{R_A(t)+H}\right) f'\left(\dfrac{K(t)}{R_A(t)+H}\right)}{f'\left(\dfrac{K(t)}{R_A(t)+H}\right)} = 1, \tag{15}$$

which we write as

$$\left(\frac{K(t)}{R_A(t)+H}\right)^* \equiv \gamma_A > 0. \tag{16}$$

Notice that this makes the instantaneous real rate of interest a constant:

$$r = m^{-1} f'(\gamma_A) - \delta = m^{-1}[f(\gamma_A) - \gamma_A f'(\gamma_A)] - \delta. \tag{17}$$

Notice also that the real wage is given by

$$v = r + \delta. \tag{18}$$

To complete the model, we note that, with the introduction of additive robots,

$$W_n(t) \equiv K(t) + R_A(t), \tag{19}$$

$$\frac{\dot{C}(t)}{C(t)} = m^{-1} f'(\gamma_A) - \delta - \theta, \tag{20}$$

$$\dot{W}_n(t) = [R_A(t) + H] f(\gamma_A) - C(t) - \delta W_n(t). \tag{21}$$

Starting from an initial steady state characterized by (9) and (10), where there are no robots, we study the conditions under which it is profitable to adopt robots that perfectly substitute for workers using the system of four equations given by (16), (19), (20), and (21) and four variables: C, W_n, K, and R_A. With some manipulation, we can show that

$$R_A + H = \left(\frac{1}{1+\gamma_A}\right)(H + W_n).$$

Using this equation in (21), the general-equilibrium system can be summarized in terms of C and W_n as

$$\frac{\dot{C}(t)}{C(t)} = m^{-1} f'(\gamma_A) - \delta - \theta,$$

$$\frac{\dot{W}_n(t)}{W_n(t)} = \left(\frac{1}{1+\gamma_A}\right)\left[1 + \frac{H}{W_n(t)}\right]f(\gamma_A) - \delta - \frac{C(t)}{W_n(t)}.$$

Before the introduction of robots, we have

$$r^K - \delta = m^{-1} f'\left(\frac{K_{ss}}{H}\right) - \delta, \tag{22}$$

$$v = m^{-1}\left[f\left(\frac{K_{ss}}{H}\right) - \left(\frac{K_{ss}}{H}\right)f'\left(\frac{K_{ss}}{H}\right)\right]. \tag{23}$$

At the moment that robots are introduced and adopted, we have $W_n \equiv K_{ss}$, so we can write

$$r^K - \delta = m^{-1} f'\left(\frac{K_{ss} - R_A}{R_A + H}\right) - \delta = m^{-1} f'(\gamma_A) - \delta, \tag{24}$$

$$v = m^{-1}[f(\gamma_A) - \gamma_A f'(\gamma_A)]. \tag{25}$$

Since the rate of return to capital before the introduction of robots is equal to the subjective rate of time preference given by (10), the condition for it to be profitable to invest in robots is

$$r^{R_A} - \delta > \theta. \tag{26}$$

If (26) is satisfied, then some of the initial capital stock in the form of conventional machines will be instantaneously retrofitted to become additive robots, so

$$\gamma_A \equiv \frac{K_{ss} - R_A}{R_A + H} < \frac{K_{ss}}{H}. \tag{27}$$

This implies that when robots are first introduced, say at time 0, it is unambiguous that

$$k_0 \equiv \frac{K_{ss} - R_A}{R_A + H} < \frac{K_{ss}}{H}.$$

This decline in $k \equiv \dfrac{K}{[R_A + H]}$, taken alone, causes the real wage to fall on impact and remain permanently lower (since k remains equal to γ_A). In the long run, the general-equilibrium system is given by

$$\frac{\dot{C}}{C} = m^{-1} f'(\gamma_A) - \delta - \theta,$$

$$\frac{\dot{W}_n}{W_n} = \left(\frac{1}{1+\gamma_A}\right) f(\gamma_A) - \delta - \frac{C}{W_n},$$

with

$$\frac{\dot{W}_n}{W_n} = \frac{\dot{C}}{C} = m^{-1} f'(\gamma_A) - \delta - \theta$$

and

$$\frac{C}{W_n} = \left(\frac{1}{1+\gamma_A}\right) f(\gamma_A) - m^{-1} f'(\gamma_A) + \theta.$$

The analysis follows that of the *AK* model of endogenous growth.[14]

After the adoption of additive robots, total (human and robotic) labor share of national income tends toward a long-run constant given by

$$\frac{v[R_A + \bar{H}]}{[R_A + H]f(\gamma_A)} = \frac{[f(\gamma_A) - \gamma_A f'(\gamma_A)]}{f(\gamma_A)}.$$

However, the (human) labor share of national income is given at each moment by

$$\frac{v\bar{H}}{[R_A + H]f(\gamma_A)} = \frac{m^{-1}[f(\gamma_A) - \gamma_A f'(\gamma_A)]\bar{H}}{[R_A + H]f(\gamma_A)}.$$

As the stock of additive robots continues to grow, with a fixed human labor force size, we find that the (human) labor share of national income tends toward zero in the long run.

2. Robots *Augment* Human Labor: Case of Multiplicative Robots, $(1 + R_M)H$

Equations (1) to (10) continue to hold in this economy *before* the introduction of robots. Suppose that advances in AI and robotics science make it possible to adopt robots that augment human labor. We now have conventional machines (denoted K) and multiplicative robots that augment human labor (denoted R_M).

The production function is now given by

$$Y(t) = F(K(t), (1 + R_M(t))H).$$

In intensive form, we can write,

$$Y(t) = (1 + R_M(t))H \, f\left(\frac{K(t)}{(1 + R_M(t))H}\right).$$

Profit maximization under imperfect competition gives the following first-order conditions:

$$r^K(t) = m^{-1} f'\left(\frac{K(t)}{(1 + R_M(t))H}\right), \tag{28}$$

$$r^{R_M}(t) = m^{-1} H \times \left[f\left(\frac{K(t)}{(1 + R_M(t))H}\right) - \left(\frac{K(t)}{(1 + R_M(t))H}\right) \right.$$
$$\left. \times f'\left(\frac{K(t)}{(1 + R_M(t))H}\right) \right], \tag{29}$$

$$v(t) = m^{-1}(1 + R_M(t)) \times \left[f\left(\frac{K(t)}{(1 + R_M(t))H}\right) - \left(\frac{K(t)}{(1 + R_M(t))H}\right) \right.$$
$$\left. \times f'\left(\frac{K(t)}{(1 + R_M(t))H}\right) \right], \tag{30}$$

where $r^K(t)$ is the rental rate on a unit of conventional machine, and $r^{R_M}(t)$ is the rental rate on a multiplicative robot that augments human labor.

If capital is malleable and perfectly mobile across its two functions, we require

$$r = r^K - \delta = r^{R_M} - \delta, \tag{31}$$

assuming the same rate of capital depreciation across the two functions. The effective capital intensity is given by

$$k \equiv \frac{K}{(1 + R_M(t))H}.$$

The effective capital intensity is a constant that satisfies

$$\frac{f\left(\frac{K(t)}{(1 + R_M(t))H}\right) - \left(\frac{K(t)}{(1 + R_M(t))H}\right) f'\left(\frac{K(t)}{(1 + R_M(t))H}\right)}{f'\left(\frac{K(t)}{(1 + R_M(t))H}\right)} = 1, \tag{32}$$

which we write as

$$\left(\frac{K(t)}{(1 + R_M(t))H}\right)^* \equiv \gamma_M > 0. \tag{33}$$

Notice that this makes the instantaneous real rate of interest a constant:

$$r = m^{-1} f'(\gamma_M) - \delta = m^{-1} H[f(\gamma_M) - \gamma_M f'(\gamma_M)] - \delta. \tag{34}$$

Notice also that the real wage is given by

$$v(t) = m^{-1} (1 + R_M(t)) [f(\gamma_M) - \gamma_M f'(\gamma_M)]. \tag{35}$$

To complete the model, we note that

$$W_n(t) \equiv K(t) + R_M(t), \tag{36}$$

$$\frac{\dot{C}(t)}{C(t)} = m^{-1} f'(\gamma_M) - \delta - \theta, \tag{37}$$

$$\frac{\dot{W}_n(t)}{W_n(t)} = \left[\frac{Hf(\gamma_M)}{1 + \gamma_M H}\right]\left[1 + \frac{1}{W_n(t)}\right] - \delta - \frac{C(t)}{W_n(t)}, \tag{38}$$

where we have used the relationship $(1 + R_M)H = \left[\dfrac{H}{1 + \gamma_M H}\right](1 + W_n)$.

Before the introduction of robots, we have

$$r^K - \delta = m^{-1} f'\left(\frac{K_{ss}}{H}\right) - \delta, \tag{39}$$

$$v = m^{-1}\left[f\left(\frac{K_{ss}}{H}\right) - \left(\frac{K_{ss}}{H}\right)f'\left(\frac{K_{ss}}{H}\right)\right]. \tag{40}$$

At the moment that robots are introduced and adopted, we have $W_n \equiv K_{ss}$, so we can write,

$$r^K - \delta = m^{-1} f'\left(\frac{K_{ss} - R_M}{(1 + R_M)H}\right) - \delta = m^{-1} f'(\gamma_M) - \delta, \tag{41}$$

$$v = m^{-1}(1 + R_M)\left[f\left(\frac{K_{ss} - R_M}{(1 + R_M)H}\right) - \left(\frac{K_{ss} - R_M}{(1 + R_M)H}\right)f'\left(\frac{K_{ss} - R_M}{(1 + R_M)H}\right)\right] \tag{42}$$

$$= m^{-1}(1 + R_M) [f(\gamma_M) - \gamma_M f'(\gamma_M)].$$

We note that, given m,

$$\frac{dv}{dR_M} = m^{-1}[f(\gamma_M) - \gamma_M f'(\gamma_M)] + m^{-1} \gamma_M f''(\gamma_M)[H^{-1} + \gamma_M],$$

so the real wage can fall or increase on impact.

The condition for it to be profitable to invest in robots is

$$r^{R_M} - \delta > \theta. \tag{43}$$

If (43) is satisfied, then some of the initial capital stock in the form of conventional machines will be instantaneously retrofitted to become multiplicative robots, so

$$\gamma_M \equiv \frac{K_{ss} - R_M}{(1 + R_M)H} < \frac{K_{ss}}{H}. \tag{44}$$

This implies that when robots are first introduced, say at time 0, it is unambiguous that

$$k_0 \equiv \frac{K_{ss} - R_M}{(1 + R_M)H} < \frac{K_{ss}}{H}.$$

This decline in $k \equiv \dfrac{K}{[(1 + R_M)H]}$, taken alone, causes the real wage to fall on impact. However, the real wage rises on account of the term $(1 + R_M)$ that multiplies $[f(\gamma_M) - \gamma_M f'(\gamma_M)]$ in (42). While the immediate impact on the real wage is ambiguous, an examination of (37) and (38) shows that the real wage now grows at a positive trend growth rate. This is because as nonhuman wealth grows and W_n^{-1} tends toward zero, (38) can be written as

$$\frac{\dot{W}_n}{W_n} = \left[\frac{Hf(\gamma_M)}{1 + \gamma_M H} \right] - \delta - \frac{C}{W_n},$$

so W_n grows in the long run at the rate $m^{-1} f'(\gamma_M) - \delta \; \theta$, maintaining a constant ratio of nonhuman wealth to consumption. Equation (42) shows that the real wage grows steadily as R_M steadily grows. We note also that after the adoption of multiplicative robots, the (human) labor share of national income is given by

$$\frac{v\bar{H},}{[(1 + R_M)H]f(\gamma_M)} = \frac{m^{-1}[f(\gamma_M) - \gamma_M f'(\gamma_M)]\bar{H},}{Hf(\gamma_M)},$$

which is a constant in steady state.

3. Both Types of Robots: Case of Imperfect Substitutes

Next, we analyze the wage effects of introducing both types of robots when there are two types of jobs that human workers perform: routine jobs that additive robots can also perform and nonroutine jobs whose productivity multiplicative robots augment. Routine jobs performed by human and robotic labor, $R_A + H_1$, substitute imperfectly for nonroutine jobs enabled by multiplicative robots, $(1 + R_M)H_2$, with a constant-elasticity-of-substitution subproduction function: $[(R_A + H_1)^\rho + ((1 + R_m)H_2)^\rho]^{1/\rho}$; $\rho < 1$. (Note that the elasticity of substitution is given by $(1 - \rho)^{-1}$.) A fixed fraction of the population performs routine jobs that additive robots can substitute and supply H_1 number of hours, while the remaining fraction of the population performs nonroutine jobs that multiplicative robots augment and supply $\bar{H}_2$ number of hours. We assume that overhead labor (H_f) is supplied only by workers performing nonroutine jobs, so $\bar{H}_2 \equiv H_2 + H_f$. With a linear homogeneous aggregate production function in its two arguments, we write,

$$F(K, \ [(R_A + H_1)^\rho + ((1 + R_m)H_2)^\rho]^{1/\rho}),$$

where K represents the stock of conventional machines. The analysis can proceed in two steps. In the first step, we note that the equality of the rate of return principle applied to additive and multiplicative robots implies that the following condition holds:

$$\left(\frac{R_A + H_1}{(1 + R_M)H_2}\right)^{\rho - 1} = H_2, \tag{45}$$

so we can write,

$$\left(\frac{R_A + H_1}{(1 + R_M)H_2}\right)^* \equiv \gamma_R > 0.$$

Using this result, we can write the aggregate production function as,

$$Y = (1 + R_M)H_2[1 + \gamma_R^\rho]^{\frac{1}{\rho}} f\left(\frac{K}{(1 + R_M)H_2[1 + \gamma_R^\rho]^{\frac{1}{\rho}}}\right).$$

Profit maximization under imperfect competition gives the following first-order conditions:

$$r^K(t) = m^{-1} f'\left(\frac{K(t)}{(1 + R_M(t))H_2[1 + \gamma_R^\rho]^{\frac{1}{\rho}}}\right), \tag{46}$$

$$r^{R_M}(t) = m^{-1}H_2[1+\gamma_R^\rho]^{\frac{1}{\rho}-1}\left[f\left(\frac{K(t)}{(1+R_M(t))H_2[1+\gamma_R^\rho]^{\frac{1}{\rho}}}\right)\right.$$
$$\left.-\left(\frac{K(t)}{(1+R_M(t))H_2[1+\gamma_R^\rho]^{\frac{1}{\rho}}}\right)f'\left(\frac{K(t)}{(1+R_M(t))H_2[1+\gamma_R^\rho]^{\frac{1}{\rho}}}\right)\right],\tag{47}$$

$$r^{R_A} = m^{-1}[1+\gamma_R^{-\rho}]^{\frac{1}{\rho}-1}\left[f\left(\frac{K(t)}{(1+R_M(t))H_2[1+\gamma_R^\rho]^{\frac{1}{\rho}}}\right)\right.$$
$$\left.-\left(\frac{K(t)}{(1+R_M(t))H_2[1+\gamma_R^\rho]^{\frac{1}{\rho}}}\right)f'\left(\frac{K(t)}{(1+R_M(t))H_2[1+\gamma_R^\rho]^{\frac{1}{\rho}}}\right)\right],\tag{48}$$

$$v_1(t) = m^{-1}[1+\gamma_R^{-\rho}]^{\frac{1}{\rho}-1}\left[f\left(\frac{K(t)}{(1+R_M(t))H_2[1+\gamma_R^\rho]^{\frac{1}{\rho}}}\right)\right.$$
$$\left.-\left(\frac{K(t)}{(1+R_M(t))H_2[1+\gamma_R^\rho]^{\frac{1}{\rho}}}\right)f'\left(\frac{K(t)}{(1+R_M(t))H_2[1+\gamma_R^\rho]^{\frac{1}{\rho}}}\right)\right],\tag{49}$$

$$v_2(t) = m^{-1}(1+R_M(t))[1+\gamma_R^\rho]^{\frac{1}{\rho}-1}\left[f\left(\frac{K(t)}{(1+R_M(t))H_2[1+\gamma_R^\rho]^{\frac{1}{\rho}}}\right)\right.$$
$$\left.-\left(\frac{K(t)}{(1+R_M(t))H_2[1+\gamma_R^\rho]^{\frac{1}{\rho}}}\right)f'\left(\frac{K(t)}{(1+R_M(t))H_2[1+\gamma_R^\rho]^{\frac{1}{\rho}}}\right)\right],\tag{50}$$

where $r^K(t)$ is the rental rate on a unit of conventional machine, $r^{R_M}(t)$ is the rental rate on a multiplicative robot that augments human labor, $r^{R_A}(t)$ is the rental rate on an additive robot, $v_1(t)$ is the real wage of a worker whose job an additive robot is a perfect substitute for, and $v_2(t)$ is the real wage of a worker whose job a multiplicative robot augments.

If capital is malleable and perfectly mobile across its three functions, we require

$$r = r^K - \delta = r^{R_M} - \delta = r^{R_A} - \delta,\tag{51}$$

assuming the same rate of capital depreciation across the three functions. The effective capital intensity is given by

$$k \equiv \frac{K}{(1+R_M)H_2[1+\gamma_R^\rho]^{\frac{1}{\rho}}}.$$

The effective capital intensity is a constant that satisfies

$$
\frac{f\left(\dfrac{K(t)}{(1+R_M(t))H_2[1+\gamma_R^\rho]^{\frac{1}{\rho}}}\right) - \left(\dfrac{K(t)}{(1+R_M(t))H_2[1+\gamma_R^\rho]^{\frac{1}{\rho}}}\right) \times f'\left(\dfrac{K(t)}{(1+R_M(t))H_2[1+\gamma_R^\rho]^{\frac{1}{\rho}}}\right)}{f'\left(\dfrac{K(t)}{(1+R_M(t))H_2[1+\gamma_R^\rho]^{\frac{1}{\rho}}}\right)}
$$

$$
= \frac{1}{H_2[1+\gamma_R^\rho]^{\frac{1}{\rho}-1}}, \tag{52}
$$

which we write as,

$$
\left(\frac{K(t)}{(1+R_M(t))H_2[1+\gamma_R^\rho]^{\frac{1}{\rho}}}\right)^* \equiv \gamma_K > 0. \tag{53}
$$

Notice that this makes the instantaneous real rate of interest a constant:

$$
r = m^{-1}f'(\gamma_K) - \delta. \tag{54}
$$

Notice also that the real wages are given by

$$
v_1 = m^{-1}[1+\gamma_R^{-\rho}]^{\frac{1}{\rho}-1}[f(\gamma_K) - \gamma_K f'(\gamma_K)], \tag{55}
$$

$$
v_2 = m^{-1}(1+R_M)[1+\gamma_R^\rho]^{\frac{1}{\rho}-1}[f(\gamma_K) - \gamma_K f'(\gamma_K)]. \tag{56}
$$

To complete the model, we note that

$$
W_n(t) = K(t) + R_A(t) + R_M(t), \tag{57}
$$

$$
\frac{\dot{C}(t)}{C(t)} = m^{-1}f'(\gamma_K) - \delta - \theta, \tag{58}
$$

$$
\frac{\dot{W}_n(t)}{W_n(t)} = \frac{f(\gamma_K)}{\gamma_K}\left[1 + \frac{1}{\gamma_K H_2[1+\gamma_R^\rho]^{\frac{1}{\rho}}} + \frac{\gamma_R}{\gamma_K[1+\gamma_R^\rho]^{\frac{1}{\rho}}}\right]
$$

$$
\times\left[1 + \frac{1+H_1}{W_n(t)}\right] - \delta - \frac{C(t)}{W_n(t)}, \tag{59}
$$

where we have used the following relationships:

$$1 + R_M = \frac{K}{\gamma_K H_2 [1 + \gamma_R^\rho]^{\frac{1}{\rho}}},$$

$$R_A = \frac{\gamma_R K}{\gamma_K [1 + \gamma_R^\rho]^{\frac{1}{\rho}}} - H_1.$$

Before the introduction of robots, we have

$$r^K - \delta = m^{-1} f' \left(\frac{K_{ss}}{(H_1^\rho + H_2^\rho)^{\frac{1}{\rho}}} \right) - \delta, \tag{60}$$

$$v_1 = m^{-1} \left[1 + \left(\frac{H_1}{H_2} \right)^{-\rho} \right]^{\frac{1}{\rho} - 1}$$

$$\times \left[f \left(\frac{K_{ss}}{(H_1^\rho + H_2^\rho)^{\frac{1}{\rho}}} \right) - \left(\frac{K_{ss}}{(H_1^\rho + H_2^\rho)^{\frac{1}{\rho}}} \right) f' \left(\frac{K_{ss}}{(H_1^\rho + H_2^\rho)^{\frac{1}{\rho}}} \right) \right], \tag{61}$$

$$v_2 = m^{-1} \left[1 + \left(\frac{H_1}{H_2} \right)^{\rho} \right]^{\frac{1}{\rho} - 1}$$

$$\times \left[f \left(\frac{K_{ss}}{(H_1^\rho + H_2^\rho)^{\frac{1}{\rho}}} \right) - \left(\frac{K_{ss}}{(H_1^\rho + H_2^\rho)^{\frac{1}{\rho}}} \right) f' \left(\frac{K_{ss}}{(H_1^\rho + H_2^\rho)^{\frac{1}{\rho}}} \right) \right]. \tag{62}$$

At the moment that robots are introduced and adopted, we have $W_n \equiv K_{ss}$, so we can write,

$$r^K - \delta = m^{-1} f' \left(\frac{K_{ss} - R_A - R_M}{(1 + R_M) H_2 [1 + \gamma_R^\rho]^{\frac{1}{\rho}}} \right) - \delta = m^{-1} f'(\gamma_K) - \delta \tag{63}$$

with per capita consumption now growing.

While the real wage for workers whose productivity is augmented by multiplicative robots might drop on impact, it enjoys a trend growth as in the pure multiplicative case. Comparing (61), which gives the real wage of workers performing routine jobs before the adoption of robots, and (55), which gives the corresponding real wage after the adoption of robots, we see that the effective capital intensity declines with the adoption of robots:

$$\gamma_K \equiv \frac{K_{ss} - R_A - R_M}{(1 + R_M) H_2 [1 + \gamma_R^\rho]^{\frac{1}{\rho}}} < \frac{K_{ss}}{(H_1^\rho + H_2^\rho)^{\frac{1}{\rho}}}.$$

Through this channel, the adoption of robots depresses the real wage of workers doing routine jobs.[15] However, the real wage for workers whose jobs are substitutable by additive robots enjoys a productivity boost from the joint adoption of multiplicative robots if the elasticity of substitution between routine and nonroutine jobs is greater than one and the following condition holds:

$$\gamma_R < \frac{H_1}{H_2}.$$

If this channel is sufficiently strong, the real wage of workers doing routine jobs can rise with the adoption of both types of robots.[16]

After the adoption of additive and multiplicative robots, the (human) labor share of national income is given by

$$
\frac{v_1 H_1 + v_2 \bar{H}_2}{[1 + R_M] H_2 [1 + \gamma_R^\rho]^{\frac{1}{\rho}} f(\gamma_K)}
$$

$$
= \frac{m^{-1}[f(\gamma_K) - \gamma_K f'(\gamma_K)][(1 + \gamma_R^{-\rho})^{\frac{1}{\rho}-1} H_1 + (1 + R_M)(1 + \gamma_R^\rho)^{\frac{1}{\rho}-1}\bar{H}_2]}{(1 + R_M) H_2 [1 + \gamma_R^\rho]^{\frac{1}{\rho}} f(\gamma_K)}.
$$

With fixed labor force sizes, the steady growth of multiplicative robots means that in the long run, the labor share of national income is given by

$$
\frac{m^{-1}[f(\gamma_K) - \gamma_K f'(\gamma_K)]\bar{H}_2}{[1 + \gamma_R^\rho] f(\gamma_K) H_2},
$$

which is a constant.

4. Conclusion

In standard neoclassical growth theory, following Solow and Swan, net investment is equal to zero in the absence of population growth and technological progress. We find that with additive robots, the growth rate of consumption, which is initially equal to zero, also jumps up to a positive number. Along this path, the consumption per capita is growing, fueled by a more rapid pace of capital accumulation that is more than sufficient to cover physical capital depreciation. Along a balanced-growth path, total nonhuman wealth is growing at the same rate as consumption per capita, with constant shares in the form of conventional machines and additive robots. However, we obtain the stark result that real wages are permanently depressed and the (human) labor share of national income asymptotically tends toward zero although total (human and robotic) labor share of national income tends toward a long-run positive constant.

We find that with the arrival of multiplicative robots, while the immediate impact is to cause the stock of conventional machines to fall when it is profitable to adopt robots, the real wage need not fall because of an offsetting labor-augmenting effect coming from the multiplicative nature of the robot. As in the case of additive robots, the real rate of interest, which is initially equal to the subjective rate of time preference, immediately jumps up to a permanently higher level. The rate of growth of consumption, which is initially equal to zero, also jumps up to a positive number. Along this path, the consumption per capita is growing, fueled by a more rapid pace of capital accumulation that is more than sufficient to cover physical capital depreciation. The real wage, even if it drops initially, continues to steadily increase along a balanced-growth path as nonhuman wealth grows even in the absence of steady technological progress. The (human) labor share in national income tends toward a long-run positive constant.

We show that the wage effects of introducing both types of robots are analytically similar to the polar case of introducing only multiplicative robots. While the real wage for workers whose productivity is augmented by multiplicative robots might drop on impact, it enjoys a positive trend growth as in the pure multiplicative case. The real wage for workers in routine jobs that additive robots substitute enjoys a productivity boost from the joint adoption of multiplicative robots if there are relatively abundant routine jobs performed by human workers compared with the number of nonroutine jobs in the economy and the elasticity of substitution between routine and nonroutine jobs is greater than one. In this case, the (human) labor share in national income is a positive constant in the long run.

9

Wage Effects of Additive and Multiplicative Robots alongside Factory Buildings and Physical Structures

Hian Teck Hoon

ABSTRACT   We study the effects of robots, additive and multiplicative, on wages in an aggregative growth model in both the short and long run. There are three factors of production in the model economy: human labor, robots, and a complementary asset that groups together factory buildings and physical structures. We identify three effects from adopting robots: a factor-intensity effect, a labor-augmenting effect, and an asset price effect. When only additive robots are introduced, the real wage gradually declines to reach a permanently lower level as a result of the factor-intensity effect—more "human and robotic labor" working on a constant stock of buildings and physical structures. However, the price of buildings and physical structures unambiguously jumps up—a positive asset price effect from adopting robots. In the long run, the higher price of the complementary asset leads to the development of more factory buildings and physical structures, which attenuates the factor-intensity effect and restores real wages in the case of additive robots and raises real wages in the case of multiplicative robots.

Introduction

In contrast to the assumption of Chapter 8 that conventional machines (being malleable) can be instantaneously retrofitted to function as additive or multiplicative robots, this chapter assumes that the co-operating factor is a slow-adjusting asset like factory buildings and physical structures, which take time to build. The adjustment cost of such investments is large. With this assumption, we write the production function as $Y = F(T, R_A + H)$ with additive robots (T representing the stock of factory buildings and structures) and $Y = F(T, (1 + R_M)H)$ with multiplicative robots.

Here is a summary of the key analytical results obtained in this chapter. We introduce two different types of robots—additive robots and multiplicative robots—into an aggregative model with human workers and a co-operating asset that groups together factory buildings and physical structures in order to study the effects on wages. The price of physical structures is endogenously determined; a surge in physical structure prices enriches the owners of nonhuman wealth. An additive robot (R_A) performs a job that a human worker (H) does, so total human and robotic labor is given by $H + R_A$ with suitable normalization. On the other hand, a multiplicative robot (R_M) augments human labor, so total effective labor is given by $(1 + R_M)H$. Robots that perfectly substitute for human labor, which are additive to human labor, correspond most closely to the process we commonly refer to as automation. More recently, with "deep learning" algorithms developed by scientists within the artificial intelligence (AI) community, machines are enabled to learn to a certain extent without human supervision. Workers in medical research can take advantage of deep learning to sift through and analyze large volumes of medical data. For example, an application called Face2Gene uses facial analysis and AI to analyze the relevant features of a patient and compare them with a database to provide clinicians with a list of possible rare diseases within a short time. Similar techniques can help scientists sift through experimental data for new discoveries. For example, a French company named CybeleTech uses AI to determine which seeds work best in particular environments.[1] Such advances in AI would more nearly correspond to the multiplicative case we study.

The wage effects of these two polar cases are dramatically different in the short run with a constant stock of factory buildings and physical structures. As in Chapter 8, we assume that labor supply is infinitely inelastic, so we abstract from any employment effect. (We leave to the appendix to this chapter to show that we can readily extend the analysis to incorporate endogenous labor supply and thus also study the employment effects of introducing additive and multiplicative robots.) When additive robots are introduced, we show that when it is profitable for firms to adopt the robots in the production process, the real wage gradually declines to reach a permanently lower level even as the price of physical structures jumps up and gradually increases to reach a permanently higher level. Thus, this polar case of additive robots confirms the fear people have that the introduction of robots hurts workers' wage earnings and enriches the owners of nonhuman wealth. In the long run, however, the stock of factory buildings and physical structures increases, thus restoring the real wage.

When multiplicative robots are introduced in the other polar case, we show that there are two offsetting effects with a constant stock of factory buildings and physical structures: a factor-intensity effect (with more effective labor working on a fixed supply of physical structures in the short run), which tends to reduce wages, and a labor-augmenting effect (with multiplicative robots making each worker more effective), which raises hourly pay. We establish the result that, given the price-marginal cost markup, if the share of factory buildings and physical structures is less than the elasticity of substitution between physical structures and effective labor, then introducing robots must raise the whole path of real wages. This condition is satisfied, for example, in the familiar case of a Cobb-Douglas production function. In the long run, the growth of real wages is further propelled by the accumulation of capital taking the form of factory buildings and physical structures.

In Section 1, we use the concept of the factor-price frontier to illustrate how an introduction of robots affects real wages through the factor-intensity effect and labor-augmenting effect. In Section 2, we introduce an asset price effect of adopting robots by conducting the full dynamic general-equilibrium analysis for the two polar cases: only additive robots, R_A, introduced; and only multiplicative robots, R_M, introduced. In Section 3, we study the long-run effects of introducing robots when the supply of factory buildings and physical structures has adjusted in response to the changes in asset prices. Section 4 concludes.

1. Robotics and Factor-Price Frontier

Consider first the case of additive robots, R_A. The aggregate production function is given by $Y = F(T, H + R_A)$, which is assumed to be homogeneous of degree one in its two arguments, T and $H + R_A$, respectively, where Y is output, T is a constant stock of factory buildings and physical structures, H is variable labor supply after overhead labor H_f has been employed with $\bar{H} \equiv H + H_f$, and R_A is the stock of additive robots. With a linear homogeneous production function, we write $Y = (H + R_A)f(T/(H + R_A))$ with $f'(T/(H + R_A)) > 0$ and $f''(T/(H + R_A)) < 0$. Firm optimization under conditions of imperfect competition leads to

$$v = m^{-1}\left[f\left(\frac{T}{H+R_A}\right) - \left(\frac{T}{H+R_A}\right)f'\left(\frac{T}{H+R_A}\right)\right], \tag{1}$$

$$r^T = m^{-1}f'\left(\frac{T}{H+R_A}\right), \tag{2}$$

$$r^{R_A} = m^{-1}\left[f\left(\frac{T}{H+R_A}\right) - \left(\frac{T}{H+R_A}\right)f'\left(\frac{T}{H+R_A}\right)\right], \tag{3}$$

where v is the real hourly wage, r^T is rental rate on factory buildings, r^{R_A} is the rental rate on an additive robot, and m is the markup of price over marginal cost. With free entry and exit of firms, the condition that total revenue covers total cost pins down m.

Equations (1) and (2) allow us to derive the factor-price frontier. Let $x \equiv T/(H+R_A)$. Using x in (1) and (2), we have

$$v = m^{-1}[f(x) - xf'(x)], \tag{4}$$
$$r^T = m^{-1} f'(x). \tag{5}$$

From (5), we obtain $dx/dr^T = m[f''(x)]^{-1}$. Using this in (4), we obtain

$$\frac{dv}{dr^T} = -x < 0. \tag{6}$$

We also have

$$\frac{d^2v}{d(r^T)^2} = \frac{-m}{f''(x)} > 0.$$

The factor-price frontier is illustrated in Figure 9.1a, given m (see the appendix for all figures). Note that in the additive robot case, $\tilde{v} \equiv v$. The effect of introducing an additive robot is to decrease x. As shown in Figure 9.1b, this has the effect of reducing the real wage (from v_1 to v_2). We call this the factor-intensity effect of introducing robots. Essentially, with more total human and robotic labor working on a constant stock of factory buildings, the marginal revenue productivity of labor falls, and lowers the wage.

Next consider the case of multiplicative robots, R_M. The aggregate production function is given by $Y = F(T, (1+R_M)H)$, which is assumed to be homogeneous of degree one in its two arguments, T and $(1+R_M)H$, respectively, where R_M is the stock of multiplicative robots. With a linear homogeneous production function, we write $Y=(1+R_M)Hf(T/(1+R_M)H)$. Firm optimization under conditions of imperfect competition leads to

$$v = m^{-1}(1 + R_M)\left[f\left(\frac{T}{(1+R_M)H}\right) - \left(\frac{T}{(1+R_M)H}\right)f'\left(\frac{T}{(1+R_M)H}\right)\right], \quad (7)$$

$$r^T = m^{-1}f'\left(\frac{T}{(1+R_M)H}\right), \quad (8)$$

$$r^{R_M} = m^{-1}H\left[f\left(\frac{T}{(1+R_M)H}\right) - \left(\frac{T}{(1+R_M)H}\right)f'\left(\frac{T}{(1+R_M)H}\right)\right], \quad (9)$$

where r^{R_M} is the rental rate on a multiplicative robot.

In the multiplicative case, we write $x \equiv T/((1+R_M)H)$. Using x in (7) and (8), and defining $\tilde{v} \equiv v/(1+R_M)$, we have

$$\tilde{v} = m^{-1}[f(x) - xf'(x)], \quad (10)$$

$$r^T = m^{-1} f'(x). \quad (11)$$

From (11), we obtain $dx/dr^T = m[f''(x)]^{-1}$. Using this in (10), we obtain

$$\frac{d\tilde{v}}{dr^T} = -x < 0. \quad (12)$$

We also have

$$\frac{d^2\tilde{v}}{d(r^T)^2} = -\frac{m}{f''(x)} > 0.$$

The factor-price frontier can once again be illustrated in Figure 9.1a, given m, noting that $\tilde{v} \equiv v/(1+R_M)$. The effect of introducing a multiplicative robot is to decrease x as in the additive robot case. As shown in Figure 9.1b, this has the effect of reducing the *adjusted* real wage (from $\tilde{v}_1$ to $\tilde{v}_2$). We call this the factor-intensity effect of introducing robots. The effect on the *unadjusted* real wage—that is, v—however, is represented by $(1 + R_M) \times \tilde{v}$. Before the introduction of the multiplicative robot, the real wage is given by $v = m^{-1}[f(T/H) - (T/H) f'(T/H)]$. With the introduction of robots, although x decreases (the factor-intensity effect), which results in a fall of $\tilde{v}$, this is offset by the term $(1+R_M)$, which multiplies $\tilde{v}$. We call this the labor-augmenting effect of introducing robots. In this case, while more "effective" labor working on a constant stock of factory buildings (taken by itself) reduces the marginal productivity of labor, there is an offsetting effect as each human worker's effective labor input is boosted by the adoption of the multiplicative robot.

2. Dynamic General-Equilibrium Analysis

Consider an economy initially without any robots. There is no technological progress. The only nonhuman asset is the stock of factory buildings and physical structures. The representative household supplies inelastically $\bar{H}$ units of labor and lives infinitely with a subjective rate of time preference given by θ. Output is given by $Y = Hf(T/H)$. The real wage is given by $v = m^{-1}\left[f\left(\dfrac{T}{H}\right) - \left(\dfrac{T}{H}\right)f'\left(\dfrac{T}{H}\right)\right]$, and the factory rental rate is given by $r^T = m^{-1} f'(T/H)$. In the closed economy, consumption, C, is equal to output so $C = Y$. The real rate of interest is given by θ and the price of factory buildings and physical structures, q, is given by

$$q = \frac{m^{-1}f'\left(\dfrac{T}{H}\right)}{\theta}. \tag{13}$$

2.1. Case of Additive Robots

With the introduction of additive robots, the aggregate production function is given by $Y = F(T, H + R_A)$. Firm optimization under imperfect competition gives rise to (1) to (3). Savers can now invest in factory buildings as well as in additive robots, so equality of rate of return gives us

$$r = r^{R_A} - \delta = \frac{r^T}{q} + \frac{\dot{q}}{q}, \tag{14}$$

where r is the instantaneous real rate of interest. Using (2) and (3) in (14), we obtain

$$\frac{\dot{q}}{q} = m^{-1}\left[f\left(\frac{T}{H + R_A}\right) - \left(\frac{T}{H + R_A}\right)f'\left(\frac{T}{H + R_A}\right)\right]$$
$$- \delta - \frac{m^{-1}f'\left(\dfrac{T}{H + R_A}\right)}{q}. \tag{15}$$

Household intertemporal optimization, assuming the log utility function, gives the familiar Euler equation

$$\frac{\dot{C}}{C} = r - \theta. \tag{16}$$

Using the expression for r, we obtain

$$\frac{\dot{C}}{C} = m^{-1}\left[f\left(\frac{T}{H+R_A}\right) - \left(\frac{T}{H+R_A}\right) f'\left(\frac{T}{H+R_A}\right)\right] - \delta - \theta. \qquad (17)$$

The time rate of change in the stock of additive robots is given by

$$\dot{R}_A = (H+R_A)f\left(\frac{T}{H+R_A}\right) - \delta R_A - C. \qquad (18)$$

Equations (17) and (18) give a system of two dynamic equations in the variables C, a control variable, and R_A, a stock variable. It is readily checked that the system exhibits saddle-path stability, which we illustrate in Figure 9.2a. Note that when $R_A = 0$, consumption is given by $Hf(T/H)$, which is denoted Point I in Figure 9.2a. Upon the introduction of robots, there is an immediate drop of consumption (to Point II), prompting a gradual buildup of the stock of additive robots. The economy travels along a positively sloped saddle path, where $C = \Phi(R_A)$; $\Phi'(R_A) > 0$. Along the adjustment path, (1) indicates that the real wage is gradually declining as the factor intensity, $x = T/(H+R_A)$, gradually decreases to reach a permanently lower level. In the new steady state, the factor intensity is pinned down by

$$m^{-1}\left[f\left(\frac{T}{H+R_A}\right) - \left(\frac{T}{H+R_A}\right) f'\left(\frac{T}{H+R_A}\right)\right] = \delta + \theta.$$

Substituting the relationship between C and R_A along the saddle path, $C = \Phi(R_A)$, into (18), we obtain

$$\dot{R}_A = (H+R_A)f\left(\frac{T}{H+R_A}\right) - \delta R_A - \Phi(R_A). \qquad (19)$$

Equations (15) and (19) form another system of two dynamic equations in the variables q, a jumpy variable, and R_A, a stock variable. It is readily checked that the system exhibits saddle-path stability, which we illustrate in Figure 9.2b. Note that when $R_A = 0$, the price of factory buildings and physical structures is given by (13), which is denoted Point I in Figure 9.2b. Upon the introduction of robots, there is an immediate upward jump of factory building price, a positive asset price effect, followed by a steady rise until it reaches the new steady state. In the new steady state, the price of factory building is given by

$$q = \frac{m^{-1}f'\left(\dfrac{T}{H+R_A}\right)}{\theta}.$$

Thus, we see that the case of introducing additive robots leads to an immiserization of real wages but an appreciation of factory building prices. With a representative household, while consumption drops initially, the introduction of the additive robot leads to a rising path of per household consumption. In the new steady state, household consumption is unambiguously higher.

2.2. Case of Multiplicative Robots

With the introduction of multiplicative robots, the aggregate production function is given by $Y = F(T, (1+R_M)H)$. Firm optimization under imperfect competition gives rise to (7) to (9). Savers can now invest in factory buildings and physical structures as well as in multiplicative robots, so equality of rate of return gives us

$$r = r^{R_M} - \delta = \frac{r^T}{q} + \frac{\dot{q}}{q}, \tag{20}$$

where r is the instantaneous real rate of interest. Using (8) and (9) in (20), we obtain

$$\frac{\dot{q}}{q} = m^{-1}H\left[f\left(\frac{T}{(1+R_M)H}\right) - \left(\frac{T}{(1+R_M)H}\right)f'\left(\frac{T}{(1+R_M)H}\right)\right]$$
$$-\delta - \frac{m^{-1}f'\left(\dfrac{T}{(1+R_M)H}\right)}{q}. \tag{21}$$

Household intertemporal optimization gives the familiar Euler equation

$$\frac{\dot{C}}{C} = r - \theta. \tag{22}$$

Using the expression for r, we obtain

$$\frac{\dot{C}}{C} = m^{-1}H\left[f\left(\frac{T}{(1+R_M)H}\right) - \left(\frac{T}{(1+R_M)H}\right)f'\left(\frac{T}{(1+R_M)H}\right)\right] - \delta - \theta. \tag{23}$$

The time rate of change of multiplicative robots is given by

$$\dot{R}_M = (1 + R_M)Hf\left(\frac{T}{(1 + R_M)H}\right) - \delta R_M - C. \tag{24}$$

Equations (23) and (24) give a system of two dynamic equations in the variables C, a control variable, and R_M, a stock variable. It is readily checked that the system exhibits saddle-path stability and can be illustrated in a diagram similar to Figure 9.2a (not shown). Upon introducing robots, there is a drop in consumption followed by a gradual buildup of robots. Substituting the relationship between C and R_M along the saddle path, $C = \Psi(R_M)$, into (24), we obtain

$$\dot{R}_M = (1 + R_M)Hf\left(\frac{T}{(1 + R_M)H}\right) - \delta R_M - \Psi(R_M). \tag{25}$$

Equations (21) and (25) form another system of two dynamic equations in the variables q, a jumpy variable, and R_M, a stock variable. It is readily checked that the system exhibits saddle-path stability, which we can illustrate in a diagram similar to Figure 9.2b (not shown). Upon the introduction of robots, there is an immediate upward jump of factory building price, followed by a steady rise until it reaches the new steady state.

We pointed out in the last section that with multiplicative robots, there are two effects on wages: a factor-intensity effect, which depresses wages, and a labor-augmenting effect, which boosts wages. We now examine the condition under which, given m, the labor-augmenting effect dominates so that, overall, the introduction of multiplicative robots raises the whole path of real wages. Taking the derivative of the real wage, v, in (7) with respect to the stock of multiplicative robots, R_M, we obtain

$$\frac{dv}{dR_M} = m^{-1}[f(x) - xf'(x)]\left[1 - \frac{\alpha_T}{\sigma}\right], \tag{26}$$

where $x \equiv T/[(1 + R_M)H]$, $\alpha_T \equiv xf'(x)/f(x)$ is the share of factory buildings and physical structures in national income, and $\sigma \equiv -\{f'(x)[f(x) - xf'(x)]/[xf''(x)f(x)]\}$ is the elasticity of substitution between factory buildings, T, and effective labor, $(1 + R_M)H$. A necessary and sufficient condition for the introduction of multiplicative robots to boost wages is $\sigma > \alpha_T$. This condition is satisfied with a conventional Cobb-Douglas production function, where the elasticity of substitution is one.[2]

3. Long-Run Equilibrium with Endogenous Supply of Factory Buildings and Physical Structures

Suppose that the number of factory buildings and physical structures that human and robotic labor work with to produce the final output is endogenously determined. We model this by supposing that resources (measured in units of output) have to be used up in order to add to the stock of factory buildings and physical structures. Let the amount of resources used be given by the function $\chi(T)$; $\chi(0) = 0$, $\chi'(\cdot) > 0$, $\chi''(\cdot) > 0$.

In the long-run equilibrium case of additive robots, with $x \equiv T/(H + R_A)$, $r = \theta$, so

$$\theta + \delta = m^{-1}[f(x) - xf'(x)]. \tag{27}$$

From (27), we write $x = \phi(\theta + \delta)$. Using this in (1) and (14) with $\dot{q} = 0$, we have

$$v = m^{-1}[f(\phi(\theta + \delta)) - \phi(\theta + \delta)f'(\phi(\theta + \delta))], \tag{28}$$

$$q = \frac{m^{-1}f'(\phi(\theta + \delta))}{\theta}, \tag{29}$$

$$\chi'(T) = q. \tag{30}$$

We showed earlier that with a constant stock of factory buildings and physical structures, the introduction of additive robots leads to a gradual decline of the real wage. However, the adoption of additive robots boosts the shadow price of factory buildings and physical structures, thus spurring investment. In the long run, the increased stock of factory buildings and physical structures restores the real wage initially depressed by the adoption of additive robots.

In the long-run equilibrium case of multiplicative robots, with $x \equiv T/[(1 + R_M)H]$, $r = \theta$, so

$$\theta + \delta = m^{-1}H[f(x) - xf'(x)]. \tag{31}$$

We write $x = \psi((\theta + \delta)/H)$. The real wage is given by

$$v = m^{-1}[1 + R_M]\left[f\left(\psi\left(\frac{\theta + \delta}{H}\right)\right) - \psi\left(\frac{\theta + \delta}{H}\right)f'\left(\psi\left(\frac{\theta + \delta}{H}\right)\right)\right],$$

and we have

$$\chi'(T) = q = \frac{m^{-1}f'\left(\psi\left(\dfrac{\theta + \delta}{H}\right)\right)}{\theta}.$$

The factor-intensity effect that tends to pull down wages when robots are introduced is absent in the long run when the stock of factory buildings and physical structures adjusts endogenously. Hence, only the labor-augmenting effect of multiplicative robots is at work.

4. Conclusion

In this chapter we first studied the case of introducing only additive robots. We showed that when it is profitable for firms to adopt the robots in the production process, the real wage gradually declines to reach a permanently lower level. Essentially, with more total human and robotic labor working on a constant stock of factory buildings and physical structures, the marginal revenue product of labor falls and thus lowers the wage. This is the factor-intensity effect.

Then, we studied the case of introducing only multiplicative robots. We showed that there are two offsetting effects: a factor-intensity effect (with more effective labor working on a constant stock of factory buildings), which tends to reduce wages, and a labor-augmenting effect (with multiplicative robots making each worker more effective), which raises hourly pay. We establish the result that, given the price-marginal cost markup, if the share of factory buildings and physical structures in national income is less than the elasticity of substitution between physical structures and effective labor, then introducing robots must raise the whole path of real wages. In this case, while having more "effective" labor working on a constant stock of factory buildings and physical structures (taken by itself) reduces the marginal revenue productivity of labor, there is an offsetting effect as each human worker's effective labor input is boosted by the adoption of the multiplicative robot.

In both cases we studied, the introduction of robots results in an upward shift in the path of the shadow value of factory buildings and physical structures, a positive asset price effect. In our model, we first assumed that the stock of factory buildings and physical structures is constant. More generally, if the stock of factory buildings and physical structures is endogenously determined at a rising marginal cost, the boost in the shadow value of factory buildings and physical structures can be expected to lead to a gradual increase in the stock of factory buildings and physical structures being used in cooperation with workers and robots. The endogenous increase in the supply of these co-operating assets can then act to offset the factor-intensity effect, which is what lies behind the wage-depressing effect of robots. In the long run, with only additive robots, the increased stock of factory buildings and physical structures restores the real wage initially depressed by the adoption of additive robots. With only multiplicative robots, the factor-intensity effect that tends to pull down wages is absent in the long run when the stock of factory buildings adjusts endogenously. Hence, only the labor-augmenting effect of multiplicative robots is at work in the long run.

The basic analysis in this chapter, which uses an aggregative model, suggests that as the stock of robots grows large, even if robots are harmless or even helpful in the long run, nations may at some point encounter resistance from workers to further introduction of robots into the economy, although it will not always be straightforward to classify machinery into additive-robot and multiplicative-robot categories. That development might not only deprive society of some of its future wage growth (and economic growth more broadly) but also stir opposition to most or all innovation, thus depriving society of the satisfactions that come with engagement in the innovation process. If robotization proceeds at a fast pace, and the outcome is these mounting tensions, social and political, these preliminary analyses would be successful.

APPENDIX

In this appendix, we introduce endogenous labor supply so that we can analyze the effects of introducing additive and multiplicative robots both on wages and on employment. To keep the analysis simple, we perform a thought experiment: What happens to the economy's wages and employment when there is a helicopter drop of additive and multiplicative robots?

Population size is normalized to one. We assume that households are identical as before but now suppose that an individual's current utility is given by $\log C + \log(1 - \bar{H})$, where the total time endowment is normalized to one, C is aggregate consumption, and $\bar{H}$ is aggregate employment.[3] With this representation of individual preferences, it is readily shown that aggregate employment is given by

$$\bar{H}(t) = 1 - \frac{C(t)}{v(t)},$$

so that aggregate employment ($\bar{H}$) is negatively related to the consumption-wage ratio (C/v).

In the closed economy that we are studying, assuming for simplicity that the depreciation rate (δ) is equal to zero, market clearing requires that aggregate consumption (C) equals output ($F(T, H + R_A)$ in the case of additive robots and $F(T, (1 + R_M)H)$ in the case of multiplicative robots). With additive robots, we can then write,

$$\bar{H} = 1 - \frac{Tf(x)}{m^{-1}x[f(x) - xf'(x)]}; \; x \equiv \frac{T}{H + R_A},$$

after noting $v = m^{-1}[f(x) - xf'(x)]$. We get from here a reduced-form function of aggregate employment:

$$\bar{H} = \eta(x, T); \; \frac{\partial \eta}{\partial x} > 0; \; \frac{\partial \eta}{\partial T} < 0.$$

It is now evident that, given T and m, a helicopter drop of additive robots, in reducing x, leads not only to a fall in real wages but also to a decrease in aggregate employment. The real wage does not fall by as much as in the case of infinitely inelastic labor supply, so that part of the downward pressure on wages brought about by the helicopter drop of additive robots is alleviated by a contraction in aggregate employment.

Now consider a helicopter drop of multiplicative robots. With multiplicative robots, we can then write,

$$\bar{H} = 1 - \frac{Hf(x)}{m^{-1}[f(x) - xf'(x)]}; \; x \equiv \frac{T}{(1 + R_M)H},$$

after noting $v = m^{-1}(1 + R_M)[f(x) - xf'(x)]$. We get from here a reduced-form function of aggregate employment:

$$\bar{H} = \eta(x),$$

where

$$\frac{d\bar{H}}{dx} = \frac{xf''(x)f(x)(\sigma - 1)}{m^{-1}\left[1 + \dfrac{f(x)}{f(x) - xf'(x)}\right][f(x) - xf'(x)]^2},$$

and

$$\sigma \equiv \frac{-f'(x)[f(x) - xf'(x)]}{xf''(x)f(x)}.$$

We get the result that, if the elasticity of substitution between physical structures and total effective labor (σ) is less than one, then, given T and m, a helicopter drop of multiplicative robots has an ambiguous effect on real wages but decreases aggregate employment. The real wage is pulled down by the fall in x but increased by the labor-augmenting effect of $1 + R_M$ on human labor. If the elasticity of substitution between physical structures and total effective labor is less than one, the helicopter drop of multiplicative robots increases the consumption-wage ratio and thus contracts employment.

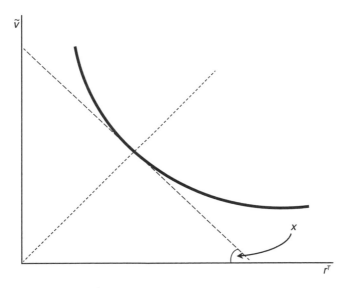

Figure 9.1a. Factor-price frontier.

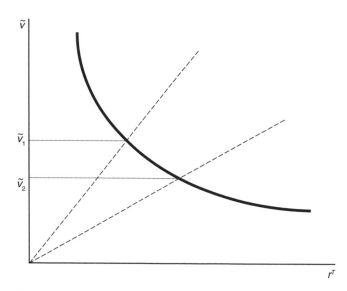

Figure 9.1b. Decrease in x due to introduction of robotics.

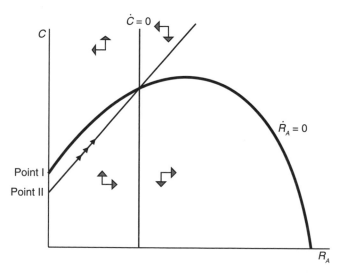

Figure 9.2a. Saddle-path stability in (R_A, C) plane.

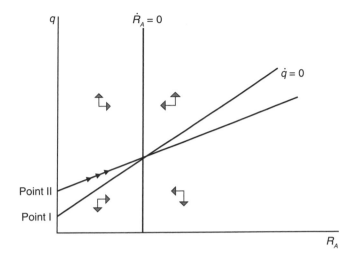

Figure 9.2b. Saddle-path stability in (R_A, q) plane.

10

Additive Robots, Relative Prices, and Indigenous Innovation

Hian Teck Hoon

ABSTRACT We formalize the idea in a two-sector model that when an influx of additive robots in the capital goods sector causes the relative price of the capital good to fall, economic incentives are created to make indigenous innovation in the consumption goods sector more profitable. This causes some workers in the economy to shift from participating in production to participating in innovative activity. Consequently, the new wage path must ultimately be rising, as long as innovation in the consumption goods sector continues undiminished, exerting its upward pull on wage rates.

Introduction

In this chapter, we study a channel through which the adoption of additive robots leads to wage growth by stimulating innovation in the consumption goods sector as the adoption of additive robots in the capital goods sector reduces the relative price of the capital good. First, we set up a two-sector model where there is *no innovation* and zero technological progress. The model has the characteristic that there is a sector that uses only human labor to produce a capital good before the arrival of robots. The capital good is used to produce a pure consumption good. With zero technological progress and no innovation, the model exhibits a stationary equilibrium where the wage rate, consumption per capita, relative price of the capital good, and stock of conventional machines are all constant. With the arrival of additive robots, we obtain the result that capital accumulation is stimulated, consumption per capita grows, and the real wage declines to a permanently lower level as the relative price of the capital good permanently declines to a lower level.

Next, we study a two-sector model where there is *indigenous innovation*, which occurs endogenously within the model. We model innovation by quality improvement of intermediate inputs used in the production of the consumption good. The model has the feature that the consumption goods sector produces a product using conventional machines and a continuum of intermediate inputs supplied by imperfectly competitive firms, which also use conventional machines as primary inputs. In reduced form, such a model is identical to the first model except for the fact that the rate of innovation is now endogenously determined. We derive two main results: (1) a drop in the relative price of the capital good stimulates indigenous innovation, which acts to boost real wages; and (2) the arrival of additive robots spurs investment in conventional machines, which also stimulates indigenous innovation. Thus, once we depart from the first two-sector model to allow for indigenous innovation that raises the productivity of the consumption goods sector, the arrival of additive robots is good for wage growth.

The chapter is organized as follows. In Section 1, we set up the two-sector model with zero technological progress and no innovation to study the effects of introducing additive robots. In Section 2, we develop the two-sector model with indigenous innovation and study the effects of introducing additive robots. Section 3 concludes.

1. The Two-Sector Model with Zero Technological Progress and No Innovation

Consider an economy initially without any robots. There is no technological progress or innovation. Production of the capital good requires only human labor. Capital, in turn, is used to produce a pure consumption good. With suitable normalization, output of the capital good is given by $Y^I = H$, and the output of the pure consumption good is given by $Y^C = K$. Let q be the relative price of the capital good measured in units of the pure consumption good. Under perfect competition, the following conditions hold:

$$v(t) = q(t), \tag{1}$$

$$r^K(t) = 1, \tag{2}$$

where v is the real wage and r^K is the capital rental rate. The asset pricing relationship is given by

$$r(t) = \frac{r^K}{q(t)} + \frac{\dot{q}(t)}{q(t)} - \delta, \tag{3}$$

which, using (2), can be written as,

$$r(t) = \frac{1}{q(t)} + \frac{\dot{q}(t)}{q(t)} - \delta. \tag{4}$$

The capital accumulation equation is given by

$$\dot{K}(t) = H - \delta K(t). \tag{5}$$

Household intertemporal optimization, assuming the log utility function, gives the familiar Euler equation

$$\frac{\dot{C}(t)}{C(t)} = r(t) - \theta. \tag{6}$$

With clearing of the pure consumption goods market, $C(t) = Y^C(t)$, and using (5) and (6) in (4), we obtain

$$\frac{\dot{q}(t)}{q(t)} = \theta + \frac{H}{K(t)} - \frac{1}{q(t)}. \tag{7}$$

Equations (5) and (7) give a pair of dynamic equations in $K(t)$ and $q(t)$ that exhibit saddle-path stability given an initial capital stock, $K(0)$. In a steady state,

$$K_{ss} = \frac{H}{\delta}, \tag{8}$$

$$q_{ss} = \frac{1}{\theta + \delta}, \tag{9}$$

with $r_{ss} = \theta$.

Now, consider the arrival of additive robots. In order for it to be profitable to adopt additive robots, the rate of return to holding robots in the saver's portfolio must be at least as great as $r_{ss} = \theta$. We note that if additive robots are adopted, then the production of the capital good is now given by $Y^I = H + R_A$. Letting r^{R_A} be the rental rate on a unit of the additive robot, we require that

$$r^{R_A} = v. \tag{10}$$

Given (1), this is equivalent to

$$r^{R_A} = q.\tag{11}$$

Moreover, the equality of the rate of return principle requires that

$$r^{R_A} = r^K.\tag{12}$$

Using (2), equations (11) and (12) imply that if it is profitable to adopt additive robots, then

$$q = 1.\tag{13}$$

Using (13) in (4), the rate of return to holding additive robots in the saver's portfolio is given by

$$r = 1 - \delta.\tag{14}$$

Therefore, if additive robots are profitable to adopt, the following condition must hold:

$$1 - \delta > \theta.\tag{15}$$

With the pure consumption-goods market clearing so $C = K$, it follows from (6), (14), and (15) that

$$\frac{\dot{C}(t)}{C(t)} = 1 - \delta - \theta > 0,\tag{16}$$

even in the absence of steady technological progress. Using (1), (9), (13), and (15), we see that when additive robots are adopted, the real wage declines from $v = (\theta + \delta)^{-1}$ to $v = 1$. Hence, we rediscover the result obtained in Chapter 8: the adoption of additive robots leads to a one-time permanent drop in the real wage even as the per capita consumption, which was stagnant before the adoption of robots, begins a trend growth without steady technological progress.

2. The Case of Indigenous Innovation Responding to Price Incentives

Before the adoption of robots, the output of the capital goods sector is given simply by $Y^I = H_I$ with suitable normalization. Here, Y^I is the output of the capital good, and H_I is the number of human workers employed in production in the capital goods sector. The output of the consumption good is given by $Y^C = K_C^{1-\alpha} \int_0^1 \Lambda_i^{1-\alpha} x_i^\alpha di; 0 < \alpha < 1$. Here, Y^C is output of the consumption good, K_C is the capital stock employed directly in the consumption goods sector, and x_i is the quantity of intermediate good i with quality denoted by Λ_i. Both the final goods are produced under conditions of perfect competition. However, each intermediate good i is produced under monopolistic competition as in Grossman and Helpman (1991) and Aghion and Howitt (1992).[1]

Let q denote the relative price of output in the capital goods sector, letting the consumption good serve as the numeraire. Profit maximization by competitive firms in the capital goods sector gives

$$v = q, \tag{17}$$

where v is the real wage. Competitive firms engaged in the production of the consumption good solve the following profit-maximization problem:

$$Maximize \ K_C^{1-\alpha} \int_0^1 \Lambda_i^{1-\alpha} x_i^\alpha \ di - r^K K_C - \int_0^1 p_i x_i di,$$

where r^K is the rental rate of capital and p_i is the relative price of intermediate good i. Solving this optimization problem gives rise to

$$r^K = (1-\alpha) K_C^{-\alpha} \int_0^1 \Lambda_i^{1-\alpha} x_i^\alpha di, \tag{18}$$

$$p_i = \alpha K_C^{1-\alpha} \Lambda_i^{1-\alpha} x_i^{-(1-\alpha)}. \tag{19}$$

Turning to monopolistically competitive firm i, the following maximization problem is solved under the assumption that producing one unit of x_i requires one unit of conventional machine:

$$Maximize \ \pi_i \equiv p_i x_i - r^K x_i,$$

subject to (19). Solving this optimization problem, we obtain

$$r^K = \alpha^2 K_C^{1-\alpha} \Lambda_i^{1-\alpha} x_i^{-(1-\alpha)}. \tag{20}$$

We can reexpress (20) as

$$x_i = \left(\frac{\alpha^2}{r^K} \right)^{\frac{1}{1-\alpha}} K_C \Lambda_i. \tag{21}$$

Integrating across i in (21), we obtain

$$\int_0^1 x_i di = \left(\frac{\alpha^2}{r^K}\right)^{\frac{1}{1-\alpha}} K_C \Lambda, \tag{22}$$

where $\Lambda \equiv \int_0^1 \Lambda_i di$. Using (21) in (22), we obtain, after further simplification,

$$r^K = (1-\alpha)^{1-\alpha} \alpha^{2\alpha} \Lambda^{1-\alpha}. \tag{23}$$

The condition that the total demand for capital is equal to the total supply of capital gives

$$K_C + \int_0^1 x_i \, di = K. \tag{24}$$

Using (22), (23), and (24), we obtain

$$K_C = \frac{K}{1 + (1-\alpha)^{-1}\alpha^2}. \tag{25}$$

Then, using (22) and (25) with the production function for the consumption good, we obtain an expression for the output of the consumption good:

$$Y^C = B\Lambda^{1-\alpha}K; \ B \equiv \frac{(1-\alpha)^{-\alpha}\alpha^{\frac{2\alpha^2}{1-\alpha}}}{1 + (1-\alpha)^{-1}\alpha^2}. \tag{26}$$

Let the growth rate of technology be expressed as $\dot{\Lambda}/\Lambda \equiv \lambda$. The general equilibrium dynamics of the economy can be summarized as follows. After setting aggregate consumption equal to output of the consumption good and taking note of (3), (6), (23), and (26), we have

$$\dot{K} = H_I - \delta K, \tag{27}$$

$$r = \frac{(1-\alpha)^{(1-\alpha)}\alpha^{2\alpha}\Lambda^{1-\alpha}}{q} + \frac{\dot{q}}{q} - \delta, \tag{28}$$

$$r = \theta + (1-\alpha)\lambda + \frac{\dot{K}}{K}, \tag{29}$$

where r is the instantaneous real interest rate and θ is the subjective rate of time preference. Using (27) and (29) in (28), and defining $\tilde{q} \equiv q/\Lambda^{1-\alpha}$, we obtain

$$\frac{\dot{\tilde{q}}}{\tilde{q}} = \frac{H_I}{K} + \theta - \frac{(1-\alpha)^{1-\alpha}\alpha^{2\alpha}}{\tilde{q}}. \tag{30}$$

If H_I is treated as exogenous, (27) and (30) can be characterized in a diagram with $\tilde{q}$ in the vertical axis and K on the horizontal axis. The stationary-K locus is a vertical line and the stationary $\tilde{q}$ locus is positively sloped in this diagram. Saddle-path stability is exhibited with a positively sloped saddle path that is less steep than the stationary $\tilde{q}$ locus.

To better understand the effects of introducing robots when the rate of technological progress is endogenously determined by the number of innovators, it would be helpful to conduct a preliminary analysis assuming that H_I is given exogenously so that, from (37), given later, λ is also given exogenously. In a steady state before the introduction of additive robots, we have

$$\tilde{q}_{ss} = \frac{(1-\alpha)^{1-\alpha}\alpha^{2\alpha}}{\delta+\theta}, \tag{31}$$

$$K_{ss} = \frac{H_I}{\delta}, \tag{32}$$

with $r_{ss} = \theta$. With the adoption of additive robots, $r^K = r^{R_A} = \upsilon$, so using (17) and (23), we obtain

$$\tilde{q} = (1-\alpha)^{1-\alpha}\alpha^{2\alpha}. \tag{33}$$

Using (23) and (33) in (3), the rate of return to holding additive robots in the saver's portfolio is given by

$$r = 1 + (1-\alpha)\,\lambda - \delta.$$

For it to be profitable to adopt additive robots, we require that the following condition holds:

$$r = 1 + (1-\alpha)\,\lambda - \delta > \theta. \tag{34}$$

Assume that $\delta + \theta < 1$ so (34) is satisfied.[2] Comparing (31), (33), and (34), we see that with the adoption of additive robots, real wage experiences an immediate decline. After the immediate impact, the real wage continues on its trend growth at the rate of $(1-\alpha)\lambda$. The growth rate of per capita consumption also increases. This is so because using (34) in (29), we have

$$\frac{\dot{K}}{K} = 1 - (\delta + \theta) > 0. \tag{35}$$

Since consumption goods market clearing means that $C = Y^C$, we have, using (26), (34), and (35), that

$$\frac{\dot{C}}{C} = (1 - \alpha)\lambda + \frac{\dot{K}}{K} > 0. \tag{36}$$

In this preliminary analysis, we have held H_I exogenously fixed. We will now show that when H_I is endogenously determined, the adoption of additive robots causes an instantaneous drop of the real wage as the relative price of the capital good, q, drops. However, the cheaper capital good stimulates innovation in the consumption goods sector so that λ increases. As a result, although the adoption of additive robots leads to an instantaneous drop of the real wage, the subsequent path of the real wage corresponds to a higher *trend* growth rate.

To determine the equilibrium allocation of human workers between production and innovation, we let λ be endogenously determined with

$$\lambda = \mu H_{IN} \,(\gamma - 1); \, \gamma > 1,$$

where H_{IN} is human labor doing innovation and μ is the constant probability (in a Poisson process) of a successful innovation. Labor-market clearing requires

$$H_{IN} + H_I = H,$$

so we can also write,

$$\lambda = \mu(H - H_I)(\gamma - 1). \tag{37}$$

The flow of profit from successful innovation for intermediate good firm i is given by

$$\pi_i \equiv \Phi \Lambda^{-\alpha} \Lambda_i K; \, \Phi \equiv \left(\frac{1 - \alpha}{\alpha} \right) \left(\frac{\alpha^{\frac{2}{1-\alpha}} \, [(1-\alpha)^{1-\alpha} \alpha^{2\alpha}]^{-\left(\frac{\alpha}{1-\alpha} \right)}}{1 + (1-\alpha)^{-1} \alpha^2} \right). \tag{38}$$

The asset pricing relationship is given by

$$r_t = \frac{\pi_{it}}{V_{it}} + \frac{\dot{V}_{it}}{V_{it}} - \mu H_{IN_i}. \tag{39}$$

Free entry into innovating is given by

$$v_t = \mu V_{it.} \qquad (40)$$

Using (1), (38), (39), and (40), we obtain

$$H_{INi} = \Phi[(1-\alpha)^{1-\alpha}\alpha^{2\alpha}]^{-1}\Lambda^{-1}\tilde{q}^{-1}K\Lambda_i - \mu^{-1}\left[r - \frac{\dot{q}}{q}\right]. \qquad (41)$$

Using (28) in (41), we obtain

$$H_{INi} = \Phi[(1-\alpha)^{1-\alpha}\alpha^{2\alpha}]^{-1}\Lambda^{-1}\tilde{q}^{-1}K\Lambda_i - \mu^{-1}\left[\frac{(1-\alpha)^{1-\alpha}\alpha^{2\alpha}}{\tilde{q}} - \delta\right]. \qquad (42)$$

Integrating over i in (42), and using $\lambda = \mu H_{IN}(\gamma - 1)$, we have

$$\frac{\lambda}{(\gamma-1)} = \mu\Phi[(1-\alpha)^{1-\alpha}\alpha^{2\alpha}]^{-1}\tilde{q}^{-1}K - \left[\frac{(1-\alpha)^{1-\alpha}\alpha^{2\alpha}}{\tilde{q}} - \delta\right]. \qquad (43)$$

From (43), we obtain the following partial derivatives:

$$\left(\frac{1}{\gamma-1}\right)\frac{\partial\lambda}{\partial\tilde{q}} = \frac{-(1-\alpha)^{1-\alpha}\alpha^{2\alpha}[\mu\Phi K - 1]}{\tilde{q}},$$

$$\left(\frac{1}{\gamma-1}\right)\frac{\partial\lambda}{\partial K} = \mu\Phi[(1-\alpha)^{1-\alpha}\alpha^{2\alpha}]^{-1}\tilde{q}^{-1}.$$

A crucial result from (43) is that, ceteris paribus, a drop in $\tilde{q}$ leads to an increase in the number of human workers innovating for sufficiently high probability of successful innovation, μ, which boosts the rate of technological progress, λ. In particular, the sufficient condition is $\mu > 1/(\Phi K)$. How do we explain this result? There are two channels through which a fall in the relative price of the capital good affects the equilibrium allocation of human labor engaged in the innovative activity. First, a fall in the relative price of the capital good reduces the demand for workers employed in the production of the capital good. This releases workers to be employed in the innovative activity, which increases the rate of technological progress. Second, a fall in the relative price of the capital good, holding other things constant, leads to a fall in the shadow value of a new innovation (V_i).[3] This second channel acts to reduce the demand for innovators. Overall, if the probability of success in innovation (μ) is sufficiently high, the first channel dominates so a fall in the relative price of the capital good leads to more workers being employed in the innovative activity and thus increases the rate of technological progress.

Another important result is that, ceteris paribus, an increase in K leads to an increase in the number of human workers innovating. Suppose that the technology to develop additive robots becomes available and that capital is malleable, so a unit of capital can be retrofitted to become an additive robot that perfectly substitutes for one human worker. Suppose that it is profitable to employ an additive robot. Then, the rental price of an additive robot cannot be higher than the current real wage. In equilibrium, with adoption of additive robots, the following condition must hold:

$$v = q = r^K. \tag{44}$$

This implies that (33) holds when additive robots are adopted even when the rate of innovation is endogenously determined. For it to be profitable to adopt additive robots, the condition expressed in (34) must hold, where λ is itself determined by (43). Real wage experiences an immediate decline if $\delta + \theta < 1$ and $\tilde{q}$ drops on impact. From (43), if $\mu > 1/(\Phi K)$ holds when additive robots are first adopted, this implies that the rate of technical progress, λ, is increased. Since (35) holds, we find that the capital stock is steadily increased. Equation (43) implies that this expansion of the capital stock stimulates the pace of innovation. This would imply that as K steadily increases, H_{IN} steadily increases so λ is also steadily increasing. In recent work, Bloom et al. (2018) show that in many sectors of the economy, it takes many more researchers to achieve a given level of success in innovation.[4] This suggests that, according to (43), even though μ, the probability of a successful innovation, is initially high when additive robots are first adopted, there is an exogenous steady decline in μ over time. Turning to (37), a decline in μ leads to a decline in λ both directly and by leading to a fall in H_{NI}, the number of people doing research.

3. Conclusion

In this chapter, we showed that with the arrival of additive robots, capital accumulation is stimulated, and consumption per capita grows at a faster pace. When there is indigenous innovation, we find that while the real wage drops on impact, the decline in relative price of capital stimulates the pace of innovation so that the initial decline in the real wage is compensated with a higher trend growth if the probability of a successful innovation is sufficiently high. Summarizing our analysis, we showed that there are at least three channels that deliver more positive results on wage growth as a consequence of adopting robots. The first channel, examined in Chapter 8, is that the introduction of multiplicative robots that augment the productivity of human labor leads to positive wage growth. The second channel, examined in Chapter 9, is that the adoption even of additive robots has a positive asset price effect that stimulates investment in slow-adjusting, nonmalleable capital (such as factory buildings and physical structures) that complements total human and robotic labor. The third channel, examined in this chapter, works by stimulating innovation in the consumption goods sector as the adoption of additive robots in the capital goods sector reduces the relative price of the capital good.

Epilogue

Edmund Phelps

With this monograph, we have reported statistical evidence supporting the thesis that grassroots innovation, economic growth, and job satisfaction are linked to the values a society embraces. Values at the core of modernism—independence, initiative, achievement, and acceptance of competition—are strong in the countries with high indigenous innovation. An index of a people's modernism accounts for virtually half of intercountry differences in productivity growth over recent decades. We have also reported theoretical analyses of the effects, long run as well as short run, of the two types of automation that have emerged.

Now, in the West, there is extraordinary discontent and division—a vast alienation and dissatisfaction with the "system" both political and economic. In this epilogue we will consider how our perspective and findings may, to some extent, illuminate what is behind these developments and what steps might be taken toward remedying the division and ending the discontent.

The Great Alienation

There is more than one discontent. And innovation, or the loss of it, plays a part in all of them.

One discontent is the widespread frustration over economic growth or the lack of it. "For most people," as Ray Dalio said about America and could have said about the West, there has been "little or no real income growth for decades."[1] Many people have not seen their earnings increase much over what their parents had earned.[2] This reflects the continuing slow-down of the West that began some five decades ago in America and later spread to Europe—a slowdown in the growth of total factor productivity.[3]

The cause of the slowdown, in our view, is a serious loss of innovation in the aggregate—relieved only briefly by the advances in information and communication that came out of Silicon Valley. Our research in this volume has shown that this deficiency is less a loss of exogenous innovation driven by scientific discovery than it is a loss of *indigenous* innovation in the long-regarded "lead economies"—those in America, Britain, and France.

The decline of innovation has brought a whole syndrome of ills: not only slower growth of wages but—ominously—a long slide in rates of return to investment. These ills have led, in turn, to a serious contraction of male labor force participation and reduced investment.[4] In some countries there has been a widespread disappearance of many rewarding jobs and satis-fying careers. In American data, this is evidenced by the long downward trend of job satisfaction reported in household surveys.[5]

This is extraordinary. One would have to go back to postwar Britain, 1945–1975, or as far back as the Weimar Republic, 1918–1933, to find such stasis in an important Western economy.[6] The nations of the West—especially those that were in the lead—are in grave need of a return to high levels of economic growth, and human flourishing.

Besides the slow growth of incomes *in general* is a different discontent that began in the 1980s and grew stronger in some countries than others. This is the fall in the *relative* wages of middle-income earners in several (though not all) Western economies—typically, workers engaged in farming, manufacturing, or mining and stranded in rural areas.

Trade may have played a part. New competition coming from farms and factories in Asia has surely had a negative impact on real wages in some industries. But whether this impact comes close to explaining the decline of relative wages in farming and manufacturing is not clear. It is interesting that the countries that have long been regarded as the "innovation nations"—America, Britain, and France—are the ones that have the newly distressed regions, while the countries that have always been regarded as "trading nations"—Germany and the Netherlands, at any rate—have not been afflicted with such regions.[7]

Less known is the new competition coming from within: highly able people in cities have managed to raise their incomes by mastering new tech-nologies while most rural people have not had the opportunity.[8] As a re-sult, these workers in the middle of the wage distribution—at the 50th percentile—have not kept up with those who climbed to the high end of the distribution—say, the 90th percentile.[9] (It appears, then, that the loss of much innovation has been a drag on all incomes, while the innovation that remained has pulled up urban wages more than rural wages. Hence the loss of relative income in rural areas.)

This failure to "keep up" has distressed working-class people in industrial and rural regions. It is thought that they have a sense of being disrespected—knowingly "left behind." In France, the farmers and truckers reacted with violent protests. In America, home of rugged individualism, they have turned to drugs and switched their votes.

In times past, workers faced with such a development would have moved to cities in the hope of finding work at their former pay. But in the present time, with innovation generally weak in most industries, these workers might judge that they could not find work quickly enough to make it worth the cost and stress. They are made less mobile still by the inability to sell their house (except at a price insufficient to buy a house elsewhere) and to take their medical insurance with them.

It must be said that it is not only the decline in relative wages that has aroused anger among middle-income workers. It is also the corruption, barriers to competition, cronyism, and other obstacles that have blocked these people's sense of having a "fair shot." They lack the connections, or "strings," that they—for the most part—would need to get ahead.

In addition, with the rise of "identity politics," some working-class regions may have come to feel they have not received their fair share of government benefits, whatever the truth of the matter. In France, the Yellow Vest protesters obviously felt alienated when their taxes were raised for projects not of their choosing.

A striking reaction is the formation over recent decades of "populist" parties in France, Italy, Germany, and Spain.[10] Now, populist strains of one kind or another have arisen in the governing parties of America, Britain, and Sweden. There have been consequences. When the Italians were governed by the Fascist Party and Mussolini ran the economy—practicing his doctrine of *corporativismo*—that was the end of their capitalism and their democracy. Now there is fear in America that extremists will replace America's capitalism and democracy with Trumpean corporatism or socialism.

Again, it is impossible not to think that the alienation and angry reactions in the West—particularly in America—would have been considerably less had there not been a serious weakening of indigenous innovation in the West.

Now, a new source of discontent has descended on the West. Advances in artificial intelligence have created expectations that further innovation will bring radically increased *automation* over the next several decades. This prospect raises the question of what kind of society we can have if automation brings an invasion of robots displacing humans from their work.

It is clear that few people in a nation can have hopes of living the good life if there is little opportunity for work that is rewarding. A nation might

fall apart if a great many people lacked the satisfactions of agency, succeeding, flourishing and, at a minimum, self-support.

Regaining Growth and Flourishing

How, then, from the perspective of the present volume, might a nation overcome these three challenges?

Clearly, regaining widespread flourishing and rapid wage growth in all
sectors will require restoring the substantial loss of indigenous innovation that
has hung over the lead economies for most of the past five decades. Our research for this volume has found evidence supporting the theory advanced in
my book *Mass Flourishing* that high indigenous innovation in a nation derives
from the dynamism of its people—their desire and capacity to innovate.[11] And
this dynamism, we confirmed here, depends on the strength of *modern* values—
values under the headings of individualism, vitalism, and self-expression—
relative to traditional values.[12] We found that modern values were generally
positive for economic performance and some traditional ones negative.

These findings point to a way forward. To regain the high "desire" to
innovate, it will be important to cultivate the "positive" values and not the
"negative" values—to "accentuate the positive," as a pop song put it. A
wide-ranging change in the books studied in high school may be essential.
It might also help to reintroduce music and art into high school and middle
school curriculums. (Students are more likely to exercise creativity in their
work if they have had the experience of expressing their creativity in their
school years.) It might also help to step up federal funding of the arts.

These steps and more will surely be necessary to inspire a revival of
modern values. Whether these steps will be sufficient is an open question.

Yet dynamism requires a "capacity" to innovate as well as a "desire."
By now, there is a vast accretion of policies, laws, and deal-making im-
peding or blocking new entrants bearing new ideas. It would be a major
step forward to restore antitrust policy. Stripping away overreaching regulation would likely be a huge help to many would-be innovators. Getting
rid of the close ties between powerful corporations and the government—
both the legislative and executive branches—would also be helpful. (That
will be an unending struggle, but progress can be made.)

Another crucial step is to minimize the bureaucracy involved in starting
a business, registering property, or obtaining building permits. Philip
Howard has documented cases of regulations so prescriptive that they reduce the role of humans to one of interpreting the regulations rather than
applying judgment and creativity.[13]

Our findings also point to initiatives that may *not* be helpful. While
some attribute the slowdown to a loss of scientific advances,[14] added to

by cutbacks in national science foundations,[15] our findings jibe with the view that (until recent decades, at any rate) most innovators have come from the grass roots on up: from ordinary people at work in an *economy* open to thinking of better ways to do things and better things to make.

That does not mean that cutting funding to governments' science foundations would be desirable. But it does mean that there are no empirical grounds for believing that increased funding of such foundations would substantially restore innovation.

Next, how might a nation best respond to the casualties of the "new competition" referred to earlier? As suggested earlier, labor markets do not work in a smooth, textbook fashion when there is little or no productivity growth creating job vacancies, so that climbing back up the ladder is more difficult for these workers at present than it was in earlier times. A return to high innovation would have the desirable side effect of facilitating their climb back to the relative wages they were earning before—back to their former rung on the ladder.

Lastly, how best to respond to the increased automation that artificial intelligence is expected to bring and is already bringing? For one thing, society will have—roughly speaking—only gainers if the total innovation brings enough capital saving that it ultimately reverses the labor saving created by the automation. Second, the government might subsidize every company's employment of low-wage workers to induce it to employ more of them and thus bid up wage rates at the low end. And we might expand the Earned Income Tax Credit to aid individuals as much as it aids families. In this way, society could protect working-class people from losing their jobs to robots.

Furthermore, it is essential to *resist* some novel directions recently proposed by a few policy advocates. *Work* is fundamental. That has been noted by many great scholars—from the economists Thorstein Veblen and Alfred Marshall to the philosophers William James, John Rawls, and Amartya Sen to the sociologists Gunnar Myrdal and William Julius Wilson. My book *Rewarding Work* discussed the manifold rewards in the workplace, particularly in a dynamic economy.[16] But the argument can be simply stated:

We must oppose the universal basic income, not only because it is a lamentable use of public revenue that would be better directed toward pulling up the wages of low-end workers to a level enabling their *self-support,* which is essential for people's self-esteem—either through earned-income tax credits or through subsidies to companies for their employment of low-wage workers, thus pulling up workers' pay—but also because it is apt to draw or keep many people and also their children *away from work,* which is—for most people, at any rate—the only available avenue to personal fulfillment and, indeed, to their involvement in the world.

NOTES

Introduction

1. The Swedish economist Knut Wicksell did pioneering work on matters of capital formation, primarily saving and investment, most of it contained in his treatise *Interest and Prices* published in 1898 in the German edition *Geldzins und Guterpreise* (Jena: G. Fischer, 1898). Joseph Schumpeter's landmark work on economic growth was his 1911/12 treatise in German, *Theorie der Wirtschaftlichen Entwicklung* (Vienna: Duncker and Humblot, 1911/12), and the much later English translation, *The Theory of Economic Development* (Cambridge, MA: Harvard University Press, 1934). (German was the second language of economics from the 1890s, when the German economy was in full bloom, to the 1920s, when the economy was weak and scholarship was in decline.)

   Arthur Cecil Pigou was a leading figure in the building of the Cambridge School of Economics, "where everything from the demand and supply curve to macroeconomics was invented," to quote personal correspondence from Antara Haldar received December 13, 2018. Among his principal books are *The Economics of Welfare* (London: Macmillan, 1920), *Industrial Fluctuations* (London: Macmillan, 1927), and *A Study in Public Finance* (London: Macmillan, 1928). An extraordinary contributor to several fields, Frank Ramsey is now recognized mainly for his seminal paper, "A Mathematical Theory of Saving," *Economic Journal* 38, no. 152 (December 1928): 543–559, though he also pioneered the theory of optimal taxation.

   Paul Samuelson's conceptual work ranged from his "revealed preference" introduced in his first paper on welfare economics, "Welfare Economics and

International Trade," *American Economic Review* 28, no. 2 (June 1938): 261–266; and his ideas on convergence to equilibrium in "The Stability of Equilibrium," *Econometrica* 9, no. 2 (April 1941): 97–120; to his "factor price frontier" introduced in "Parable and Realism in Capital Theory: The Surrogate Production Function," *Review of Economic Studies* 29, no. 3 (June 1962): 193–206; his seminal work on overlapping generations in "An Exact Consumption Loan Model of Interest with or without the Social Contrivance of Money," *Journal of Political Economy* 66, no. 6 (December 1958): 467–482; and his concept of a continuum of goods in R. Dornbusch, S. Fischer, and P. A. Samuelson, "Comparative Advantage, Trade and Payments in a Ricardian Model with a Continuum of Goods," *American Economic Review* 67, no. 5 (December 1977): 823–839.

There were others who made basic contributions to the neoclassical edifice, some of the most important being Gustav Cassel, J. B. Clark, Irving Fisher, J. R. Hicks, and Kenneth J. Arrow. Note also that the body of neoclassical theory introduced here is not fundamentally monetary, so there are no references to advances in monetary economics.

This neoclassical framework was broadened to the open economy by Bertil Ohlin's work on trade, *Interregional and International Trade* (Cambridge, MA: Harvard University Press, 1933) and "Mechanisms and Objectives of Exchange Control," *American Economic Review* 27, no. 1 (March 1937): 141–150; papers on factor prices by Paul Samuelson, notably Wolfgang F. Stolper and Paul Samuelson, "Protection and Real Wages," *Review of Economic Studies* 9, no. 1 (November 1941): 58–73, and Paul Samuelson, "International Trade and Equalisation of Factor Prices," *Economic Journal* 58, no. 230 (June 1948): 163–184; the paper by Robert A. Mundell, "The Pure Theory of International Trade," *American Economic Review* 50, no. 1 (March 1960): 67–110; and others.

2. Many applications and extensions of the intertemporal framework appeared in the 1960s and succeeding decades, among them Edmund Phelps, "The Golden Rule of Accumulation," *American Economic Review* 51, no. 4 (September 1961): 638–643; Franco Modigliani, "Long-Run Implications of Alterative Fiscal Policies and the Burden of the National Debt," *Economic Journal* 71, no. 284 (December 1961): 730–755; Robert E. Lucas and Leonard A. Rapping, "Real Wages, Employment and Inflation," *Journal of Political Economy* 77, no. 5 (September-October 1969): 721–754; Janusz Ordover, "Distributive Justice and Optimal Taxation," *Journal of Public Economics* 5, no. 1–2 (January-February 1976): 139–160; Carl Shapiro and Joseph Stiglitz, "Equilibrium Unemployment as a Discipline Device," *American Economic Review* 74, no. 3 (June 1984): 433–444; and Phelps, *Structural Slumps: The Modern Equilibrium Theory of Unemployment, Interest and Assets,* with Hian Teck Hoon, George Kanaginis, and Gylfi Zoega (Cambridge, MA: Harvard University Press, 1994).

3. Their books were both started in 1915 and delayed by WWI. See Frank H. Knight, *Risk, Uncertainty and Profit* (Boston: Houghton Mifflin, 1921); and John Maynard Keynes, *A Treatise on Probability* (London: Macmillan,

1921). In his later book *The General Theory of Employment, Interest and Money* (London: Macmillan, 1936), Keynes wrote of firms and speculators endeavoring to gauge the "average opinion" prevailing in the markets. This discussion of "what average opinion expects the average opinion to be" and, further, "what average opinion expects average opinion to be" is on p. 156.

4. The latter book by Keynes is *General Theory of Employment*. Keynes later observed that following a drop of demand in a town or country, workers might not leave, owing to each worker's speculation that the other workers will move away—a lack of coordination among the workers. See *The Collected Writings of John Maynard Keynes*, vol. 14, *The General Theory and After*, pt. 2, *Defence and Development*, ed. Donald Moggridge (London: Macmillan, 1973).

5. Perhaps the earliest use of the term *standard* to describe the state of economics in the past several decades is in Roman Frydman and Michael Goldberg, *Beyond Mechanical Markets: Asset Price Swings, Risk, and the Role of the State* (Princeton, NJ: Princeton University Press, 2011), 199.

6. See Robert M. Solow, "A Contribution to the Theory of Economic Growth," *Quarterly Journal of Economics* 70, no. 1 (February 1956): 65–94.

7. Some models are interpreted as describing an endogenous *source* of self-sustained growth—one governed or governable by society. For example, several economists have formed hypotheses about the influence of *education* on technical progress. The paper by Richard R. Nelson and Edmund Phelps, "Investment in Humans, Technological Diffusion and Economic Growth," *American Economic Review* 56, no. 1/2 (March 1966): 69–75, proposes that education is "important to those functions requiring adaptation to change" (69) and thus helps to speed the diffusion of innovations. But this model does not imply that a higher education level would generate a sustained steepening of the growth path—only a one-time shift.

8. In the textbook growth models, the long-run grown rate is *equal* to the rate of technical progress. Although far from essential in this book, the following algebra may be worth adding. For convenience, let Λ denote the level of total factor productivity and λ denote its growth rate. In this notation, the long-run growth rate of *total output* would be *equal* to λ if there were to be no further capital accumulation. It would be equal to λ times a "multiplier," given by the reciprocal of labor's share, if there were to be investment to keep capital growing as fast as output. Nevertheless, technical progress remains the sine qua non for long-run growth.

For many years, there had been a belief among economic historians that capital formation was somehow a *larger* contributor to productivity growth than was technological progress. That belief came under discussion in several papers beginning in 1956. See, for example, Benton F. Massell, "Capital Formation and Technological Change in United States Manufacturing," *Review of Economics and Statistics* 42, no. 2 (May 1960): 182–188; Robert M. Solow, "Investment and Technical Progress," in *Mathematical Methods in the Social Sciences*, ed. K. Arrow, S. Karlin, and P. Suppes (Stanford, CA: Stanford University Press, 1960), 89–104; and Edmund

Phelps, "The New View of Investment: A Neoclassical Analysis," *Quarterly Journal of Economics* 76, no. 4 (November 1962): 548–567.

9. Schumpeter, in his 1911/12 classic *Theorie der Wirtschaftlichen*, made the point that he never met anyone in the economies he knew who possessed any "creativity." In his 1939 book he is explicit that the entrepreneur is capitalizing on the work of an inventor or discoverer. See Schumpeter, *Business Cycles: A Theoretical, Historical and Statistical Analysis of the Capitalist Process* (New York: McGraw-Hill, 1939).

   Robert Solow appears to have viewed the standard theory in the same spirit: in reflective remarks made toward the end of his paper "A Contribution to the Theory of Economic Growth"—the last pillar of the standard theory—he characterizes his growth model as a "frictionless, competitive, *causal* system" (91; italics added). What he meant by "causal," I think, is that the model has no place for any events or actions springing up *within* the economy modeled.

10. See Nicholas Conard, Maria Malina, and Susanne C. Münzel, "New Flutes Document the Earliest Musical Tradition in Southwestern Germany," *Nature*, August 2009, 737–740.

11. See the charts in figures 7.1 and 7.2 in Edmund Phelps, *Mass Flourishing: How Grassroots Innovation Created Jobs, Challenge, and Change* (Princeton, NJ: Princeton University Press, 2013), 183–184. They permit the reader to take into account that some countries have high levels of employment, which tend to reduce conventional measures of productivity such as real gross domestic product per employee and output per man-hour. Although these measures are from 1996 data, it is doubtful that results from 2017 data will be found to differ.

   The implication of the "standard theory" that factor prices, such as wage rates and thus productivity measures as well, are equalized among countries was proved in a celebrated paper by Paul A. Samuelson, "The Gains from International Trade," *Canadian Journal of Economics and Political Sciences* 5, no. 2 (May 1939): 195–205.

12. See Schumpeter, *Theory of Economic Development*. Schumpeter uses the word "obviously" on p. 88 of the Harvard edition.

13. Some economists deny there has been a slowdown of productivity in recent times, properly measured. This volume will bring some important data to bear on the question.

14. This summary of early models of endogenous growth draws on Richard R. Nelson, Merton J. Peck, and Edward Kalachek, *Technology, Economic Growth and Public Policy* (Washington, DC: Brookings Institution, 1967); and Edwin Mansfield, *Industrial Research and Technological Innovation: An Econometric Analysis* (New York: Norton, 1968). It would be difficult to do justice to the variety of insights presented by this first generation of model builders. Some of the prominent contributions were Richard Nelson, "The Simple Economics of Basic Scientific Research," *Journal of Political Economy* 67, no. 3 (June 1959): 297–306; Kenneth J. Arrow, "The Economic Implications of Learning by Doing," *Review of Economic Studies* 29,

no. 3 (June 1962): 155–173; and Mansfield, *Industrial Research*. Around 1970 Nelson and Sidney Winter began years of interchange and collaboration culminating in the expositions and models of "Schumpeterian competition" in *An Evolutionary Theory of Economic Change* (Cambridge, MA: Harvard University Press, 1982).

Another early model of endogenous growth takes global progress to be a function of the proportion of the labor force allocated to produce it. See Edmund Phelps, "Models of Technical Progress and the Golden Rule of Research," in *Golden Rules of Economic Growth* (New York: Norton, 1966), 137–157. This model, in turn, suggested another model in which exponential growth of the labor force, far from diminishing the productivity of labor, speeds it up if some fixed share of the labor force is allocated to raising productivity. See Phelps, "Population Increase," *Canadian Journal of Economics* 1, no. 3 (August 1968): 497–518.

It may be worth adding that in these same years the notion of "defensive investment" and thus "defensive innovation" arose and Kenneth Arrow introduced what might be called "offensive innovation"—an innovation motivated by the expectation that it would enable the innovator to take over a whole industry and gain the whole of the monopoly profit.

15. See Arrow, "Economic Implications of Learning." Arrow pointed out in this paper that an entrepreneur would have an incentive to invest in the development of the new thing only if the enterprise were allowed to erect barriers to entry or a protection like patent rights.

16. Nelson also inspired work on the diffusion of new methods across competitive industries, such as the spreading use of fertilizer and the moldboard plow in farming. See Nelson and Phelps, "Investment in Humans."

17. In this latter model, the long-run growth rate of productivity is positive under some conditions even if the population does not grow. A 1986 paper by Romer presents a model in which steady growth results from learning by doing. See "Increasing Returns and Long-Run Growth," *Journal of Political Economy* 94, no. 5 (October 1986): 1002–1037. In this model, learning by doing brings some growth that brings more learning by doing and so forth in an endless spiral of growth.

18. Philippe Aghion and Peter Howitt, "A Model of Growth and Cycles through Creative Destruction" (Working Paper No. 527, Economics Department, MIT, May 1989); Philippe Aghion and Peter Howitt, "A Model of Growth through Creative Destruction," *Econometrica* 60, no. 2 (1992): 323–351. See also the stupendous textbook by Aghion and Howitt, *Endogenous Growth Theory* (Cambridge, MA: MIT Press, 1998).

19. See Paul M. Romer, "Endogenous Technical Change," *Journal of Political Economy* 98, no. 5 (January 1990): 71–103.

20. Nelson, Peck, and Kalachek write that "in the absence of new technological knowledge, sooner or later these possibilities would be exhausted. As returns to additional capital and education declined, not only would their contribution to further expansion diminish; their rate of expansion probably would decline as well." *Technology, Economic Growth*, 16.

21. What I mean by "dynamism" is indicated in Phelps, *Mass Flourishing,* ix, 20. In my use of the term, a decrease of innovation owing to some weakening in the market for goods is not a decrease of dynamism.

22. See Edmund Phelps, "The Dynamism of Nations," *Project Syndicate,* December 2003; Phelps, "Macroeconomics for a Modern Economy" (Nobel Prize Lecture in Economics, Royal Swedish Academy of Sciences, December 2006); Phelps, "The Economic Performance of Nations," in *Entrepreneurship, Innovation, and the Growth Mechanism of Free Enterprise Economies,* ed. E. Sheshinski, R. J. Strom, and W. J. Baumol (Princeton, NJ: Princeton University Press, 2007), 342–356; Phelps, "In Search of a More Dynamic Economy," *Financial Times,* July 20, 2008; Phelps, "What Is Wrong with the West's Economies?," *New York Review of Books,* August 13, 2015, 54–56; and Phelps, "The Dynamism of Nations: Toward a Theory of Indigenous Innovation," *Capitalism and Society* 12 (May 2017): article 3.

23. Walt Rostow's wonderful coinage, "take-off into sustained economic growth," or productivity growth, appearing in *The Process of Economic Growth* (New York: Norton, 1952), was amended to "self-sustained" growth in his paper "The Take-Off into Self-Sustained Growth," *Economic Journal* 66, no. 261 (March 1956): 25–48. By "self-sustained" I think he meant not deriving and thus depending on a series of outside forces that kept the growth going for some time.

24. The consensus of scholars poring over much of the available data is that output per head began a sustained climb in Britain and America around 1820. With the national income data provided by Angus Maddison—see Maddison, *The World Economy: Historical Statistics* (Paris: OECD, 2003)— we can see that Britain lost ground in the latter decades of the 19th century, though Germany and France did not. Incredible as it appears now, tens of economic historians and economists were far from identifying what was behind the takeoffs in Britain and America after the end of the Napoleonic Wars in 1815.

25. Paul Johnson, *The Birth of the Modern: World Society 1815–1830* (New York: HarperCollins, 1991).

26. See Phelps, *Mass Flourishing;* for summaries and restatements, see Edmund Phelps, "Mass Flourishing: How It Was Won, Then Largely Lost," pts. 1 and 2, *OECD Insights,* August 19 and 20, 2013; Phelps, "What Is Wrong?"; and Phelps, "Dynamism of Nations: Toward a Theory."

27. See Phelps, *Mass Flourishing,* 66. The term *getting on* in 1840s London meant making a success of one's life. See Rick Rylance, *The Cambridge Companion to the Brontës* (Cambridge: Cambridge University Press, 2002), 157–158.

28. See Emma Griffin, *Liberty's Dawn* (New Haven, CT: Yale University Press, 2013).

29. See Friedrich Hayek's presidential address delivered before the London Economic Club on November 10, 1936: "Economics and Knowledge," *Economica* 4, no. 13 (February 1937): 33–54; it takes up imperfect

knowledge-creating opportunities (which the market unfailingly and rather quickly identifies!). See also his much-cited paper "The Use of Knowledge in Society," *American Economic Review* 35, no. 4 (September 1945): 519–530, in which he refers to "adaptations" to changing circumstances. Both are in Hayek's *Individualism and Economic Order* (Chicago: University of Chicago Press, 1948). See also the influential book by Chester I. Barnard, *The Functions of the Executive* (1938; Cambridge, MA: Harvard University Press, 1968).

30. Hence cities were a by-product of the ferment of new ideas, not the cause of the ferment, as the famed urban economist Jane Jacobs maintained. See Jacobs, *The Death and Life of Great American Cities* (New York: Random House, 1961). See also Saskia Sassen, *The Global City* (Princeton, NJ: Princeton University Press, 2001).

31. The passage by Marshall, which I have been quoting since as early as my 1985 textbook *Political Economy,* is from his early textbook *Elements of Economics* (London: Macmillan, 1892), 5. Marshall knew of what he spoke. Born in 1842, he had been observing business life for five decades when he wrote those lines.

32. Alexis de Tocqueville, *Democracy in America,* 2 vols. (London: Saunders and Otley, 1835–1840).

33. Marx harshly criticizes Adam Smith for seeing the experience of one's work as a cost to one's tranquility, freedom, and happiness—far from a vehicle to freedom and happiness. "For Smith," Marx writes, "labor is a curse. 'Tranquility' appears as an adequate state, identical with 'freedom' and 'happiness.' It seems far from Smith's mind that the individual, 'in his normal state of health, strength, activity, skill, facility,' also needs a normal portion of work, and of the suspension of tranquility. . . . Smith has no inkling whatsoever that overcoming obstacles is in itself a liberating activity—hence as self-realization, . . . hence real freedom." Karl Marx, *Grundrisse der Kritik der Politischen Okonomie* (New York: Penguin, 1993), 611, written 1857–1861, published originally in German (1939–1941) and in English by Penguin in 1973.

It is unsurprising that Smith did not notice these rewards of work, since they were certainly not prevalent in the British economy of the 1700s. The architects of the standard theory, 1893–1965, must have noticed them, however—certainly Marshall did and so did the mavericks Thorstein Veblen and Gunnar Myrdal—but apparently these architects did not see the harm of treating labor as simply leisure lost.

34. See David Hume, *An Enquiry Concerning Human Understanding* (London: Clarendon, 1748), for his discussion of how knowledge is increased.

35. This speculation has been voiced by Diana Coyle in "Rethinking GDP," *Finance and Development* 54, no. 1 (March 2017): 17–19. The statistical study and quote referred to here can be found in M. L. Cropper and A. S. Arriaga-Salina, "Inter-city Wage Differentials and the Value of Air Quality," *Journal of Urban Economics* 8, no. 2 (September 1980): 248. It draws on Robert M. Solow's "On Equilibrium Models of Urban Location," in *Essays*

in Modern Economics, ed. Michael Parkin and A. R. Nobay (London: Longman, 1973), 2–16.

Another point on the material benefits brought by the takeoffs is that the resulting national income gains soon enabled governments to take public health and hygiene measures that saved many working-age people from early death.

36. Abraham Lincoln, "Second Lecture on Discoveries and Inventions," February 11, 1859.

37. The economist Kenneth Boulding was heard at an unpublished lecture given in Philadelphia around 1967 to place great importance on "obtaining better terms of trade."

38. This satisfaction, which certainly seems important, I first added at a joint conference, "The Future of Europe," cohosted by the Oxford Martin School and the Center on Capitalism and Society at Oxford University in April 2016. The others cited here are pointed to in Phelps, *Mass Flourishing.*

39. There are other sorts of models. In 1949, the celebrated engineer and statistician W. A. Phillips, when a student at the London School of Economics, built in the basement a hydraulic model of the workings of the British economy. Made a lecturer and later a professor at LSE, he went on to discover a statistical relationship between the rate of wage inflation and the unemployment rate, dubbed the Phillips Curve.

40. See Douglass North, *Institutional Change and American Economic Growth* (Cambridge: Cambridge University Press, 1971); and Daron Acemoglu and James A. Robinson, *Why Nations Fail: The Origins of Power, Prosperity and Poverty* (New York: Currency, 2013).

41. These signs of slowdown were not always immediate noticed, owing to a surge of increased investments following a steep rise of oil prices and the end of fixed exchange rates, not to mention the violence that broke out around 1968, notably in New York, Los Angeles, and Paris. It took the whole decade or more to sense the new developments, though they seem clearer by now. See Assar Lindbeck, "The Recent Slowdown of Productivity Growth," *Economic Journal* 93, no. 369 (March 1983): 13–34; and Stanley Fischer, "Symposium on the Slowdown in Productivity Growth," *Journal of Economic Perspective* 2, no. 4 (Fall 1988): 3–7.

Those economists were referring to labor productivity—that is, output per worker or per hour worked. In 2012, Robert J. Gordon, poring over data he had constructed on the growth rate of total factor productivity in the American economy, noticed far slower growth rates from 1972 with some ups and downs. (At my suggestion, he calculated the growth rate in the periods 1922–1972 and 1972–2012, which showed far slower growth over the latter period. The latter growth rate was approximately *half* the earlier growth rate. Phelps, *Mass Flourishing* displays the bar chart on pp. 220–221. In another bar chart, contained in his book *The Rise and Fall of American Growth: The U.S. Standard of Living since the Civil War* [Princeton, NJ: Princeton University Press, 2016], Gordon presents decadal averages showing reduced growth in the 1970s and far slower growth since then. It had been my impression for some time that 1968 saw the first signs of a sea change in attitude and orientation in the nation.) The present volume uses data constructed by the Banque de France after Gordon's construction of data and extended to a large set of countries.

42. Phelps, *Mass Flourishing,* 222–225, reported that the growth rate of total factor productivity in the United States in the span 1972–2012 was *half* the rate in the span 1922–1972, based on earlier annual estimates in Penn World Tables.

43. For prominent accounts, see Tyler Cowen, *The Great Stagnation* (Boston: Dutton, 2011); Phelps, *Mass Flourishing;* and Gordon, *Rise and Fall.*

44. It may be noted that the standard theory does not leave room for a decline of entrepreneurship; the latter is baked into the prevailing model of the economy. Hayek, as noted at the outset, did move away a little from the standard theory in injecting the notion that insightful managers might, over years of experience, develop a sense of unexploited opportunities arising from exogenous developments in population, climate, and so forth. See Hayek, "Use of Knowledge in Society."

45. One source is the data reported in the General Social Survey, known as the GSS. This time series goes back only to 1972, so it cannot support (or refute) the implication of the hypothesis that job satisfaction was buoyant in the 1950s and well into the 1960s compared with its level after the slowdown of indigenous innovation in the years around 1970—and, one might add, the investment boom in the 1970s. One *can* see that the proportion of respondents who feel "a little dissatisfied" or "very dissatisfied" with the "work they do" *rose* from 177 and 134, respectively, in 1985 and 1986, after the worst of the early 1980s recession was over, to 188 and 281 in 2004 and 2006. The dissatisfaction was even worse in the latest year, 2016.

    Another source of data is the degree of "life satisfaction" reported in household surveys by the Pew Research Center. We know that, statistically, job satisfaction is a huge part of life satisfaction in household surveys. And even if it were not, people's sense of satisfaction with their lives in a modern society is germane to the theory articulated and tested in this volume. (It is also of interest per se.) The resulting time series, from its start in the early 1970s, shows a *downward trend* in the reported degree of life satisfaction.

46. See the extensive investigation in the forthcoming volume by Anne Case and Angus Deaton, *Deaths of Despair and the Future of Capitalism* (Princeton, NJ: Princeton University Press, March 2020). See also Jeffrey D. Sachs, "America Is Falling Far Behind on Key World Goals," CNN, July 11, 2018, https://www.cnn.com/2018/07/11/opinions/america-ranks-low-sustainable -development-sachs/index.html. Sachs also referred to a decline in the sense of "well-being" and "longevity." (It is not clear whether longevity is to be categorized as nonmaterial, since it is heaven-sent, not earned, but it also increases leisure and consumption possibilities, which are in the material category.)

47. Christopher Lasch, *The Culture of Narcissism* (New York: W. W. Norton, 1979).

48. Caddell is quoted in Stuart E. Eizenstaat, *President Carter: The White House Years* (New York: St. Martin's, 2018), 690.

49. The line appears in the biopic *The Iron Lady* (2011), directed by Phyllida Lloyd.

50. Jimmy Carter, "Energy and the National Goals," Malaise Speech, televised July 15, 1979, https://www.americanrhetoric.com/speeches /jimmycartercrisisofconfidence.htm. Vice President Walter Mondale said, "We wanted a government as good as the people; now we tell them we need a people as good as the government." Eizenstaat, *President Carter,* 679.

51. I like to think of this economy as the Hollywood model. Many writers are producing screenplays chosen from a stock of scripts, and a number of these writers are producing materials that can be developed into screenplays. (I think of F. Scott Fitzgerald's *Great Gatsby* and Budd Schulberg's *On the Waterfront.*)

52. Where, it might be wondered, are the prices in this model? Viewing the two aggregates, *K* and *D*, as fairly homogenous, it is reasonable to conceive this economy as near to having just one relative price, the real price of capital, *K*, denoted *q*—the notation commonly found in two-sector aggregative models. In such an extended model, the price, *q*, might be lower than average if there were a large overhang of *K* in the economy. But the model might be built in such a way that participants struck by new ideas would not be deterred from developing them by the depression in the price received for the resulting product. Hence, it does not appear to be impermissible to abstract here from the price.

1. Innovation: The Source of Rapid Growth

1. Charles W. Cobb and Paul H. Douglas, "A Theory of Production," in "Papers and Proceedings of the Fortieth Annual Meeting of the American Economic Association," supplement, *American Economic Review* 18, no. 1 (March 1928): 139–165.

2. Robert Barro and Xavier Sala-i-Martin, "Public Finance in Models of Economic Growth," *Review of Economic Studies* 59, no. 4 (1992): 645–661.

3. Richard R. Nelson and Edmund Phelps, "Investment in Human, Techno-logical Diffusion, and Economic Growth," *American Economic Review* 56, no. 1–2 (March 1966): 69–75; Philippe Aghion and Peter Howitt, "A Model of Growth through Creative Destruction," *Econometrica* 60, no. 2 (1992): 323–351; Philippe Aghion, Peter Howitt, and Fabrice Murtin, "The Rela-tionship between Health and Growth: When Lucas Meets Nelson-Phelps," *Review of Economics and Institutions* 2, no. 1 (2011): article 1.

4. See João Amador and Carlos Coimbra, "Characteristics of the Portuguese Economic Growth: What Has Been Missing?" (Working Papers w2007708, Banco de Portugal, Economics and Research Department, 2007); Robert Barro, "Economic Growth in a Cross Section of Countries," *Quarterly Journal of Economics* 106, no. 2 (May 1991): 407–443; William Baumol,

"Productivity Growth, Convergence, and Welfare: What the Long-Run Data Show," *American Economic Review* 76, no. 5 (December 1986): 1072–1085; Robert E. Lucas, "On the Mechanics of Economics Development," *Journal of Monetary Economics* 22, no. 1 (July 1988): 3–42; Paul Romer, "Increasing Returns and Long-Run Growth," *Journal of Political Economy* 94, no. 5 (October 1986): 1002–1037; Paul Romer, "Endogenous Technological Change," in "The Problem of Development: A Conference of the Institute for the Study of Free Enterprise Systems," *Journal of Political Economy* 98, no. 5, pt. 2 (October 1990): S71–102; and Xavier Sala-i-Martin, "I Just Ran Two Million Regression," in "Papers and Proceedings of the Hundred and Fourth Annual Meeting of the American Economic Association," *American Economic Review* 87, no. 2 (May 1997): 178–183.

5. Daron Acemoglu, Ufuk Akcigit, and William Kerr, "Innovation Network," *Proceedings of the National Academy of Sciences* 113, no. 41 (October 2016): 11483–11488.

6. Ufuk Akcigit, John Grisby, and Tom Nicholas, "The Rise of American Ingenuity: Innovating and Investors of the Golden Age" (NBER Working Paper No. 23047, National Bureau of Economic Research, Cambridge, MA, January 2017).

7. Pierre Mohnen and Rene Belderbos, "Intersectional and International R&D Spillovers" (UNU-MERIT Working Paper 7, Maastricht, Netherlands, 2013).

8. Petra Moser, Alessandra Voena, and Fabian Waldinger, "German-Jewish Émigrés and US Invention," *American Economic Review* 104, no. 10 (October 2014): 3222–3255.

9. Joseph Zeira, "Workers, Machines, and Economic Growth," *Quarterly Journal of Economics* 113, no. 4 (November 1998): 1091–1117.

10. Nicholas Kaldor, "Capital Accumulation and Economic Growth," in *The Theory of Capital,* ed. F. A. Lutz and D. C. Hague (New York: St. Martin's, 1961), 177–222.

11. Pietro Peretto and John Seater, "Factor-Eliminating Technical Change," *Journal of Monetary Economics* 60, no. 4 (May 2013): 459–473; David Hémous and Morten Olsen, "The Rise of the Machines: Automation, Horizontal Innovation and Income Inequality" (CEPR Discussion Paper No. 10244, Center for Economic Policy Research, London, 2016); Philippe Aghion, Benjamin F. Jones, and Charles I. Jones, "Artificial Intelligence and Economic Growth" (NBER Working Paper No. 23928, National Bureau of Economics, Cambridge, MA, October 2017).

12. Zeira, "Workers, Machines, and Economic Growth."

13. William Baumol, "Macroeconomics of Unbalance Growth: The Anatomy of Urban Crisis," *American Economic Review* 57, no. 3 (June 1967): 415–426.

14. Daron Acemoglu, Simon Johnson, and James Robinson, "The Colonial Origins of Comparative Development: An Empirical Investigation," *American Economic Review* 91, no. 5 (December 2001): 1369–401; Daron Acemolgu and James Robinson, *Why Nations Fail: The Origins of Power, Prosperity, and Poverty* (New York: Crown, 2012).

15. Finn E. Kydland and Edward C. Prescott, "Business Cycles: Real Facts and a Monetary Myth," *Quarterly Review* (Federal Reserve Bank of Minneapolis) 14, no. 2 (Spring 1990): 3–18.

16. Hian Teck Hoon and Edmund Phelps, "Growth, Wealth and the Natural Rate: Is Europe's Jobs Crisis a Growth Crisis?," *European Economic Review* 41, nos. 3–5 (1997): 549–557.

17. Edward C. Prescott, "Why Do Americans Work So Much More than Europeans?," *Quarterly Review* (Federal Reserve Bank of Minneapolis) 28, no. 1 (July 2004): 2–13.

18. Philippe Aghion and Peter Howit, *Endogenous Growth Theory* (Cambridge, MA: MIT Press, 1998); Philippe Aghion and Peter Howitt, "Appropriate Growth Policy: A Unifying Framework," *Journal of the European Economic Association* 4, no. 2–3 (2006): 269–314. The later paper was delivered as the 2005 Joseph Schumpeter Lecture, 20th Annual Congress of the European Economic Association, Amsterdam, August 25, 2005.

19. Edmund Phelps, *Mass Flourishing: How Grassroots Innovation Created Jobs, Challenge, and Change* (Princeton, NJ: Princeton University Press, 2013).

20. Friedrich A. Hayek, *Individualism and Economic Order* (Chicago: University of Chicago Press, 1948). This book contains "Socialist Calculation, I, II" of 1935, "Economics and Knowledge" of 1937, and "The Use of Knowledge in Society" of 1945.

21. Henri Bergson, *Creative Evolution,* trans. Arthur Mitchell (New York: Henry Holt, 1911).

22. Antonin Bergeaud, Gulbert Cette, and Rémy Lecat, "Productivity Trends in Advanced Countries between 1890 and 2012," *Review of Income and Wealth* 62, no. 3 (September 2016): 420–444. Additional related work can be found at http://www.longtermproductivity.com/post.html.

23. Bergeaud, Cette, and Lecat, "Productivity Trends."

24. Angus Maddison, *The World Economy: Historical Statistics* (Paris: OECD, 2003), https://www.oecd-ilibrary.org/development/the-world-economy_9789264104143-en.

25. Bergeaud, Cette, and Lecat, "Productivity Trends."

26. Gilbert Cette, Yusuf Kocoglu, and Jacques Mairesse, "Productivity Growth and Levels in France, Japan, the United Kingdom and the United States in the Twentieth Century" (NBER Working Paper No. 15577, National Bureau of Economic Research, Cambridge, MA, December 2009).

4. A Case Study of Iceland's Successful Innovators

This chapter was written in collaboration with Ágúst Arnórsson.

1. See http://www.solfar.com/.

2. See https://www.facebook.com/vanillagames.

3. See http://www.ossur.is/.

4. See https://www.sabreairlinesolutions.com/home/.

5. See https://startupiceland.com/2014/12/02/oz-a-startup-profile-founder
   -spilling-the-beans/.
6. See, for example, https://www.eveonline.com/?gclid=EAIaIQobChMItYH54v
   HN2QIV5pPtCh02_wzTEAAYASAAEgJUZfD_BwE&gclsrc=aw.ds&dclid
   =CIfnkuTxzdkCFYWNGwod_WgOXw.

5. The Force of Values

Ágúst Arnórsson assisted with research for this chapter.

1. William Baumol, "Entrepreneurship: Productive, Unproductive, and Destructive," *Journal of Political Economy* 98, no. 5 (October 1990): 893–921.
2. Friedrich A. Hayek, "Competition as a Discovery Procedure," in *New Studies in Philosophy, Politic, Economics and the History of Ideas* (London: Routledge, 1978), 179–190. Hayek wrote this piece in 1967/68 and delivered it as a lecture in 1968 at the University of Kiel.
3. Edmund Phelps, "The Dynamism of Nations: Toward a Theory of Indigenous Innovation," *Capitalism and Society* 12, no. 1 (May 2017): article 3, https://ssrn.com/abstract=2963105.
4. Edmund Phelps, *Mass Flourishing: How Grassroots Innovation Created Jobs, Challenge, and Change* (Princeton, NJ: Princeton University Press, 2013).
5. Edmund Phelps and Gylfi Zoega, "Corporatism and Job Satisfaction," *Journal of Comparative Economics* 41, no. 1 (February 2013): 35–47.
6. Joseph Schumpeter, *Theorie der Wirtschaftlichen Entwicklung* (Vienna: Duncker and Humblot, 1911/12).
7. David C. McClelland, *The Achievement Society* (Princeton, NJ: Princeton University Press, 1961).
8. Robert H. Brockhaus, "The Psychology of the Entrepreneur," in *Encyclopedia of Entrepreneurship* (Englewood Cliffs, NJ: Prentice-Hall, 1982), 39–57.
9. Donald L. Sexton and Nancy Bowman, "The Entrepreneur: A Capable Executive and More," *Journal of Business Venturing* 1, no. 1 (1985): 129–140.
10. Amir N. Licht and Jordan I. Siegel, "The Social Dimensions of Entrepreneurship," in *The Oxford Handbook of Entrepreneurship*, ed. Mark Casson and Bernard Yeung (Oxford: Oxford University Press, 2006), 511–539.
11. Stanley Cromie, "Assessing Entrepreneurial Inclinations: Some Approaches and Empirical Evidence," *European Journal of Work and Organizational Psychology* 9, no. 1 (March 2000): 7–30.
12. Richard Lynn, *The Secret of the Miracle Economy: Different National Attitudes to Competitiveness and Money* (London: Social Affairs Unit, 1991).
13. Scott Shane, "Cultural Influences on National Rates of Innovation," *Journal of Business Venturing* 8, no. 1 (January 1993): 59–73.
14. Edward C. Banfield, *The Moral Basis of a Backward Society* (Glencoe, IL: Free Press, 1958).

15. Robert D. Putnam, Robert Leonardi, and Raffaella Y. Nanetti, *Making Democracy Work: Civic Traditions in Modern Italy* (Princeton, NJ: Princeton University Press, 1993).

16. Stephen Knack and Philip Keefer, "Does Social Capital Have an Economic Payoff? A Cross-Country Investigation," *Quarterly Journal of Economics* 112, no. 4 (November 1997): 1251–1288.

17. Guido Tabellini, "Culture and Institutions: Economic Development in the Regions of Europe," *Journal of the European Economic Association* 8, no. 4 (June 2010): 677–716.

18. See Paul J. Zak and Stephen Knack, "Trust and Growth," *Economic Journal* 111, no. 470 (March 2001): 295–321. They offer examples of trust relationships. One is that of Thomas Hobbes, who claimed that trust between strangers was derived from the government alone, and thus had nothing to do with goodwill, while John Stuart Mill stated that the fear of being exposed motivated members of society to hold to their obligations because otherwise they would harm their reputation, which doesn't really rely on goodwill either.

19. See Knack and Keefer, "Does Social Capital?"; Zak and Knack, "Trust and Growth"; Yann Algan and Pierre Cahuc, "Trust, Growth and Happiness: New Evidence and Policy Implications," in *Handbook of Economic Growth*, vol. 2A, ed. Philippe Aghion and Steven Durlauf (Amsterdam: North-Holland, 2013), 49–120; and Christian Bjørnskov, "How Does Social Trust Lead to Economic Growth?," *Southern Economic Journal* 78 (2012): 1346–1368. A study by Brueckner, Chong, and Gradstein (2015) finds that the causality is the other way around, such that a fall in income makes trust fall. See Markus Brueckner, Alberto Chong, and Mark Gradstein, "Does Economic Prosperity Breed Trust?" (Discussion Paper 10749, Centre for Economic Policy Research, London, August 3, 2015).

20. Edmund Phelps, "Economic Culture and Economic Performance: What Light Is Shed on the Continent's Problem?" (Working Paper No. 17, Center on Capitalism and Society, Columbia University, New York, July 2006).

21. Tabellini, "Culture and Institutions."

22. Edmund Phelps and Gylfi Zoega, "Entrepreneurship, Culture and Openness," in *Entrepreneurship and Openness: Theory and Evidence,* ed. David B. Audretsch, Robert Litan, and Robert Strom (Cheltenham, UK: Edward Elgar, 2009), 101–130.

23. Raicho Bojilov and Edmund Phelps, "Job Satisfaction: The Effects of Two Different Cultures" (Working Paper No. 78, Center on Capitalism and Society, Columbia University, New York, September 2012).

24. Phelps, *Mass Flourishing.*

25. Agust Arnorsson and Gylfi Zoega, "Social Capital and the Labor Market," *Capitalism and Society* 11, no. 1 (June 2016): article 1, https://ssrn.com/abstract=2788829.

26. On canonical correlations, see Harold Hotelling, "Relations between Two Sets of Variates," *Biometrika* 28, no. 3–4 (December 1936): 321–377; and Alissa Sherry and Robin K. Henson, "Conducting and Interpreting Canonical

Correlation Analysis in Personality Research: A User-Friendly Primer," *Journal of Personality Assessment* 84, no. 1 (2005): 37–48.

27. Hotelling, "Relations between Two Sets."

28. For a more thorough discussion, see Jacques Tacq, *Multivariate Analysis Techniques in Social Science Research: From Problem to Analysis* (Thousand Oaks, CA: Sage, 1997).

29. Sherry and Henson, "Conducting and Interpreting."

30. These are Australia, Austria, Belgium, Canada, Denmark, Finland, France, Germany, Greece, Ireland, Italy, Japan, the Netherlands, Norway, Portugal, Spain, Sweden, Switzerland, the United Kingdom, and the United States.

31. Other functions than the first one were not statistically significant.

32. They are standardized because of the constraint that the variance of the pair of canonical variables in a canonical function are equal; $var(X^*) = var(Y^*)$.

33. It might, for example, be the case that the effect of the standardized coefficient for a certain variable is picked up by another variable. Theoretical insight is thus needed for explanation.

34. The measures of economic freedom and freedom from corruption are from the Heritage Foundation index for 2008. The measures of people values are taken from the European Values Study conducted in 2008 and 2009.

35. The innovation variables are an average from 1993 to 2013.

36. Phelps, "Economic Culture and Economic Performance"; Bojilov and Phelps, "Job Satisfaction."

6. Individual Values, Entrepreneurship, and Innovation

1. Yann Algan and Pierre Cahuc, "Inherited Trust and Growth," *American Economic Review* 100, no. 5 (December 2010): 2060–2092.

2. Jeffrey V. Butler, Paola Giuliano, and Luigi Guiso, "The Right Amount of Trust," *Journal of the European Economic Association* 14, no. 5 (October 2016): 1155–1180.

3. See Raquel Fernandez, "Does Culture Matter?," in *Handbook of Social Economics,* vol. 1A, ed. Jess Benhabib, Alberto Bisin, and Matthew Jackson (Amsterdam: North-Holland, 2010), 481–510.

4. Edward Banfield, *The Moral Basis of a Backward Society* (New York: Free Press, 1958); James Coleman, *Power and the Structure of Society* (New York: W. W. Norton, 1974); Robert D. Putnam, *Bowling Alone: The Collapse and Revival of American Community* (New York: Simon and Schuster, 2000).

5. Miguel Jiménez and Sébastien Jean, "The Unemployment Impact of Immigration in OECD Countries," *European Journal of Political Economy* 27, no. 2 (June 2011): 241–256.

6. Alberto Bisin and Thierry Verdier, "The Economics of Cultural Transmission and the Dynamics of Preferences," *Journal of Economic Theory* 97, no. 2 (April 2001): 298–319; Luigi Guiso, Paola Sapienza, and Luigi Zingales, "Long-Term Persistence," *Journal of the European Economic Association*

14, no. 6 (August 2016): 1401–1436; Guido Tabellini, "Culture and Institutions: Economic Development in the Regions of Europe," *Journal of the European Economic Association* 8, no. 4 (June 2010): 677–716.

7. Algan and Cahuc, "Inherited Trust and Growth."
8. Raicho Bojilov and Edmund Phelps, "Career Choice and Economic Innovation: A Comparison between China, Germany and the USA" (Working Paper No. 80, Center on Capitalism and Society, Columbia University, New York, November 2013).
9. For more details on the survey design and methodology, see Roland Inglehart, *World Values Surveys 1981–2004* (Ann Arbor: University of Michigan Press, 2006).
10. Algan and Cahuc, "Inherited Trust and Growth."

7. Innovation, Job Satisfaction, and Performance in Western European Countries

1. The countries included are Australia, Canada, Finland, France, Germany, Italy, Japan, the Netherlands, Norway, Spain, Sweden, Switzerland, the United Kingdom, and the United States.

8. Growth Effects of Additive and Multiplicative Robots alongside Conventional Machines

1. See Alfred Marshall, *Elements of Economics of Industry*, 3rd ed. (London: Macmillan, 1899), 19; italics added for emphasis.
2. Paul Samuelson, "Mathematical Vindication of Ricardo on Machinery," *Journal of Political Economy* 96, no. 2 (April 1988): 276. In the third edition of his *Principles of Political Economy and Taxation*, Ricardo had written a chapter titled "On Machinery," where he discussed whether the application of machinery (with the arrival of the Industrial Revolution) would benefit all classes of society, including the working class. Ricardo presented a scenario in which the demand for labor falls as machinery substitutes for human labor. See Agnar Sandmo, *Economics Evolving: A History of Economic Thought* (Princeton, NJ: Princeton University Press, 2011). Following his analysis, Ricardo concluded "that the opinion entertained by the laboring class, that the employment of machinery is frequently detrimental to their interests, is not founded on prejudice and error, but is conformable to the correct principles of political economy." David Ricardo, *The Principles of Political Economy and Taxation* (1821; London: Everyman's Library, 1911), 267.
3. See International Federation of Robotics, *World Robotics Report 2016*, https://ifr.org/ifr-press-releases/news/world-robotics-report-2016.
4. International Federation of Robotics.

5. Robert M. Solow, "A Contribution to the Theory of Economic Growth," *Quarterly Journal of Economics* 70, no. 1 (February 1956): 65–94; Trevor W. Swan, "Economic Growth and Capital Accumulation," *Economic Record* 32, no. 2 (November 1956): 334–361; Edmund Phelps, *Golden Rules of Economic Growth* (New York: W. W. Norton, 1966); Hirofumi Uzawa, "Optimal Growth in a Two-Sector Model of Capital Accumulation," *Review of Economic Studies* 31, no. 1 (January 1964): 1–24; Erik Brynjolfsson and Andrew McAfee, *The Second Machine Age: Work, Progress, and Prosperity in a Time of Brilliant Technologies* (New York: W. W. Norton, 2014).

6. Daron Acemoglu and Pascual Restrepo, "The Race between Man and Machine: Implications of Technology for Growth, Factor Shares and Employment," *American Economic Review* 108, no. 6 (June 2018): 1488–1542.

7. Georg Graetz and Guy Michaels, "Robots at Work" (Discussion Paper 1335, Centre for Economic Performance, London School of Economics, London, March 2015, updated 2017).

8. Daron Acemoglu and Pascual Restrepo, "Robots and Jobs: Evidence from US Labor Markets" (NBER Working Paper No. 23285, National Bureau of Economic Research, Cambridge, MA, March 2017).

9. Maarten Goos, Alan Manning, and Anna Salomons, "Explaining Job Polarization: Routine-Biased Technological Change and Offshoring," *American Economic Review* 104, no. 8 (August 2014): 2059–2526.

10. Solow, "Contribution to the Theory"; Swan, "Economic Growth and Capital Accumulation."

11. We make the assumption that additive robots can substitute for an assembly-line worker doing a routine job but cannot substitute for a research scientist whose nonroutine job is made more productive with an AI-enabled robot plowing through huge databases.

12. Note that $(1 - \rho)^{-1}$ gives the elasticity of substitution.

13. For an early discussion of capital theory and the rate of return, see Robert M. Solow, *Capital Theory and the Rate of Return* (Amsterdam: North-Holland, 1963).

14. Robert J. Barro and Xavier Sala-i-Martin, *Economic Growth*, 2nd ed. (Cambridge, MA: MIT Press, 2004), 205–210.

15. More specifically, the real wage declines on account of the term $f(x) - xf'(x)$ where x is the relevant effective capital intensity, in (55) and (61).

16. More specifically, this channel works through the term $[1 + \gamma_R^{-\rho}]^{\frac{1}{\rho}-1}$ in (55) and the term $\left[1 + \left(\dfrac{H_1}{H_2}\right)^{-\rho}\right]^{\frac{1}{\rho}-1}$ in (61). With the elasticity of substitution between routine and nonroutine jobs being greater than one, the relative abundance of routine jobs performed by human workers acts, ceteris paribus, to depress the real wage of workers doing routine jobs before the adoption of robots, as can be seen from (61).

9. Wage Effects of Additive and Multiplicative Robots alongside Factory Buildings and Physical Structures

1. See https://www.cybeletech.com/en.
2. See William D. Nordhaus, "Lethal Model 2: The Limits to Growth Revisited," *Brookings Papers on Economic Activity* 2 (1992): 1–59. He shows that a neoclassical constant-returns-to-scale aggregate production function with an elasticity of substitution between pairs of factors of production not equal to one can be written as a *generalized* Cobb-Douglas production function where the exponent on a factor of production is equal to the factor share.
3. With population normalized to one, C and $\bar{H}$ also represent per capita consumption and employment, respectively.

10. Additive Robots, Relative Prices, and Indigenous Innovation

1. Gene M. Grossman and Elhanan Helpman, *Innovation and Growth in the Global Economy* (Cambridge, MA: MIT Press, 1991); Philippe Aghion and Peter Howitt, "A Model of Growth through Creative Destruction," *Econometrica* 60, no. 2 (March 1992): 323–351.
2. As an example, suppose that the rate of time preference is 20 percent and the rate of capital depreciation is 10 percent. Then $\delta + \theta = 0.30$.
3. Note that, from (17), (39), and (40), we can write $r - \dot{q}/q = (\pi_i/V_i) - \mu H_{INi}$. From (28), we have $r - \dot{q}/q = \dfrac{(1-\alpha)^{1-\alpha}\alpha^{2\alpha}}{\tilde{q}} - \delta$.
4. See Nicholas Bloom, Charles I. Jones, John Van Reenen, and Michael Webb, "Are Ideas Getting Harder to Find?" (NBER Working Paper No. 23782, National Bureau of Economic Research, Cambridge, MA, September 2017, updated March 2018).

Epilogue

1. Ray Dalio, "Why and How Capitalism Needs to Be Reformed (Part 1 & 2)," LinkedIn, April 5, 2019, https://www.linkedin.com/pulse/why-how -capitalism-needs-reformed-parts-1-2-ray-dalio/.
2. Much of the discussion here is in Richard Reeves and Isabel Sawhill, "Modeling Equal Opportunity," *Russell Sage Foundation Journal of the Social Sciences* 2, no. 2 (May 2016): 60–97. See also Raj Chetty et al., "The Fading American Dream: Trends in Absolute Income Mobility since 1940" (NBER Working Paper No. 22910, National Bureau of Economic Research, Cambridge, MA, December 2016).
3. See Assar Lindbeck, "The Recent Slowdown of Productivity Growth," *Economic Journal* 93, no. 369 (March 1983): 13–34; and Stanley Fischer,

"Symposium on the Slowdown in Productivity Growth," *Journal of Economic Perspective* 2, no. 4 (Fall 1988): 3–7. The "great slowdown" should not be confused with "secular stagnation" or "structural slumps."

4. Interestingly, these trends from 1970 to 2018 have *not* been accompanied by a worsening trend of the unemployment rate in America, Britain, Canada, Germany, and Sweden, which constitute more than half of the West. The bulge of the unemployment rate in Italy and France, for example, can be attributed to the presence of institutions that have impeded or failed to facilitate the reemployment of workers in the years following the global financial crisis of 2009–2011. In the aforementioned countries, the labor market has always recovered from adverse shocks.

5. The existing time series on job satisfaction was instituted by the General Social Survey in 1972, and fortunately it has continued to the present time.

6. To be sure, the Great Depression of the 1930s was more recent than Weimar. But it was a different phenomenon—caused by different developments and marked by different ills.

7. Edmund Phelps, "Dangers in a Repeat of Historic Corporatism," *Journal of Policy Modeling* 39, no. 4 (July-August 2017): 611–615. Previously published as "Trump, Corporatism, and the Dearth of Innovation," *Project Syndicate*, January 17, 2017; and as Working Paper No. 93, Center on Capitalism and Society, Columbia University, New York, January 2017 (presented at the 129th Annual Meeting of the American Economic Association, Chicago, January 2017).

8. In the US, many young men and a large number of women, overcoming discrimination and urban slums to gain a college education, obtained positions where they had greater productivity, hence greater pay, than their predecessors in those positions had, thus pulling up productivity and pay in the upper stratum of jobs, while no such development occurred in the middle stratum. That development raised wage rates in the upper quartile of the distribution, for example, while doing nothing to raise the wage rates of those still doing relatively low-skilled work.

9. In just the past 20 years, the ratio of the wage at the 90th percentile to the wage at the 50th percentile rose from 2.2 in 1997 to 2.4 in 2017—a rise of about one-tenth. (Perhaps the rise between 1977 and 1997 was another one-tenth.) See the discussion of the data by Edward P. Lazear, "Mind the Productivity Gap to Reduce Inequality," *Wall Street Journal*, May 5, 2017.

10. Among the most notable are the Alternative for Germany, Marie Le Pen's National Rally, and Mario Salvati's Lega on the right and, somewhat to the left, Spain's Vox and Italy's 5-Star Movement.

11. This definition of dynamism comes from the earlier iteration, "the appetite and capacity for innovation," found in Edmund Phelps, *Mass Flourishing: How Grassroots Innovation Created Jobs, Challenge, and Change* (Princeton, NJ: Princeton University Press, 2013), ix.

12. These are the values instilled in a torrent of books in the 19th century and the first half of the 20th, books by Charlotte Brontë, Emily Brontë, Charles Dickens (the Dickens of *David Copperfield*), Herman Melville, Jules Verne,

Mark Twain, Robert Louis Stevenson, H. Rider Haggard, Arthur Conan Doyle, H. G. Wells, Laura Ingalls Wilder, Willa Cather, Jack London, Virginia Woolf, and H. P. Lovecraft—all undoubtedly influenced by some giants of the past such as Homer, Aristotle, Pico della Mirandola, Luther, Cervantes, Shakespeare, Hume, and Voltaire.

13. See Philip K. Howard, *Try Common Sense: Replacing the Failed Ideologies of Right and Left* (New York: W. W. Norton, 2019).

14. Deirdre McCloskey gives an admirable discussion of the matter in her *Bourgeois Dignity* (Chicago: University of Chicago Press, 2010), 355–365.

15. See Mariana Mazzucato, *The Entrepreneurial State: Debunking Public vs. Private Sector Myths* (London: Anthem, 2013); and Joseph Stiglitz, *People, Power and Profit: Progressive Capitalism for an Age of Discontent* (New York: W. W. Norton, 2019).

16. Edmund Phelps, *Rewarding Work: How to Restore Participation and Self-Support to Free Enterprise* (Cambridge, MA: Harvard University Press, 1997; 2nd ed. 2007). See also my critique of Philippe van Parjis, "A Basic Income for All," *Boston Review,* October 2000. In his *Basic Income: A Radical Proposal for a Free Society and a Sane Economy* (Cambridge, MA: Harvard University Press, 2017), he offers a rebuttal to my critique.

ACKNOWLEDGMENTS

It is a great pleasure to acknowledge, as the senior author, the enormous intellectual contributions of the three coauthors of this volume, Raicho Bojilov, Hian Teck Hoon, and Gylfi Zoega. For more than three years, we held a team call over Skype every Wednesday morning—Bojilov in Paris, Hoon in Singapore, Zoega in Reykjavik, and I in New York. They brought to the task huge skills in econometrics, statistics, and mathematical modeling—skills central to the research our project required.

Some of the most scintillating conversations of my career occurred in those calls. Also, it is remarkable that we did not end with any disagreements—certainly no important ones. I am proud that they were early collaborators of mine. Bojilov worked with me on values in 2006, Zoega worked with me on innovation as early as 2008, and Hoon joined me in analyzing innovation and employment in 2011. (Both he and Zoega were coauthors of my 1994 book *Structural Slumps*.) I am extremely fortunate to have worked with all of them anew, beginning with the shift in my research toward innovation around 2000.

This intensive project could not have gone far without some substantial financing. The Ewing Marion Kauffman Foundation enabled the start of new research on innovation with repeated grants beginning in 2004. Later, the Alfred P. Sloan Foundation provided a grant to fund research on the effects of robots on the path of wages and employment. The Smith Richardson Foundation provided from 2015 to 2018 the principal funding of the three-year project—now more nearly a four-year project—that has brought about this book. I am most grateful for this support.

I also want to thank Ian Malcolm for guiding this project on the road to its publication at Harvard University Press.

Finally, I would like to say that this effort has been an activity of the Center on Capitalism and Society, of which I am the director; and the huge efforts of Catherine Pikula, my executive assistant, and Lizzie Feidelson, the Center's administrative manager, have been essential to the achievement of this project. I am also grateful to Richard Robb, a stalwart of the Center, for our many conversations on the realm of this book.

INDEX